# SCENES FROM AN AFTERLIFE

# Scenes from an Afterlife
## The Legacy of George Orwell

**John Rodden**

ISI Books
2003

Cataloging-in-Publication Data

    Scenes from an afterlife: the legacy of George Orwell / John Rodden — Wilmington, DE : ISI Books, 2003.
        p. ; cm.
    Includes index
    ISBN: 1-932236-01-5
        1. Orwell, George, 1903–1950 — Criticism and interpretation.
    I. Title.
    PR6029.R8 Z763 2003 2003102919
    828/.91209—dc21    CIP


*Published by:*        ISI Books
                Intercollegiate Studies Institute
                3901 Centerville Road
                Wilmington, Delaware 19807
                www.isibooks.org


*Interior design by Kara Beer*

Portions of Part II previously appeared in *Repainting the Little Red Schoolhouse: A History of Eastern German Education, 1945–95* (Oxford: Oxford University Press, 2002). Several passages in Parts I and III are derived from *George Orwell: The Politics of Literary Reputation* (New Brunswick, N.J.: Transaction, 2002) and from articles in *Media Studies Journal, College English, Kenyon Review, Canadian Journal of History*, and *Four Quarters*, with the permission of the editors. This material has been substantially revised for inclusion in the present work. The cartoon on page 7 is by Charles Schulz, © 1983 United Features Syndicate, and is used by permission of the copyright owner; the illustration on page 17 is used by permission of the American Newspapers Publishers Association. All photos and illustrations pertaining to Germany are from the Deutsches Historisches Museum, Berlin, and are used by permission.

FOR LYNN HAYDEN
*mit Dankbarkeit*

# Contents

## III.
### Man and Mentor, Myth and Monument

# Preface

The following chapters reflect on George Orwell's heritage since the passing of 1984. Having lived at close intellectual quarters with Orwell for more than two decades, I conceived this work as a centennial tribute to his life and legacy. When I completed a previous study of Orwell in 1989—a watershed year that witnessed the dismantling of the Berlin Wall and the death throes of Soviet-style communism throughout Eastern Europe—numerous commentators forecast Orwell's own imminent cultural eclipse. With the arrival of what pundits proclaimed the most important year in modern history since the French Revolution exactly two centuries earlier, the work of George Orwell would supposedly cease to possess relevance in the "New World Order."

That prophecy has not been realized. Whether or not "the end of history" once confidently (and imminently) anticipated by political philosophers is just around the corner, Orwell is alive and well in the twenty-first century. One encounters his legacy not only in the pages of academic journals and intellectual quarterlies, but also in popular periodicals and on the airwaves—including television hits such as the reality show, *Big Brother*. And then there is the ceaseless attention accorded him by scholars and biographers: *The Com-*

*plete Works of George Orwell* has been issued (in twenty volumes consisting of a total of 8,500 pages) and the fifth biography within a dozen years will soon be published.[1]

Perhaps Orwell and his work will gradually recede from the headlines as the new century unfolds. And yet, in 2003, not only is the announcement of his literary obituary utterly premature, but so also is the implication that he is culturally and politically dated. Instead, the lament "If Orwell were alive today" continues to be voiced. Editorialists declare: "What we need is an Orwell for our time." He is still loved and hated by numerous intellectuals, claimed and disclaimed by the Left, quoted and misquoted (even by the last British prime minister). He is still invoked regularly to address public controversies ranging from America's "war on terrorism" to the policies of the British Labor Party. News columnists at the *Times* of London and the *New York Times Book Review* still make frequent reference to him and his work—and even speculate about his possible successors among Anglo-American intellectuals, with specific candidates being proposed and debated. Orwell has become such an oracle for secular intellectuals that one expects "W.W.G.O.D.?" soon to be a greeting among them. (Indeed an actual 2002 headline in the *New York Times Book Review* was typical: "What Would Orwell Do?")

Even in the non-Anglophone world, Orwell is cited, saluted, and annexed anew: an opposition newspaper in Zimbabwe satirizes the country's dictator, Robert Mugabe, by serializing *Animal Farm*; a Beijing theatre stages a showcase adaptation of the fable; a Polish stamp bears Orwell's face; a German conference of intellectuals meets to discuss "Der Grosse Bruder"; so too do writers and critics convening in Barcelona, where a square has recently been named in Orwell's honor.

Indeed the diverse scenes of Orwell's afterlife straddle two centuries and traverse the globe. If Orwell is less visible today than he was twenty years ago, when the countdown to 1984 was under way, it is not because his influence has waned. It is rather an ironic tribute to the writer as legislator of humankind, attesting to the fact that our culture has even more fully absorbed the vision and sensibility of his work and life.

\*\*\*\*\*\*\*\*\*

# Preface

My thanks go first to my editor at ISI, Jeremy Beer, who provided sharp insight, ceaseless encouragement, and good humor. "You're our only author who writes for *Dissent*," he once said to me with a laugh. That a conservative publishing house is willing to sponsor the work of a "liberal" writer, some of whose positions are decidedly to the left of its own, speaks well of its editor and his ISI colleagues—and of their genuine regard for Orwell's broad-minded example.

Other colleagues and friends also assisted this work in its pilgrim's progress. Jeff Nelson, Kara Beer, Doug Schneider, and Eileen Ridge expertly guided the book from conception through production. Jay Alejandre proved the ideal student assistant, one blessed with a vigilant eye and titanic energy. Paul Rodden was a brother not only to the author but to his delicate brainchild as he patiently cradled worthwhile insights into literary form. Irving Louis Horowitz mentored this book with a keen eye for its possibilities as he prodded ceaselessly and vigorously in behalf of scholarly excellence. Beth Macom intervened with providential timing to exert decisive influence, not simply by her characteristically assiduous editorial care, but also by her bracing challenge to honor fully both the reader's capacities and my own.

For their intellectual stimulation and random acts of kind, practical advice, I am also grateful to Morris Dickstein, Mark Krupnick, Jeffrey Meyers, Jonathan Rose, Thomas Cushman, Jonathan Imber, Jack Rossi, John Vella, and George Panichas. And for their indispensable emotional support, I am greatly indebted to Tanya Oneil, Cristen and Daniel Reat, Scott and Erica Walter, Peter Dougherty, Jean Harrison, Mitch Baranowski, Michael Levenson, Monica Alejandre, Juanita Solis, Tara and Kailey Rodden, and John and Rose Rodden.

And for her wondrous generosity, quiet inspiration, and spiritual nourishment, I dedicate this book to Lynn Hayden.

# Prologue

# The Orwell Centenary—
# and the Orwell Century

# I

The "Orwell Decade" was how Günter Grass once characterized the 1980s. But it may turn out that the entire twentieth century—what Henry Luce so famously dubbed the "American Century"—will be known as the "Orwell Century." (Or, more ominously, "the Orwellian Century.") The centennial of George Orwell's birth—the date was June 25, 2003—has furnished cultural and intellectual historians as well as news journalists with renewed occasion for staking Orwell's title to that claim—just as news reporters of the war on terrorism find increasing and urgent reason to invoke Orwell's dystopian vision. The advertisement for an international conference on Orwell held in early May 2003 at Wellesley College in Massachusetts—for which celebrity intellectuals, political figures, and numerous admiring professors gathered in his name—epitomizes the honorific terms in which Orwell's name is now discussed. The ad began: "Orwell anticipated, criticized, or warned against the key developments that would mark the 1900s: the legacy of imperialism, the tragedy of homelessness and poverty, the Cold War, the Bomb, the specter of totalitarian superstates and ceaseless proxy wars, the betrayals of the Left, the advent of mass culture and the 'media age,' the rise of the 'organization man.'" Or as a PBS show on Orwell that ran in 2002–03 opened: "Called by some the most important writer of the twentieth century," Orwell's "writing pierced intellectual hypocrisy . . . from the far ends of the British Empire to the heart of European conflicts, from imperialism and fascism to socialism and communism. . . ." The PBS program was titled: "The Orwell Century."

As such sweeping tributes suggest, commentators and critics have, almost reflexively, and almost from the moment of his premature death in January 1950 at the age of 46, exalted Orwell in terms far greater than those commonly applied to a writer. Even old acquaintances still marvel at how their once "almost unknown" literary colleague has become a historical totem that seems today to straddle Anglo-American intellectual life, how the writer George Orwell suddenly metamorphosed into "the Orwell legend."

The present study is thus about a life that became a legend. My chief intention is not, however, to debunk or decimate, but rather to indicate the astounding diversity and divergence of Orwell's public images, with a particular focus on his posthumous reputation, i.e., the phenomenon of his fame and its vicissitudes.

# II

Biographers and scholars have thoroughly chronicled the life of Orwell. But the story of the unique afterlife of "Orwell"—not just the man or writer or even the persona or literary personality, but the cultural icon—is a much more ambitious and complex drama: part tragedy, part farce, part slapstick comedy, part Broadway extravaganza—indeed miracle, mystery, and morality play rolled into one. "George Orwell, an Afterlife" is no one-acter, but rather a still-running, one-man variety show composed of myriad—and still untold—scenes. In a previous study, I undertook to depict two dozen scenes from the gallery of "Orwell," which resulted in a book about both the writer's achievement and historical reception.[1] Yet I must confess that, though I hoped (and still hope) to have presented the climactic scenes, I did not come close to rounding out the narrative of Orwell's sprawling posthumous history. Nor does this book offer a full-stage dress production: these are scenes from "a," not "the," afterlife. But the following chapters do both review and pursue further the story of Orwell's complex heritage.

And here a word about the conceptual issues that have shaped my thinking may be apposite. This book reflects no commitment to a particular critical method, let alone to a theoretical apparatus or literary doxology. Still, as the previous paragraph suggests—as indeed the book's title suggests—this study is guided by a trope. I hope that my conscious embrace of a dramaturgical metaphor in this study helps capture the dynamic, controversial character— indeed the factious, disputatious quality—of Orwell's discordant afterlife. My first book made extensive use of a metaphorical vocabulary derived from art history: the portrait gallery. Yet however valuable that figural language proved for relating the gallery of Orwell's public images, its static nature suggests a fixity quite at odds with my intent here. While I have retained the idea of sketching Orwell's "reception scenes," I hope that my shift from still-life drawings to *dramatic* sketches better facilitates a dramatic imagination of Orwell's posthumous story and thus helps it come more fully to life. For I aim in this book to present not just pictures, but moving pictures—a dramatized, indeed animated, cinematic "Orwell *en route*." Or rather: not just a play script but a shooting script, not just a stage show but a newsreel of the afterlife. Indeed I aspire here to become a scholarly scenarist who envisions and crafts select scenarios of "Orwell on the Telescreen."

And so this book is a sequel that adapts and updates a few previously sketched scenes of "Orwell" and also presents several new scenarios of his posthumous reception. Occasionally I take up this irregularly serialized narrative of "Orwell" by revisiting briefly a salient scene from my study of the portrait gallery, thereby orienting the reader for the current installment of our episodic docudrama.

This "scenic" approach to cultural history—telling the story of a person's "afterlife"—may be considered a new way of writing the traditional "Life-and-Times" biography. Each section of the book highlights a dimension of the "afterlife and times" of "Orwell," showing not just his fascinating costume changes but illustrating how the man and writer ballooned into a world-historical actor who seemed to take part in every major issue during what became the "Orwell century."

# III

This book is thus a kind of "Orwell revue" in the form of seventeen scenes across three acts. Act I revisits the 1980s, the "Orwell decade." It addresses Orwell's evolving reputation in the former communist world as well as in the West. It spotlights how differently the Cold War superpowers treated Orwell's most famous dystopian visions, *Animal Farm* and *Nineteen Eighty-Four*, under conditions of advanced capitalism and declining communism. Moving from the "countdown" to 1984 to the meltdown of 1989, it examines the bizarre commercial and ideological abuses to which Orwell was subjected, from hilarious ad campaigns spun off by carpet manufacturers and pro-gun lobbyists, to forbidding attack ads launched by the regional Bell Telephone companies and their adversaries, to the Soviet publication of *Nineteen Eighty-Four* in the dying days of the USSR and the rescripting of Orwell's renegade role there. These shifting East-West perspectives illuminate why *Nineteen Eighty-Four* has stood for a half-century as an ever-expanding, universal metaphor, indeed as an all-purpose critique of capitalism, totalitarianism, socialism, modern technology, mass advertising, the welfare state, the (Left) intelligentsia, consumerist culture, the alienation of modernity, and the triviality of postmodern life.[2] Act I concludes with a shift in focus to the other major work associated with Orwell's Cold Warrior reputation, *Animal Farm*. This closing scene discusses how perceptions of *Animal Farm* have altered in the last decade, both in light of the collapse of the USSR and the popularity of the 1999 film adaptation of the fable.

Act II, "Orwell's GDR? or Post-Mortems on 'the Better Germany,'" further explores the Cold War, the "unfreeze," and the unlessons contributed by the West's leading literary Cold Warrior. The setting shifts to "Orwell" in Germany, offering an extended look at his status in East Germany and post-reunification Germany from an intensely personal standpoint. As I surveyed the tottering GDR in 1990 after the toppling of the Berlin Wall, it was indeed as if I were visiting a movie set for *Nineteen Eighty-Four*—just as the production was being shut down. And so this act concentrates on my own experience of the role and relevance of *Nineteen Eighty-Four* in the German Democratic Republic (GDR), which proudly proclaimed itself *das bessere Deutschland*. The scenes range from Orwell to the Orwellian, i.e., from Orwell's own place in the eastern German mindscape to the insidious Newspeak and shocking abridgment of personal freedoms in the self-proclaimed "Land of Reading," a.k.a. the "Land of Little Brother." One scene portrays the tragicomedy of "academic unfreedom" on the high stage: the wretched fate that befell an outspoken dissident intellectual and his family. Another scene concerns judicial doublethink on the low stage in "Orwell's GDR," as one convicted "thought criminal" titled his horrifying memoir about his imprisonment for procuring *Nineteen Eighty-Four* in the 1950s. These and other stories emerge from my encounters with faculty and students in the GDR educational system, the institution Stalin had proclaimed the "citadel of learning" that "must be captured at any price."

The spotlight shifts directly to Orwell's life and afterlife in Act III, seeking to illuminate how they became, in Erik Erikson's phrase about Luther, "half-legend, half-history." Titled "Man and Mentor, Myth and Monument," Act III outlines the extraordinary growth of a reputation—not how the man Eric Blair became the writer Orwell, but how Orwell became the headliner "Orwell."

Whereas the Cold Warrior was the cynosure of all eyes in earlier sections, other roles that "Orwell" has played now enter the limelight: Old Etonian, prose guardian and laureate, literary prophet, "St. George." Among the topics addressed are the history of attempts to write his life and the biographical issues and controversies they have raised; Orwell's canonization as a school-approved author and its ramifications on his reputation; and the origins and appeal of his public images, ranging from the schoolboy "failure" to the macho militiaman to the intellectuals' Don Quixote.

The disputes about Orwell's legacy also receive extended attention in Act III. The admiring grave-robbers—and, sometimes, the contemptuous grave-defacers—range from approving Catholic conservatives seeking to "convert" Orwell such as Christopher Hollis, to hostile Left critics aiming to disinherit him such as Raymond Williams. The final two scenes deal with the history of intellectual skirmishes for his mantle and present an overview of the key factors responsible for Orwell's fame, respectively, both of which evince that the culture wars for "Orwell" continue unabated to the present. Intellectuals continue to speculate on how the author of *Nineteen Eighty-Four* would have responded to events since his death. Or as the news headlines still prattle, pronounce, predict, and ponder: "If Orwell Were Alive Today . . ."

And so here again, as we look back on the Orwell century and forward beyond the Orwell centenary, this prodigious, perplexing array of Orwell scenes discloses, as Malcolm Muggeridge once wrote about his friend, "how the legend of a human being is created."[3]

# IV

Whatever else may be said, the still-running spectacular of George Orwell's afterlife is a unique tale of contemporary fame. It is the implausible yet true story of a literary second act that knows no comparison. For Orwell is "alive today" in a way that his intellectual contemporaries—and even noteworthy successors who have only recently passed away—are no longer. His significance is not just historical; both his life and his work still exert a shaping influence upon contemporary culture. Indeed, more than a half-century after his death, his very name wields a rhetorical and political force sufficient to stimulate public argument.

The saga of "Orwell" is a biodrama of the contemporary world. As we shall see, the following scenes from this implausible afterlife tell us much about our own lives.

# I.

# Glimpses of the World of
# *Nineteen Eighty-Four* and 1984
# —and After

# The Hype and Hilarity of "Orwellmania"

*Hegel has remarked somewhere that all great historical facts and personages occur twice. He has forgotten to add: the first time as history, the second as farce.*

—Karl Marx, *The Eighteenth Brumaire of Louis Bonaparte*

## I

As we gaze on the world stage of "Orwell," we first encounter a scene of low comedy, or perhaps *opéra bouffe*. For in the early 1980s, the otherwise quite serious "Orwell Century" experienced a brief moment of waggery and whimsy, as "Orwell" played the *farceur*. Especially in the U.S., History witnessed the explosion of an outlandish, market-driven "Orwellmania," the hype and hilarity of which is the subject of this opening chapter.

It is perhaps not so surprising that Orwell's work became grist for vaudeville slapstick and was then promoted with entrepreneurial zeal. Orwell was not only a pioneering cultural critic; he also became a commercial object of popular culture. Probably no other writer's work has so decisively contributed to the development of popular culture studies as a formal domain of academic inquiry—and so widely penetrated the international imagination—that it qualifies as a substantial body of material for popular culture analysis.

This unusual achievement is partly attributable to the variety of Orwell's oeuvre. Indeed, one notices that different works have accounted for his dual status as culture "critic" and culture "object." Whereas his essay collections (especially *Inside the Whale* and *Critical Essays*) and some of his journalism have exerted influence on postwar culture critics, *Animal Farm* and *Nineteen Eighty-Four* have been mined in diverse ways, particularly during the "countdown to 1984," by commercial and ideological interest groups.

# II

In order to appreciate the origins, emergence, and dimensions of "Orwellmania" in the 1980s, we should first consider Orwell's trailblazing role as a serious student of popular culture a half-century earlier. Orwell was not a cultural relativist. Although his critical interests ranged perhaps more widely than those of any other literary intellectual of his day, from *Ulysses* to *The Gem* and *The Magnet*, he never pretended that high and popular culture were of comparable *aesthetic* value. In this conviction he was very much an intellectual of his time. Orwell was a defiant, but not a radical, pluralist. By no means did he advocate that culture critics *totally* abandon what Evelyn Waugh referred to as "the hierarchic principle." Instead he condemned, in Paul Fussell's phrase, "generic snobbery." Literature, like society, had its underclasses, but postcards, comics, thrillers, and pamphlets still deserved critical attention, Orwell held, since the business of the critic was language and its relation to human beings.

Orwell's governing attitude toward culture was therefore a rebel's; he did not so much proselytize about the worth of penny postcards as he opposed the mandarin school of art and aesthetic pretentiousness in general. Largely as a result of his boyhood immersion in popular culture, and unlike even the most sympathetic Anglo-American intellectuals in the postwar period, Orwell seems to have felt no deep conflict between the claims of "culture" and "democracy," or to have harbored any doubts about the value of popular culture. He could comfortably assert in one breath the immense *sociological* value of boys' papers while conceding in the next the aesthetic superiority of traditional, "high" culture—and do all this while feeling neither the intellectual's

guilt for his "elitist" tastes nor the intellectual's shame for his lowbrow preferences. For many readers, Orwell's easy embrace of popular culture has constituted another powerful source of his own popular appeal. It is an attitude that
seems to provide an accessible, immediate way to bridge the gulf between the
intellectual and the public—a way to be an intellectual's "common man."

Orwell's popularity among serious readers recalls his admiration for the
appeal Dickens had for popular tastes. Indeed, Orwell's assessment of Dickens's
popularity is a fair estimate of important aspects of his own wide appeal. To
Orwell, Dickens's continued popularity was due to his remarkable affinity
with the Victorian mind, significant features of which had lingered on into
Orwell's adulthood. Orwell saw that Dickens's work (as has Orwell's in our
day) fitted the needs of his age and those of several generations to follow.
Orwell also noted that Dickens's artistic limitations were not negligible. And
yet Dickens, as Orwell wrote in his essay "Charles Dickens" (1939), possessed "a native generosity of mind" that "was probably the central secret of
his popularity." In literary terms, observed Orwell, the secret is revealed in
Dickens's capacity to express "in comic, simplified, and therefore memorable
form the native decency of the common man," who even in the 1930s—
partly due to the power of Dickens's imagination—was "still living in the
mental world of Dickens." Like other artifacts of popular culture—comic
strips, Mickey Mouse, and Popeye the Sailor—Dickens's work embodied,
according to Orwell, "the feeling that one is always on the side of the underdog, on the side of the weak against the strong." Severe artistic limitations, a
sense of decency, impassioned sympathy for the underdog—most readers of
Orwell find his work characterized by these very same shortcomings and
strengths.

# III

By the early 1980s, however, Orwell the public writer had gone a step beyond
Dickens. Not only had Orwell's writings, as he had remarked of Dickens's,
"entered even into the minds of people who do not care about" books; his
work had also come to serve as raw material for popular and mass cultural
artifacts. And as we turn now to this remarkable development, let us shift

focus from Orwell as "critic" to "object" of popular culture, and from his reception by literary intellectuals to his use by commercial and ideological interest groups. Our chief concern in the remainder of this chapter is with the formal use of his name and work in all kinds of promotional activities.

The extraordinary degree to which "Orwell" was employed in such promotional campaigns, sometimes even before the 1980s, is yet another indication of his enormous public reputation—as well as a comment on Orwell's own writing practices. For Orwell himself liberally used the popular and mass art of his day as background and motif for his fiction; reciprocally, his work itself has in turn become part of popular and mass culture. For example, the well-known Animal Farm greeting cards, featuring a piglet straddling a wall (caption: "Some cards are more equal than others"), were popular since the early 1970s. Orwell wrote about postcards and comic strips; the 1984 countdown witnessed Orwell-inspired postcards, comic strips, T-shirts, and pop songs (Van Halen's "1984"). Campaign buttons ("Orwell in '84!!") came from a Pennsylvania advertising company, which launched an Orwell for President campaign on April Fools' Day, 1983.

Some spinoffs pegged to *Nineteen Eighty-Four* laced their humor with political invective. The left-slanted *Big Brother Book of Lists*, with a sinister Thought Police agent in a black trench coat on the cover, used *Nineteen Eighty-Four* as a handy hook for its numerous compilations (e.g., J. Edgar Hoover's eight ways to spot a car driven by a communist). Similarly, the *1984 Calendar: An American History* noted about 250 dates in history that the creators considered anniversaries of government intrusion into the lives of individuals. In addition, the national campaign committees of both the Democratic and Republican parties, in soliciting funds from party supporters, sent out cover letters referring to the "Orwellian spectre" on issues ranging from defense spending to abortion.

So in 1984 the socialist author was exploited not only as an ideological patron but also as a capitalist money-maker. "Orwell" was a hot item; the date's approach ignited a conflagration that lasted for several months. Orwell's popular reputation blazed like a shooting star, radiating far beyond the literary-academic world. An in-depth analysis of his treatment in hundreds of popular periodicals in 1983–84—a number quite possibly unprecedented for a literary figure—would probably offer insight into the relation between com-

*Even Snoopy succumbed to "Orwellmania" in 1984.*

mercialism and celebrity. A partial list of the specialized magazines and trade journals that ran stories on Orwell and *Nineteen Eighty-Four* in late 1983 and early 1984, some of them with utterly outlandish angles, gives a hint of the phenomenal range of Orwell's reception among non-intellectual audiences during this time: *Roofing Spectator, Four Wheeler, Art Material Trade News, Cruising World, National Clothesline Monthly, Ohio Farmer, Racing Wheel Times, Tennis Monthly, Construction Equipment Distribution News, Cablevision, Computer Decisions Monthly, Hospitals, Electronic Packaging and Production Monthly, Metal News, American Medical News, Insulation Outlook Monthly.*

The presentation of Orwell and *Nineteen Eighty-Four* in these organs indicates how a writer's image can be transformed—sometimes beyond recognition—as his name and work penetrate beyond the sphere of the serious literary community into the wider public. Take, for example, the following banal use of *Nineteen Eighty-Four* by the *Welding Journal*. Addressed to industry employees, the February 1984 article ("1984 Is Here!") began by confusing *Nineteen Eighty-Four* with *Animal Farm*:

*Are you more equal than others?* This is your chance to become one who is more equal than others, more expert in the welding field. . . .

Is Big Brother watching you? If to you Big Brother is your boss, a board of directors, a steering committee, or a review board, they too will be watching—and they will be wondering if you are keeping aware of today's fast-moving welding technology.

Such examples of commercial defacement suggest the difference between the popularization and vulgarization of a work of art, a line hard to draw conceptually but often easy to identify in practice. Two trade journal editorials that appeared in 1983–84 underline this point even more clearly. They also show how Orwell's public image as a "dark prophet" readily served as a pretext for industry spokesmen to counterpose themselves as "true," optimistic prophets. By treating *Nineteen Eighty-Four* as a historical forecast, rather than as a warning against totalitarian thinking, they were able to "trump Orwell" with sunny counter-forecasts about their own industries. The first editorial is from *Casual Living Monthly*; the second is from *Shooting Industry*:

If I were to play George Orwell for one brief fleeting moment, I would predict a bright future for the casual furniture industry in 1984. My prediction is based on fact and empirical observation, leaving fantasy and hypothesis to Orwell and his like.

Unless George Orwell's predictions come true and 1984 sees Big Brother remove the accessibility of handguns from the majority of citizens, the handgun business should recover at least as fast as the general economy.

As one might expect, however, the commercialization of Orwell and *Nineteen Eighty-Four* was chiefly the work of the American mass media. By late 1983, the American press was shrieking that "Orwellmania!" had seized the U.S. and Britain. One headline in January 1984 summed up the ubiquity of Orwell's name: "Where Will the Orwellian Fascination End?" In the opening months of the year, christened "The Year of the Book" by Penguin Books, *Nineteen Eighty-Four* made publishing history, topping the *New York Times* and *Publisher's Weekly* lists of best-selling mass market fiction for five weeks, the first time any book several (let alone thirty-five) years old had ever risen to occupy the number one position. The promotional campaigns associated with *Nineteen Eighty-Four* and the book's sales explosion in 1983–84 were actually the culmination of a decade-long trend. By 1979, popular magazines such as *Time* and *Playboy* were warning readers that "1984" was "only" five years away.

The first signs that the countdown was turning *Nineteen Eighty-Four* into a mass culture object came in 1980–81. The 1980 Yale University freshman "facebook" for the class of 1984 featured dozens of photographs of George Orwell, which were included to replace those "faceless" student "unpersons" who had failed to include a snapshot with their college applications. In the next year "Orwell" and *Nineteen Eighty-Four* appeared in numerous advertisements. "We're Betting $2.3 Million that Orwell Was Wrong" ran an ad headline in early 1981 in *Time* for the Boise Cascade paper company. The full-page ad pictured a scene reminiscent of the Golden Country in *Nineteen Eighty-Four*. A husband, wife, and little boy stroll arm-and-arm through a quiet glen, and then step lightly through the pages of a titanic calendar labeled "1984": "We see a sunnier future than George Orwell did in 1948," the ad copy begins, "which is one reason why we've launched our most ambitious capital investment program ever."

In succeeding months other firms and stores spun ambitious ad campaigns off *Nineteen Eighty-Four*. In January 1984, Apple Computers kicked off its Macintosh computer promotion using *Nineteen Eighty-Four*. Directed by Ridley Scott, who had already directed *Alien* (1979) and *Blade Runner* (1982), the controversial $500,000, sixty-second TV spot was seen by 60 million football fans during halftime of the 1984 Super Bowl.[1] (It aired only once.) The Apple commercial was clearly targeted at archrival IBM, or "Big Blue," which Apple stopped just short of labeling "Big Brother."

The commercial's climax was stunning. A television image of rows of marching, chanting, zombie-like citizens ("We are one people with one will, one resolve, one cause!")—presumably IBM patrons tutored in Room 101—was shattered when a beautiful woman in Olympic uniform hurled a sledgehammer through the screen. Her richly textured gesture represented both a nod to David's slingshot and an appropriation of the Soviet emblem as an anti-totalitarian weapon.

All this was carefully designed. The identification of Big Brother with IBM/ Big Blue was a deliberate symbolic reversal, since IBM is the embodiment of capitalism. And what then? Q.E.D.: Equating IBM with Stalinism invites the viewer to associate Apple with capitalist democracy and freedom.

*Advertising Age* noted immediately that no commercial in recent memory had aroused such widespread public and industry discussion. Pundits, critics, and scholars concurred. Thereafter the "1984" ad was showered with prizes. It became the first American commercial to capture a Grand Prix award at Cannes. *Advertising Age* honored it as Commercial of the Decade and later proclaimed it the "greatest commercial" of the half-century. *TV Guide* went even further and declared it at century's end the "best commercial" ever produced. Or as one communication scholar pronounced it in 1999: "the biggest single splash in the history of advertising."[2]

# IV

Yet nothing recedes like success. "Orwellmania" proved to be short-lived. With the exception of the Animal Farm cards and a few promotions associated with *Nineteen Eighty-Four*, the gimmickry was over by March 1984. By the date on which Winston Smith makes his first fateful diary entry, 4 April 1984, the "Orwellian fascination" had ended. The mutability of the present had rendered *Nineteen Eighty-Four* as obsolescent as any other mass-cult object.

O'Brien's declaration to Winston—"We shall squeeze you empty, and then we shall fill you with ourselves"—could very well serve as a gloss on the making of Orwell into a cultural object, and indeed on Orwell's entire afterlife. For "Orwell" and *Nineteen Eighty-Four* have been molded to fit nearly every conceivable commercial promotion and political cause, according to changes in the cultural climate. His reception history during the 1980s exemplifies how one gets "unpersoned" in a new way: not by primitive speakwrites but by the ravenous maw of commodity fetishism. Under advanced capitalism you go down the memory hole by becoming your claimant's rhetorical billboard or effigy. You are drained of your identity—and then filled with our hype.

That Orwell—the so-called intellectuals' Common Man—became "common property" in the 1980s, of course, says less about Orwell and *Nineteen Eighty-Four* than about our culture, especially about the nature of celebrity and the price—"unpersonhood"—at which it is bought. During the 1984 countdown, Orwell the common man became a "mass man." Society gave Orwell transitory fame in exchange for annexing and depersonalizing his name and work. The barter clarifies the terms of Orwell's peculiar dual status as cultural critic and object. Partly because of his fascination with ordinary culture, Orwell shaped his work from it, and partly on that account it has been highly assimilable and susceptible to societal reappropriation. In 1983–84 the vast circle connecting writer and culture was completed. Orwell had drawn on the cultural life and materials of his day, remolding them to forge his uniquely personal, searing vision of the future: *Nineteen Eighty-Four*. At last, History "reclaimed" the cultural materials, now brilliantly transformed and exalted in Orwell's finished work, and trivialized and exhausted their meaning by associating his masterpiece with new, ephemeral cultural artifacts. The socialist author of *Nineteen Eighty-Four* was granted, in return, a moment of collectivized glory.

# V

So the ironies abound: the socialist hero as capitalist poster boy. Perhaps Orwell should have seen it all coming; after all, even before he died, *Nineteen Eighty-Four* had become known not by its original and proper title, but simply as "1984," a billboard (or sound byte) distillation ideally suited to slick ads and blaring headlines. This abridgement both reflected and facilitated the encapsulation, oversimplification, and distortion of his work in the decades to follow. (Whatever Orwell's anger at the use of *Animal Farm* as "propaganda for capitalists," as he once called it in a letter to his agent, he appears to have taken no special steps to avoid the same fate for *Nineteen Eighty-Four*.)[3]

The identification of the socialist tribune Orwell (or "Orwell") with capitalism is an ironic reversal, one that is congruent with, yet diametrically opposed to, that of Ridley Scott's "1984" commercial, which inverted the signifiers "Big Blue" and capitalism. Of course, such a transposition reflects a cultural process not uncommon in the era of late capitalism, postmodernism, and poststructuralism. Nonetheless, it is also a surprising turn of events that invites a final reflection on Orwell's reputation as a prophet and on his critique of capitalism—and indeed on capitalism's extraordinary, oft-noted resilience: its astonishing, hydra-headed capacity to survive economic downturns and social upheavals and somehow to sustain and even strengthen itself.

Certainly Orwell doubtless never envisioned that his work would serve ad campaigns and corporate sloganeering. But his insight into and ambivalence towards capitalism did reflect his awareness that capitalism possessed an indispensable virtue: economic liberty. As he observed in a surprisingly positive review of Friedrich Hayek's *Road to Serfdom* (1944), economic collectivism might snuff our individual liberty, including the freedom of an author to write "as he pleased." By 1944, Orwell the libertarian radical had come to agree, albeit reluctantly, with the conservative Hayek that "free" enterprise might indeed constitute a necessary foundation for safeguarding personal freedoms of a non-economic kind. Or as Orwell wrote in "Literature and Totalitarianism": "The economic liberty of the individual and to a great extent his liberty to do what he likes . . . comes to an end now. Till recently, the implications of this were not foreseen. It was never fully realized that the disappearance of economic liberty would have any effect on intellectual liberty." And yet, such a concession did not turn Orwell into an advocate of capitalism—or even make him reconsider his prediction that it was "doomed to extinction" in the post-totalitarian age.

Orwell, then, was no economic prophet. He did not see capitalism as resilient but rather as doomed. He believed and feared that totalitarian dictatorships and collectivist "utopias" represented the wave of the future.[4]

Orwell remained a self-described "democratic socialist" until his dying day. But it is notable that the capitalist era preceding the totalitarian empire of Oceania is portrayed in quite positive, nostalgic terms in *Nineteen Eighty-Four*. In the scene where he and Julia meet O'Brien, Winston Smith chooses to toast not a socialist future, but the past. Orwell despised capitalism for its social injustices, but he was willing to concede that capitalist societies had important virtues: freedom of thought, respect for human rights, even freedom of speech. In *The Lion and the Unicorn* (1941), Orwell admits that capitalism has spread prosperity much further down the social scale than was previously ever thought possible. And in "Will Freedom Die with Capitalism" (1941), he writes, "I think we ought to guard against assuming that as a system to live under socialism will be greatly preferable to democratic capitalism." Capitalism, says Orwell, has been "humanized."[5]

Orwell thus acknowledged the development of what might be called "capitalism with a human face." He thereby anticipated the radical sensibility of two decades later when Czech President Alexander Dubcek spoke of "socialism with a human face."[6] Yet whereas Dubcek and western leftists sought a "Third Way" in May 1968 between the advanced capitalism of the West and the state socialism of the East, Orwell the Cold Warrior believed, as he wrote in "Toward European Unity" (1947), that one might have to choose between them if a united Europe failed soon to emerge. Orwell said that he would unhesitatingly choose American capitalism over Stalinist collectivism—even though he continued to believe that some form of socialism represented the shape of things to come.

Orwell never relinquished his socialist ideals. And he never took a sanguine view of capitalism. Limited by his historical horizon, he did not anticipate globalization and the new economic conditions posed by postmodernity and "identity politics"—nor the psychological conditions, given his temperamental distaste for Freudianism and social science. Nonetheless, in one respect one might argue that Orwell was inadvertently prescient—not in his essays but in the ingenious psychodrama of *Nineteen Eighty-Four.*

Critics of popular culture often note that consumerist excesses in postmodern society and in the reigning global capitalist economy represent a near-totalitarian power akin to O'Brien's torture of Winston in Room 101.[7] The only difference is, we co-conspire more overtly with our torturers, i.e., our artificial desires, which kindle into compulsions and fan into addictions that dominate our dreams. The forces of postmodernism and globalization provoke us to become inner émigrés, to flee the external world and escape within—and then they relentlessly colonize our inner lives. We exchange politics for psychopolitics, as does Winston in his utter fascination and obsession with O'Brien. Ultimately, like Winston, we too are broken down—not our bodies but our souls. We are atomized into fragmented, performing selves consisting of diverse social roles and pumped up to stay frenetically active—which thereby ensures that the consumerist frenzy (which Adorno termed "consumer totalitarianism") continues undisturbed and the "free" market hums merrily along.[8]

"Social alienation" is one much-decried consequence of all this. But the term is clichéd and inadequate. Alienation takes a form different today than it did in Orwell's era, let alone in the nineteenth century of Karl Marx. Nowadays our alienation is, as the neo-Marxists argue, less a matter of politics and economics than consciousness: we are estranged from ourselves through psychological self-blockage. Inner and outer realities blur. The collective international psyche displaces our inner conflicts into global warfare that erupts in various "trouble spots" around the globe. So an identity crisis becomes a "capital" crisis, and commodity fetishism becomes a psychic and political condition, not just an economic one. The outcome: We are captivated, not liberated.

However much hype the commerce of this psychopolitics feeds on, it is ultimately hard to find any hilarity in it. Nonetheless, one imagines that Orwell, the socialist believer and the psychological skeptic, would hold that to combat the depersonalizing Unfreedom wrought by postmodernism and globalization, we need not more therapy—but more community.

# Ma Bell and Big Brother

## I

Although the crudest commercial manifestations of "Orwellmania" may have ended in 1984, Orwell and *Nineteen Eighty-Four* have continued to be bandied about by corporate players eager to bask in the radiance of George Orwell's halo—and resolved to annihilate their rivals with the novel's arsenal of big-brotherly catchwords.

So this scene emerges as another episode marking the descent of *Nineteen Eighty-Four* from tragedy into farce. It devotes extended attention to the most notorious example of the practice within the past two decades, indeed perhaps the most blatant instance in Orwell's entire afterlife—the case of "Ma Bell," a.k.a. AT&T. We shall explore here in detail the remarkable way in which *Nineteen Eighty-Four* anticipates and sketches the war games of a segment of the American communication industry. As we shall see, the story of the use of *Nineteen Eighty-Four* in these ad campaigns is more than merely an interesting historical vignette. It is a cautionary tale that provokes reflection on the relationship between art and advertising—and on Orwell's own dim view of the direction that technological advances were taking the modern world.

It all started, fittingly enough, in 1984—the year, not the novel. "It" is the "Great Phone Company Debate," the "Giant Tug of Wire," "Guerrilla Warfare with the Baby Bells," or the "Wire War," as various American editorialists headlined it during the 1980s. The year 1984 witnessed the occurrence of two formerly separate but now converging events—the breakup of AT&T for illegally restraining competition, and the passage of the 1984 Cable Act, which banned Bell Telephone from owning cable franchises or offering competing services. Phone companies, newspapers, and cable companies soon began positioning themselves to compete for control of two mushrooming markets that are today valued at more than $2 trillion: electronic publishing and television. "It" thus became "the biggest telecommunications issue of the 1990s," as *Business Week* characterized it. The controversy continues as the Orwell centennial passes by.[1] But the most heated stage of the controversy occurred in the early part of the last decade, and so I focus my analysis on that period.

Let's review what the so-called telecommunications revolution has meant during the last dozen years for consumers: vastly more sophisticated options for home shopping—e.g., an electronic yellow pages that allows people to look up store listings and order goods on their computers; medical information services that can relay patient information and even X-ray images over the phone lines; news services offering narrow-casted information on stocks, sports, or other topics; the ability to plug your TV into an upgraded telephone line carrying 300 or more data and video channels; and far more. It has meant, in other words, that the telephone companies are becoming our chief news and entertainment provider, which has been precisely the fear of the American newspaper and cable industries.

The rapid speed and scale of these developments have transformed the way in which millions of Americans conduct business and spend their leisure hours—and it has stunned the news and cable industries as well as many consumers. From the start, numerous business interests vied for market share. Beginning in the mid-1980s, there were three groups lobbying Congress to regulate access to the emerging electronic markets: the parent company AT&T, or Ma Bell, confined since 1984 to the long-distance phone market, together with the seven regional Bell operating companies (RBOCs), also known as the "Baby Bells"; leading American newspapers and publishers, represented most vocally by the American Newspapers Publishers Association (ANPA); and the major cable companies, or "cable cos," led by the National Cable Television Association (NCTA).

*Castigating Ma Bell and her offspring as representatives of Newspeak, the American Newspaper Publishers Association portrayed them as a monopoly that would undermine rather than promote competition and could not be effectively regulated. The alleged victims were the zombie-like duckspeakers—i.e., consumers.*

The issues were the following: Should the Baby Bells be permitted to send news, advertising, and television programs over the same wires that provide 95 percent of U.S. homes with basic phone service, possibly allowing the Bells a competitive advantage on the basis of their local monopolies? Should newspapers be safeguarded from direct competition with phone companies for advertising and information services? Should cable companies be protected from the emerging fiber-optic technologies, which would enable the phone companies to send TV signals to consumers over phone wires?

The turf war raged over a single question: Is this a First Amendment debate or an antitrust case? The Bells maintained the former, the newspapers and cable companies the latter. The Bells claimed a First Amendment right to offer information services to anyone who wanted them, even hiring constitutional scholars such as Laurence Tribe of Harvard University to testify in Congress on their behalf. The ANPA and NCTA insisted that it was unfair to allow the companies that owned the phone lines to compete against other service providers for business. They argued as follows: To be information providers as well as common carriers would give the Bells the incentive and ability to sabotage other providers, thereby turning the Baby Bells into baby bullies. Not if we're regulated, insisted the Bells. But the government can't regulate the telcos' use of their own phone wires effectively, answered their antagonists. And so on.

Veterans on Capitol Hill claimed that they had never seen a lobbying campaign so heated, dirty, and well-financed. "A new chapter in the annals of lobbying," said the *Washington Post* of the wire wars. And to a remarkable extent, the information services' war of words drew repeatedly on the arsenal of slogans in *Nineteen Eighty-Four*. Again and again, the catchwords of *Nineteen Eighty-Four* cropped up in op-ed columns and full-page advertisements. Most often it was the newspaper companies trying to hang the monikers of *Nineteen Eighty-Four* on the Baby Bells—though occasionally RBOC spokespersons responded in kind. In the business press, news reports of the feuding also repeated the Orwellian war cries.

"Slouching Toward Big Brother" ran an August 1990 headline in *Business Month*, in which the author took a pro-Bell free-market position to support the Bells' right to compete without restrictions for a share of the new markets. "Big Brother or just the Baby Bells?" asked the *Baltimore Business Journal* in an August 1991 editorial, worrying about the Bells' potential abuse of their local telephone monopolies as they entered the electronic advertising and publishing industries. "The implications are Orwellian," warned David Easterly, president of Cox Newspapers, of the Baby Bells' planned entry into information services. Cathleen Black, president of the ANPA, called the prospect "an Orwellian nightmare." To hear the newspaper industry tell it, Ma Bell was Big Brother—or Big Mama. And her brood of Baby Bells represented a whole troop of child spies, or even junior Thought Police.

Soon the Orwellian language moved beyond the business and trade journals into the editorial columns and advertising pages of the major daily newspapers. "Baby Bells as Big Brother," read the headline of a November 1991 *New York Times* editorial. Arguing that the telephone companies should not be allowed to transmit information over the very phone lines they own and operate, the *Times* feared that court decisions permitting the Bells' entry into information services would enable them to "exploit their monopolistic stranglehold over residential phone lines and dictate what information reaches nearly every home." Not to be outdone, a vice-president for AT&T lashed out in a *Los Angeles Times* column against the "Orwellian logic" of the newspaper industry, which aimed merely to "confuse the public by arguing that greater choice means less information. . . . This debate is not about control of information. It's about freedom of choice and competition." If any organization wields regional monopoly power, concluded the phone company executive, it is the *Los Angeles Times*.

Enough to make the author of *Nineteen Eighty-Four* turn over in his grave, you say? And yet, the "Orwellian" dimension of that media struggle extended far beyond the polemical use of his dystopian novel. Indeed, although the controversy grew out of the AT&T divestiture and the deregulation of cable TV in 1984, so intense did it become in the early 1990s that it also began to resemble, quite uncannily, the texture and shape of *Nineteen Eighty-Four*.

In other words, the electronic war games were far more "Orwellian" than the partisan executives realized. Indeed, what emerges as most stunning is the incredible, galling irony of it all—how these corporate players adopted baldly Orwellian tactics even as they claimed to be exposing the menacing Orwellian threat posed by their rivals. The paradox—flinging Orwell's catch-words while one behaves in starkly Orwellian terms—would be laughable if it were not so outrageous. It represents a powerful confirmation of Orwell's warnings and ongoing relevance—and an equally powerful self-condemnation of corporate America from its own ad pages. Extended attention to the deeper congruences with *Nineteen Eighty-Four* proves illuminating, for it both clarifies the corporations' rival agendas and highlights *Nineteen Eighty-Four's* relevance as a warning about the over-concentration of economic as well as political power. Tracing the parallels between Orwell's world and ours also suggests how *Nineteen Eighty-Four* serves as a model of warfare not merely among competing nation-states, but also among rival conglomerates.

# II

Recall the basic schema and setting of Orwell's fictional masterpiece. Written in the wake of World War II and published in 1949, *Nineteen Eighty-Four* portrays a world divided into three superpowers: Oceania, Eurasia, and Eastasia. Each superstate has its own sphere of influence, operates according to a rigidly hierarchical structure, and pursues continuous phony wars against its rival empires. Each superstate (probably modeled on the U.S., the Soviet Union, and China, respectively) is unable—or, more likely, unwilling—to subdue the others. In fact, alliances often change; their constant warfare is a means whereby the superstates collude with one another to confuse their populaces and consume the surplus product that otherwise could be distributed to make universal peace and plenty possible.

An important department in Oceania's Ministry of Truth is Teledep, the Teleprograms Department, which creates and distributes telescreen programming. One can describe the combatants in the information services wire war as Teledep superstates—the war metaphors are apt. Bell had a $21 million "war chest," as *Business Week* termed it; the newspapers and cable companies reportedly spent about a quarter of that amount between them, though many publishers donated free space for ANPA ads.

Why did Orwell portray three power blocs? The obvious reason is that postwar history was moving in that direction. Three separate spheres of influence were emerging: the western "free" world, the communist world, and the Third World (led by China), all of which controlled vast populations and were fighting border skirmishes with each other through proxy nations. But Orwell also had a subtler point: alliances change. The Soviet Union was Nazi Germany's ally between 1939 and 1941, fought under "Uncle Joe" Stalin on the Allied side from 1941 to 1945, and by 1949 was again an enemy of Britain and the United States.

Analogously, even as the halls of Congress and industry advertisements echoed with the information service behemoths' angry recriminations, alliances were shifting. Given the mutual interests of newspaper and cable companies to disconnect Ma Bell, the information services war chiefly witnessed the telephone companies positioned against all comers. But a surprise occurred in late February 1991 when Ma Bell turned against the Baby Bells. AT&T and the ANPA joined forces against the Bells to push for protective legislation to prevent the Bells from offering information services.

As if that weren't enough, a new twist was that the bitterest enemies—the newspapers and the Bells—were also finding ways of cooperating behind the scenes. Thus, in March 1991, even as the ANPA was launching its newest *Nineteen Eighty-Four* ad against the Bells ("Keep Big Brother at Bay!") and urging newspapers to support legislation that would restrict the Bells' ability to develop information services, ANPA executives were pursuing alliances with the Bells. *Mediaweek* characterized the newspaper-Bell negotiations as "secretive meetings . . . to map future alliances."

To look at such corporate intrigue through the two-way telescreen of George Orwell's dystopia gives one pause. In *Nineteen Eighty-Four* Orwell showed how, despite apparent rivalries, the world in fact suffered under one huge state monopoly. (Indeed, perhaps the charges and counter-charges of "monopoly" in the information services debate were all too accurate.) Orwell attacked the arrogant supposition of superpowers that they could carve up the world among them, much as the papacy parceled out the New World between Spain and Portugal in the sixteenth century. What might he have said about the casual assumption that economic conglomerates should be able to decide among themselves how to divide up the "new world" of information services? That is a question that aficionados of the "If Orwell Were Alive Today" game—the details of which I reserve for our penultimate scene from Orwell's afterlife—might also ponder.

# III

The official language of Oceania is Newspeak, the purpose of which is "not only to provide a medium of expression for the world view and mental habits proper to the devotees of *Ingsoc* [the Party organization], but to make all other modes of thought impossible." Indeed, Newspeak renders opposing ideas "unthinkable." The corruption of language, Orwell believed, could fatally undermine freedom and open the door to tyranny.

Doublethink is a special form of Newspeak and a particular vice of wordsmiths and intellectuals. One practices doublethink by "holding two contradictory beliefs in one's mind simultaneously, and accepting both of them." The Party hack—the doubleplusgood duckspeaker—knows in which direction the Party wishes his or her views to be altered, and thus "knows he is playing tricks with reality." And yet, writes Orwell, "by the exercise of doublethink he also satisfies himself that reality is not violated." The duckspeaker has no trouble affirming the Party slogan featured on all state banners in Oceania: "War Is Peace, Freedom Is Slavery, Ignorance Is Strength."

At times, it seemed as if both the Bells and their opponents used these Party slogans as a blueprint for their ad campaigns. "War Is Peace": Each side claimed that its own effort in the lobbying war was just an attempt to enlighten the public and was not spurred by selfish motives. "Freedom Is Slavery": "Free" competition would lead to the enslavement of captive consumers and of the information services industry generally, argued the ANPA. "Ignorance Is Strength": "They" are deliberately keeping consumers ignorant of the wonders of the new technologies, claimed the Bells; "they" are just floating smokescreens to confuse the public, claimed the Bells' adversaries. The newspapers and cable companies specifically charged that, amidst the overwhelming information overflow generated by the Bells' media blitz, it was impossible to sort out the truth, with the result that consumers were bewildered into passivity and simply accepted the Bells' entry into information services. Several Baby Bell spokespersons made similar accusations. Indeed, what was so unusual was not such charges and counter-charges, said industry observers, but the scale, directness, and fierceness of the campaigns—and, I might add, the brazenness of flinging Orwell's catchwords for Orwellian ends.

Wire war commentators and newspaper industry ads also freely used the "Big Brother is watching you" tag. One ANPA ad claimed that the telcos will soon "know more about you than the IRS"—that they already knew who you phoned and when, and that they would share that information with businesses of all kinds. Meanwhile, RBOC ads charged that the newspapers were practicing thought-control, since they were often the only news source in town. So Bell controlled the phone lines and the newspapers controlled expensive ad space (which the Bells were eagerly buying up). But, given recent legislative and judicial victories, the Bells were in the driver's seat. The restrictive legislation that their opponents proposed was not enacted: it was much easier to block new legislation than to pass it.

Two ANPA ads of the early 1990s offered choice instances of the role that Orwellian strategies—and even Orwell himself—ironically played in the propaganda struggle. The 1991 ANPA convention featured a videotaped ad that could have been a "Two-Minute Hate" spot during Oceania's Hate Week. In it, the Baby Bells were portrayed much as a 1950s McCarthyite comic strip might have described communists: bloated and powerful marauders aiming to exploit their monopoly advantages to crush the free flow of information. The same insinuation was advanced more explicitly in a winter 1991 ad run by the ANPA. The ad appeared in the *New York Times*, the *Washington Post*, and other major newspapers, and it pulled no punches in the by-now familiar ANPA tactic of painting the Baby Bells as Big Siblings—though the ad implied, doubtless inadvertently, that American consumers are themselves little more than gullible Oceania duckspeakers. In the ad, a Bell logo flashes up on the telescreen, which is surrounded by dozens of transfixed zombie-like citizens, shrouded in darkness. Under the Bell logo runs the alleged piece of RBOC doublethink: "MONOPOLY IS COMPETITION." The phrase summed up the newspapers' position that the Bells were a monopoly that would undermine rather than promote competition and could not be effectively regulated. Headlined "Big Brother Is Alive and Well," the ad copy features an exchange between two voices, "Doublespeak" and "Plainspeak," with the latter refuting each and every claim of the former, e.g., that the Bells' entry into information services would spur competition, that they had consumer support, that they were regulated and would not abuse their monopoly position, and so forth. The ad merits quoting at length:

> Now, in Big Brother fashion, the seven regional Bell telephone companies are trying to foist a version of doublespeak on the American public.... The $80 billion Bell monopolies are no longer satisfied with controlling the telephone wires that go into our homes. They want to own and control the news, entertainment, medical, financial, and sports information services that flow over those wires. But, as George Orwell would warn us, whoever controls the telephone wires may well control access to American minds. The only way to keep Big Brother at bay is to separate control of the telephone pipeline from the information that flows through it. ...

The ad closed: "DON'T BABY THE BELLS. KEEP COMPETITION ALIVE."

As with so many claims in the information services wars, this ad promulgated a half-truth. Competition *can* lead to monopoly, by wiping out competition, if competition is too "free," i.e., unregulated or poorly regulated. But since 1984, AT&T had been on a short congressional leash to prevent Ma Bell from gobbling up small fry in the long-distance phone market. While telcos were indeed guilty of price-gouging, regulation had limited AT&T's reach—the company's share of the long-distance market shrank from 90 percent in 1984 to 64 percent in 1990, while long-distance telephone rates had dropped 40 percent since divestiture. In this sense, as George Orwell could indeed affirm: "Freedom is Regulation."

# IV

The corruption of language reflected and promoted the corruption of values and character, Orwell maintained. So we should not forget that the main protagonist of *Nineteen Eighty-Four*, Winston Smith, is a journalist—as was George Orwell. Winston's lover, Julia, is also a popular writer; she works in a section of the Ministry of Truth ("Minitrue") that churns out cheap porn for the masses. She likes her work, but is "not interested in the final product.... Books were just a commodity that had to be produced, like jam or boot-laces." Winston's coveted job is that of leader-writer for the *Times* of Airstrip One (London), which is another department in Minitrue. Winston's "greatest pleasure is his work." He especially enjoys his "delicate pieces of forgery," for they furnish the keen pleasure of an intellectual challenge. Both Winston and Julia concoct "prolefeed," which is defined, according to "The Principles of Newspeak" in the novel's appendix, as "rubbishy entertainment and spurious news which the Party handed out to the masses." Although they are not members of the Inner Party elite, they are Outer Party members holding prestigious positions as Minitrue functionaries.

Some critics of *Nineteen Eighty-Four* prefer to see Winston and Julia as heroic, but it must be emphasized that, by Orwell's high standards, they betray their vocations as writers and public servants. (Indeed it is interesting to compare *Nineteen Eighty-Four* with *Keep the Aspidistra Flying* [1936], an early Orwell novel featuring an autobiographical hero who works in an ad agency. In these and other works, Orwell suggested that most journalists have an uneasy relationship to the truth—but that ad writers too often have none at all.) Orwell was himself a well-known London journalist, a BBC wartime broadcaster, and an editor for the left-wing weekly *Tribune*, and he argued time and again in essays such as "The Writer and Politics" and "Politics and the English Language" that journalists bear a special responsibility since their work shapes a nation's views and values. Winston and Julia betray their calling as journalists because the literary vocation demands holding fast to one's intellectual integrity—i.e., to clear writing, disinterested reporting, and fearless truth-telling.

Did the lobbyists, public relations officers, and editorial writers—many of them journalists or former journalists—in the information services war meet Orwell's high standard of professional integrity? Or were their standards closer to those of Winston and Julia? The evidence suggests that much of their activity was deceptive and self-compromising. While all sides put forward high-toned principles to back their opposing causes, often their public arguments merely masked an unsavory political campaign.

Take, for instance, the First Amendment position of the newspapers. As observers ranging from the *Wall Street Journal* to the *New Republic* pointed out, the newspaper industry's stand was disingenuous. It claimed that restrictions on the Baby Bells' entry into electronic publishing guarded the First Amendment by preventing the Bells from squelching other electronic publishers. And yet, during the 1980s, newspapers had done virtually nothing to develop information services. From what, then, did they need congressional protection?

Their evident objective was to protect the newspaper industry from emerging telecommunications and computer technologies and—more to the point—to protect their classified advertising revenue (which constitutes almost half of most newspapers' revenues). In 1980, ANPA chair Katharine Graham, publisher of the *Washington Post*, declared in *Presstime* that Ma Bell "could siphon off so much revenue from some newspapers that it could endanger their economic viability and, therefore, their strength." That same year, in a meeting with senators sponsoring legislation to deregulate Ma Bell, she was asked: "What you're really worried about is an electronic Yellow Pages that will destroy your advertising base, isn't it?" Graham answered: "You're damn right."

Allen Neuharth, Freedom Forum chair and former ANPA chair—and thus hardly a telco lobbyist—similarly warned against the doublethink rhetoric of the newspaper lobby: "What you have is the champions of the free press saying, 'Stop free enterprise!'" Neuharth dismissed the idea that ANPA was not trying to preserve its marketplace position, that it was only trying to prevent a dangerous concentration of power among information providers. Michael Kinsley's observation in the *New Republic* about ANPA Newspeak was well taken: "When an interest group asks for special legislation in the name of competition, competition is usually what it is trying to prevent." Kinsley also noted that the ANPA was striving to transform the "formerly comforting" image of the telephone into the newest "Orwellian menace."[2]

All three factions claimed that they were more sinned against than sinning. Whatever the scorecard, however, the telcos and their opponents were both guilty of trading on the widely accepted idea that technological advance and the "progress" it represented were automatically good. Do consumers really benefit from thousands more "choices"? Or does an expanded range of options sometimes merely mean that we have more illusory freedoms, more clutter in our lives, and more distractions thanks to high-tech gadgetry?

# V

> [T]he denial of reality . . . is the special feature of
> Ingsoc and its rival systems of thought. If one is to
> rule, and to continue ruling, one must be able to dis-
> locate the sense of reality.
>
> —Nineteen Eighty-Four

George Orwell was not hesitant to call attention to the misfortunes of technological Whiggery—or to challenge the liberal and Marxist shibboleth that "progress = improvement." In *The Road to Wigan Pier* (1937), Orwell condemned what he referred to as "the glittering Wells world." This heralded cornucopia of industrial delights would, as H. G. Wells prophesied in his scientific romances, supposedly transform the earth into a horn of plenty. But Orwell rightly perceived that the realization of the Wellsian utopia would instead bring a plethora of pseudo-choices, a wealth of distinctions without a difference.

"The streamlined men are coming"—was this not Orwell's forecast in *Coming Up for Air* (1939) of the advent of "the organization man," voiced years before the publication of William H. Whyte's 1950s bestseller? Even more central to Orwell's warning about technocracy and utopia is his image of the Ministry of Truth in *Nineteen Eighty-Four*. Orwell depicted corporate regimentation and social conformity in the extreme case of bureaucratic, corporate, oligarchical collectivism. But the main features are the same in both state socialism and corporate capitalism.[3]

And what about today? Does not the young techie glued to his flickering telescreen eerily resemble Winston Smith in his little cubicle at the Ministry of Truth? Winston busily fabricates a Comrade Ogilvy in the hope that his creative distortion will be more serviceable to Oceania's rulers than that of the propagandist colleague in the next cubicle. But is not the cyberspace surfer and the obsessive video gamer a postmodern "organization man" also in thrall to the dictates of his virtual-reality world?

Commenting on one extreme version of this phenomenon, the Slovenian social critic Slavoj Zizek remarks of the Microsoft empire and the "deracinated microserf": "The hired hacker is paid to indulge his so-called individuality. The employer's demand is no longer: 'Behave well and wear gray suits.' Instead it is: 'Be as idiosyncratic as you can and indulge your crazy ideas. You will lose your job if you don't.' You are paid not to slave away at a job you hate, but on the contrary, to 'enjoy' yourself. Yet the psychic pressure is much worse."[4]

The computer geek, the webslinger, the round-the-clock, bleary-eyed beta-tester "enjoys" himself in his "dream job." He (let us admit: it is usually a "he") feels "fulfilled." But let us not forget: Winston Smith "loved his work" too. Admittedly, Winston's work is (from our society's viewpoint) illegal and base, consisting as it does of the falsification, bowdlerization, and "rectification" of history. Nonetheless, are the feverish lucubrations of the socially alienated teenage techie—like Winston's joyful toil—not a splendid, ironic realization of Marx's dream of a labor liberated from alienation? His work fosters self-corruption, if not political corruption; it has a brilliant, gamey, meaningless character. The techie's *joie de vivre* derives from his delight in his own cleverness and ingenuity, quite often a spirit of playful sadism aimed at crushing or crippling all rival players in the medieval (or Nazi or sci-fi) fantasy world of his video screen.

Such pseudo-fulfillment exemplifies a paradox under advanced capitalism that Orwell grasped in *Nineteen Eighty-Four*: ersatz satisfaction via technology. For only in his work—in the absorbing "flow" induced by the creative challenges of professional distortion in the meticulous labor of "rectifying" facts—does Winston feel fully alive. Similarly, the frenzied pace and gambling fever of Internet day traders—or of the corporate "players" in the (now-collapsed) world of dot.com start-ups—often prove so utterly absorbing that they too experience a distorted realization of Marx's vision of de-alienation. They face no apparent split between their jobs and their private pleasures. Yet their work is a whirl of motion without meaning, a game of pseudo-adventure characteristic of the sterile, buzzing activity of contemporary social life.

And what could better illustrate Orwell's warning about such empty living amid technological over-stimulation than the CBS television hit, *Big Brother*?[5] This "real-life" adventure show presents twelve strangers competing in a fake Darwinian competition to "survive." They live in a house outfitted with hidden cameras and microphones. Their actions are monitored around the clock for three months. The houseguests are cut off from the outside world, and each week they eject one of their number. The game's $500,000 jackpot goes to the last player standing—i.e., the one who "survives the struggle." The *Big Brother* show has even witnessed threats of violence. (A *Big Brother* player was expelled midway through the show's summer 2001 season after he put a knife to the neck of a fellow contestant.)

The example of *Big Brother* takes us far beyond the Orwellian machinations of the Baby Bells and their immediate offspring. *Big Brother* is part of a global environment that has generated a new ethos of visibility, voyeurism, and exhibitionism in which technology peers into everything from a child's nursery to military installations. We display the most intimate details of our psyches and physiques on the Internet, and we readily acquiesce to government encroachments on our privacy, which (in the wake of "9/11") we rationalize as "anti-terrorist protection." Commenting on this latter trend, a German newspaper observed: "In the name of security, we permit this to happen to ourselves—and since September 11, more than ever. We wouldn't submit ourselves to a totalitarian ruler today. But without remarking on it, we are almost always supervised, thanks to the most modern cameras in open places—in front of bank ATM windows and discos."

The German article was headlined: "Big Brother Is Everywhere."[6] The headline might well have added: "And we love Big Brother." For it was surely fitting that "Big-Brother-Haus"—the German name for that top-rated "media spectacle," the *Big Brother* television show—had just been nominated for "Unword of the Year."[7]

# Glasnost, Gorby, and the Strange Case of Comrade Orwell

*When shrimps learn to whistle, the Cold War will end.*

—attributed to Nikita Khrushchev

## I

Today George Orwell's face adorns a postage stamp in Poland, a country where, little more than a dozen years ago, he was an unperson. Ah, the mutability of the past!

Let us cast our minds back to the summer of 1989, back to a time when there was still a Union of Soviet Socialist Republics, a time when the Berlin Wall still stood. If we do this, we can begin to fathom the sea change in Orwell's reputation in the formerly communist world, a transformation that became fully visible in June 1989.

That summer the leading Soviet literary journal, *Novy mir* (New World), published *Nineteen Eighty-Four*. Its serialization followed the printing several months earlier of a full-page extract from *Nineteen Eighty-Four* in the chief organ of the Soviet Writers Union, *Literaturnaya gazeta* (Literary Gazette). The extract was accompanied by a stunning half-page drawing of a jackboot stomping on Winston Smith's upturned face. The years 1988–89 also witnessed the publication of several chapters of Orwell's *Animal Farm* in three different Soviet organs, among them *Nedelya*, the literary supplement to the official government newspaper *Izvestia*.

Those publication events were only three of the many cultural initiatives undertaken in the phenomenal reform campaign of Mikhail Gorbachev. Nevertheless, given Orwell's status as the keenest Western critic of the Soviet system under Stalin, their publication possessed much wider significance. When it comes to *samizdat*, some books are more equal than others.

We look in this scene at these complicated issues through the lens of the present and with the advantage of historical hindsight.[1] Obviously, the belated appearance in the USSR of *Nineteen Eighty-Four* and *Animal Farm* represented a new epoch both for the dying USSR and for Orwell's reputation in the communist world. By June 1989, glasnost had moved far beyond the realm of literature and art to include Soviet history and politics; that year had already witnessed not only the spectacle of multiple candidate elections to form the Congress of People's Deputies, but also public criticism of everything ranging from the Soviet space program to Stalin's tyranny and even the fundamentals of Marxism-Leninism.

But the Soviet presentation of certain literary artworks—especially the disingenuous treatment of Orwell's books by the Soviet press—also served as timely "criteria for gauging the credibility of glasnost," in the phrase of Milan Simecka, the Czech translator of *Nineteen Eighty-Four* who had spent 1981–82 in prison for translating Orwell. His words were a cautionary reminder that the ballyhooed reform of Soviet political life was a calculated affair partly designed to preserve the Communist Party's hold on power by obtaining Western loans, trade, and technology transfers.

Likewise, as we shall soon see, the Soviet press discussions of *Animal Farm* and *Nineteen Eighty-Four* possessed ambiguous implications for Soviet efforts to come to terms with the Lenin-Stalin era, for the future conduct of Soviet cultural policy, for reconciliation of the deep philosophical split between Party reformers and hard-timers, and for the much-discussed prospects for a Russian "cultural revolution." Despite the respect that some Western historians and policymakers still harbor for Gorbachev today, it is worth remembering that glasnost literally means "publicity" as well as "openness." The Soviet response to Orwell in 1988–89 was ambivalent. From the perspective of the present, we can see that the truths about Stalinism and the history of Soviet communism in Orwell's satires represented an explosive too powerful for the shaky Soviet system to withstand. In any case, the Soviet reception of Orwell's work should not be, *à la* Winston Smith's "rectifying" of the past at the Ministry of Truth, "lifted clean out of history."

# II

Certainly the *Literaturnaya gazeta* drawing could well have portrayed Orwell's history of reception in the USSR: his dissident democratic socialism and anticommunism repeatedly earned him *Pravda*'s prize epithet, bandied with special gusto during the Stalin years, "Enemy of Mankind." Until the early 1980s, it was always Hate Week for Orwell in the Soviet Union. Not the least of the wry ironies of his Soviet reputation has long been that, despite the frequent castigation of his work in Party organs, none of his books had until 1988 ever been officially published in the communist world. Numerous references to and even reviews of *Animal Farm* and *Nineteen Eighty-Four* had appeared in the Soviet press since the late 1940s. But an official import ban existed on Orwell's work until the late 1980s. Soviet citizens were jailed for possessing his books, and tourists had their copies seized on entry to the USSR.

We can now see that the publication of *Nineteen Eighty-Four* opened a fourth, unprecedented stage in Orwell's Soviet reputation: official recognition. In the 1950s, "Orwell" had been a bogeyman word in the communist press—like Oceania's villainous "Goldstein" (named after Leon Trotsky, a.k.a. Lev Bronstein). *Pravda* and *Izvestia* misidentified Orwell in 1950 as an American and called him "a literary police agent" and "a venal writer on orders . . . from Wall Street." With the thawing out of the Cold War in the 1960s, a new line on Orwell had emerged, during which he was usually ignored as an "unperson." Meanwhile, *Nineteen Eighty-Four* was trumpeted as a satirical portrait of the United States—with the Thought Police as J. Edgar Hoover's FBI, the Ministry of Peace as the Pentagon, and so on.

By the early 1980s, a third phase of Orwell's Soviet reception had crystallized: the "mutability of the past" had become complete. The erstwhile Enemy of Mankind had emerged, *mirabile dictu*, as Comrade Orwell. (As if to sharpen the ironies—as chapter 13 discusses at greater length—Orwell's Soviet canonization occurred just as the Anglo-American Left, including leading avant-garde critics and Marxists, were loudly disowning him and laying much of the blame for the postwar failures of Western socialism at his feet.)

The "rectified" Orwell of Moscow's speakwrites was not just a loyal Party man, but a communist *beau ideal*. Soviet critics transformed Orwell into a Comrade Ogilvy, the Party hero in *Nineteen Eighty-Four* whom Winston Smith invents *ex nihilo* at the Ministry of Truth. Acknowledging that it would be an "exaggeration" to say that Orwell was "a convinced adherent of the Communist outlook," a January 1983 issue of the weekly *New Times* nevertheless hailed Orwell as a worker's hero who "shared dry crusts with the clochards of Paris" and in *Nineteen Eighty-Four* took "the exact measure of capitalism." Anticipating the Evil Empire of "Reaganism," Orwell's (remarkably prescient) message, said the *New Times* reviewer, was that "B.B." is "R.R."

Although the accelerated U.S.–USSR nuclear arms race and the heated rhetorical volleys between the Soviets and Reaganites had at this time sent the Cold War into a new deep freeze, the Andropov regime exempted the West's prize Cold Warrior from blame. In fact, Soviet leaders even approved the publication of a limited edition of *Nineteen Eighty-Four.* (Copies were carefully restricted to the Party elite.) In 1985, the Inner Party itself stepped in with an unprecedented endorsement of Orwell's vision in *Nineteen Eighty-Four*, framed via an argument rather different from that of the *New Times* review of two years earlier: Yes, *Nineteen Eighty-Four* got it right—about capitalism—but its author didn't know it. Georgii Shakhnazarov, a Central Committee official, published an essay praising Orwell for the prescience of his criticism. But he maintained that Orwell, suffering from "bourgeois individualism," mistook the evils of Western capitalism and fascism for the shortcomings of communism and socialism.

Here again, communist reviewers of *Nineteen Eighty-Four* were in the curious position, much like Winston Smith in his job as Party censor at the Ministry of Truth, of falsifying history even as they discussed a book about the falsification of history—and of referring to a work that their audiences had surely never read (except as *samizdat*).

Soviet dissident intellectuals also began to pay public tribute to Orwell's vision in smuggled-out *samizdat*. Unlike the Soviet literary *nomenklatura*, they had no doubts about Orwell's target—though they found it incredible that Orwell was an Englishman who never set foot inside the Soviet empire.[2] Andrei Sakharov, a Moscow dissident intellectual, commented upon reading *Nineteen Eighty-Four* that he was incredulous that "Orwell" was not the pseudonym of a Soviet dissident. The novel possessed such verisimilitude, he said, that he could "not imagine that someone who was not Russian could have written it." German Andreev, in a Moscow *samizdat* journal edited by the historian Roy Medvedev, agreed. Andreev wrote that the USSR of the 1980s exhibited "the contours of the society foreseen by George Orwell in *Nineteen Eighty-Four*."

A personal testament to *Nineteen Eighty-Four*'s power and continuing relevance to Soviet life came from Liudmila Alexeevna, an original member of the international Helsinki Watch Committee, which was formed in the mid-1970s to support freedom of movement across borders and to monitor applications for legal emigrations. Alexeevna stated that Orwell's novel, which she first encountered in *samizdat* in the 1950s, had been a key milestone in her journey toward becoming a dissident. *Nineteen Eighty-Four* was not just a nightmare of the USSR under Stalin, but "prophetic," an accurate portrait of trends still current.

In the fourth stage of Orwell's Soviet reception, readers could finally read him without fearing reprisal. The glasnost game changed things significantly—though not entirely, as we shall soon see. After May 1988 Orwell was no longer being excoriated in the Soviet press as a "troubadour of the Cold War" and his novel treated as a "nonbook,'" noted the anonymous introduction to the excerpt in the *Literaturnaya gazeta*. Indeed the introduction not only conceded, if somewhat obliquely, that Stalinist Russia itself had served as a model for *Nineteen Eighty-Four*, but also frankly criticized the Party for its long-standing proscription of the novel. "Of all the old taboos regarding foreign literature, [the banning of *Nineteen Eighty-Four*] was one of the firmest and least problematical," said the *Literaturnaya gazeta*. The cause of the taboo, implied the editors, wasn't hard to guess: Soviet censors recognized that "B.B." was really "J.S.":

> On the novel's first pages, the reader gets a portrait of a person with a
> moustache looking at other citizens from each corner. This panicky

moment was sufficient to make the book, which was read by the whole world, illegal in our country. . . .

Suggestions to translate the novel (it is reliably reported that there were suggestions in the 1970s) were, as before, swept aside without discussion.

And why, exactly? . . . It should have been translated and analyzed a long time ago, no matter whether Orwell's dissenting political position was flawed or whether he slandered socialism (this was the most widespread accusation). . . . Alas, in the cacophony of the Cold War, the dying voice of the author was not heard. Year after year, his novel became distorted by myths and commentaries to the myths, as if it had fallen into a hall of crooked mirrors. And if one is not afraid to call things by their names, one must admit: By virtue of our biased relationship to Orwell, with all our labels against him, we did not at all hinder—but rather aggravated—this.

The Soviet move to publish *Nineteen Eighty-Four* followed similar strategic gestures in 1987–88 toward several long-suppressed anti-Stalinist novels by Soviet writers. These included the serialization of Yevgeni Zamyatin's *We*, Boris Pasternak's *Dr. Zhivago*, Vasily Grossman's *Life and Fate*, Andrei Platonov's *Chevengur*, Anatoly Rybakov's *Children of the Arbat*, and even excerpts from Aleksandr Solzhenitsyn's early work. Anti-Stalinist movies such as *Repentance* were wildly popular. In 1989 glasnost even included the rehabilitation of Bukharin and other victims of Stalin, the exposure of the 1936–38 Moscow "show trials" as judicial frameups, and the first officially approved criticism of Lenin's policies as a key cause of Stalinism.

Gorbachev's staunchest advocates could be found within the Soviet intelligentsia. And these welcome cultural events of 1987–89 must today be appreciated as part of Gorbachev's calculated program to enlist Soviet and Western intellectuals in his campaign to revamp the Soviet bureaucracy and the Communist Party. Numerous questions about the nature and limits of this campaign therefore arise for the literary historian. Was glasnost aiming at a more open society or more favorable foreign public relations? Was Gorbachev's age of perestroika no more than a relative thaw, comparable to the Khruschev years of the late 1950s—out of the cultural Siberia of the Brezhnev-Andropov-

Chernenko years and into a mild Moscow winter?

If the example of Orwell is any guide, the answer is that Gorbachev sought to muffle the truths embodied in *Nineteen Eighty-Four*, fully aware that those truths could undermine both him and the Party. Unlike the case with the earlier phases of Orwell's reception in the USSR, however, when he was either falsely celebrated, airbrushed out of literary history, or routinely smeared, Gorbachev and the official Soviet intelligentsia adopted a nuanced strategy that entailed approaching *Nineteen Eighty-Four* less as a propaganda sheet, simply to be assaulted or claimed, and more as a politically committed novel inviting Soviet self-criticism.

So, in the idiom of Watergate Newspeak, the Soviet response to *Nineteen Eighty-Four* was at best a "limited hang-out," with plenty of threatening "expletives deleted." For example, even as the introduction to the *Literaturnaya gazeta* extract, titled "The Ministry of Truth," acknowledged that *Nineteen Eighty-Four* bore relevance to Stalinist Russia, it suggested that Orwell's main target was fascism. ("He asked a difficult question: Couldn't fascism find fertile ground in England and, if so, how soon? How will it appear? What form will it take? Thus arose the shape of the novel.") Indeed, neither Stalin nor Stalinism is specifically mentioned in the *Literaturnaya gazeta* or *Novy mir* introductions, although—*mutatis mutandis*—Big Brother is likened to Chairman Mao, Minitrue fabrication of national heroes is associated with the Chinese Cultural Revolution (with Comrade Ogilvy explicitly compared to Ley Fen), Hate Week is identified with Islam, and the "totalitarian shadowing" of the population by means of "the newest electronic equipment" is called a "reality precisely in the advanced countries of the West, most of all America."

So the old habits of Stalinism were to die hard even in the Gorbachev era. "The time has come," concluded the *Literaturnaya gazeta*, "to free ourselves from the stagnant prohibitions, to discard the myths, to shatter the crooked mirrors, and to read George Orwell thoughtfully and without prejudice."

But that time had not yet come.

Sergei Zalygin, editor of *Novy mir*, wrote: "It's possible that Orwell wrote his book with a concrete address—the address of socialism. But the time has passed when the book, to put it delicately, embarrasses us."

No, that time had not yet passed.

# III

Perhaps even more embarrassing for the Soviets was *Animal Farm*, whose "concrete address" could not be clearer. Indeed one might have assumed that the one-to-one correspondences between historical events and this biting allegory of the Bolshevik Revolution and post-revolutionary era would have been inescapable in the age of glasnost. But the September 1988 *Nedelya* notes only that *Animal Farm* is "surprisingly contemporary." It is "directed against those who make a mockery of [socialist] ideals, openly or in a disguised way, against political demagoguery and political adventurism." No mention was made of the fable's historical referents.

Likewise the March and July 1988 issues of *Rodnik*, published by the Latvian Communist Party, blatantly contradicted Orwell's famous statement (in the original *samizdat* Ukrainian preface of 1947) that his main goal in *Animal Farm* was to "expose the myth" that "Russia is a socialist country." Instead the March *Rodnik* noted (falsely) that *Animal Farm* alludes to the Night of the Long Knives in Nazi Germany (Hitler's June 1934 purge of Ernst Rohm and the S.A.) and to the 1937–38 liquidation of the anarchist militias in the Spanish Civil War. In a single passing phrase the editors mentioned that *Animal Farm* also refers to "the Moscow trials of 1937." But then come the old appeals to historical realism. Readers who "can well imagine the true picture of that period, with all its tragedies, and with the great stress and strain of the struggle," will find it "impossible to support" the fable's portrait of a time of "exultant tyranny."

Indeed, the *Rodnik* editors concluded by pointedly arguing for the "universality" of *Animal Farm* as a fable about tyranny in general. "People have tried many times to connect *Animal Farm* to our history, but such efforts are biased, not to mention that they water down the author's intention." Orwell's "grotesque animal paradise" is "multifaceted," possesses special (though unspecified) "contemporary relevance," and is "by no means open to a single interpretation."

These exegetical dodges involved much more than misleading literary criticism or historical inaccuracies. The case of "Comrade Orwell" was significant precisely because it became a site where the anxious jumble of hopes, fears, and tensions pressing upon Soviet attempts to confront the past converged and convoluted. The result was a good deal of strenuously acrobatic doublethinking.

Opening the books on the Soviet past, that is, was not just a matter of dumping "stagnant prohibitions." Orwell's writings had everything to do with the Soviet present of the 1980s. For history legitimates and disinherits. Credibility in politics depends to no small degree on one's political genealogy. Eminent ancestors make one's causes respectable; disreputable ancestors taint and disgrace. Virtue and guilt by association are central to the conduct of political life.

The "embarrassment" about *Nineteen Eighty-Four* and *Animal Farm*, then, was nothing less than about how to connect the Leninist-Stalinist past with the Gorbachevite present of the 1980s. Orwell's work raised the fearful questions: How far can Gorbachev's "new thinking" proceed before it undercuts the family tree traceable to the Revolution and thereby threatens the foundations of the Soviet political system? How long will Gorbachev be able through the glasnost campaign to exploit *samizdat* so as to bolster his political position against his main opponents, the Party's hard-line conservatives? Or will the demands fueled by the recovery of a national memory overtake and undermine him? How far can the unwriting of the rewritten history go before it subverts the Party's very claim to embody and interpret "historical truth"?

Notably, even when a book like Arthur Koestler's *Darkness at Noon* (1941), based on the Moscow show trials of the 1930s, was explicitly acknowledged (in the Leningrad monthly *Neva* in 1988) to pertain to "the Stalinist terror," the editors insisted that only "dogmatic shortsightedness" makes it "possible to consider this outstanding work of literature as anti-Soviet." Such deceitful introductions to Orwell and Koestler were representative of much Soviet cultural criticism during the glasnost age. They alert us to how far glasnost had still to go before it truly signified "openness"—and also to what never happened in the USSR, the glasnost fanfare notwithstanding. The Soviet leadership never permitted a free press. (The USSR's "Index" of forbidden literature had shrunken by a third before the regime's collapse in 1991, but it existed to the bitter end. Nor was the state's fundamental right to suppress "undesirable" material ever put in question.)

In hindsight, we can see that Gorbachev mainly presented cultural "glasnostrums." But ideas *do* have consequences. And they are not so easily calibrated. In 1989, just weeks after *Rodnik* published the secret codicils of the Molotov-Ribbentrop pact, which revealed the sordid details of Stalin's clandestine deal with Hitler that led to the illegal 1940 annexation of the Baltic republics, the sitting parliament of the Estonian Republic declared its sovereignty and its independence from Moscow. (The Supreme Soviet of the Union subsequently quashed this declaration of independence, and the Congress of People's Deputies formed a special commission to investigate the events of 1940.) Throughout the spring of 1989, Latvians, Lithuanians, and Georgians protested loudly against recently passed amendments to the Soviet constitution, which gave the Supreme Soviet in Moscow the right to declare martial law throughout the nation and to overrule all decisions by the republican parliaments (such as Estonia's secession vote).

Gorbachev would come to see that, in touting glasnost, he had unleashed a Frankenstein's monster that would destroy his credibility. "The protests are part of perestroika," Gorbachev lamely explained. "Glasnost and perestroika have permitted people to express their opinions on problems which have accumulated over the years." In 1989 the "expressions of opinion" included massive nationalist demonstrations in Georgia, ethnic riots by native Uzbeks in Uzbekistan against Meskhetian Turks, and an Azerik-fomented civil war in Azerbaijan and Armenia that claimed hundreds of lives. The violence would continue—in Chechnya above all—and take thousands more lives in the 1990s, even after all these states had gained their independence and the USSR had collapsed in December 1991.

Gorbachev could not afford to let these "protests" go on indefinitely. He tried to head off a Chinese-style political upheaval by providing a safety valve for dissent. But he failed. Gorbachev found that starting a counter-revolution was far easier than controlling its direction. The avalanche of discontent toward perestroika from angry Party conservatives, inflamed ethnic nationalists, and striking workers eventually brought down his great experiment in managing a counter-revolution from the top.

# IV

Life does not begin at seventy-two. And yet, it was seven decades until the Soviet Union at last seriously confronted what the Germans refer to as *die unbewältigte Vergangenheit*, "the unmastered past." Unlike the case of Germany and the Nazi revolution, however, Soviet authorities have no watershed event by which to disclaim continuity and thus disavow their past: the Soviet Communist Party had ruled without a break since 1917. Thus, the Party and the Soviet system, not just one man and his "cult of personality," were in some sense responsible for "vaporizing" seventeen million Enemies of Mankind in the 1930s and '40s.

No amount of official duckspeaking could ultimately evade the dilemma: the Party's claims to legitimacy rested on its continuity with the past, which the Party speakwrites had rewritten and re-rewritten since Lenin and Stalin; but the more that the historical truth emerged and clearly evinced an unbroken string of Party coverups, the more difficult became Party efforts to "contain" the horrific past—and the less secure became Party claims to legitimacy in the present.

"There should be no forgotten names and blank pages in Soviet history," declared Gorbachev in a much-quoted statement in 1988. The task of remembering and blankfilling, however, was not so easy as he implied. (In 1987, Soviet schools even canceled Russian history exams because the Soviet education ministry could not agree on a satisfactory explanation of post-1917 events.)

Until 1989, Gorbachev and other supporters of rapid cultural liberalization calculated that they could resuscitate unpersons and fill in memory holes as needed to build public trust and improve the performance of the Soviet system. They figured that they could master the present by leaving the past unmastered—i.e., by circumscribing the Stalin era and merely adjusting the official record. More concerned with economic reconstruction and Party reform than with artistic policy, they reasoned that any harm done to Soviet claims of legitimacy by the publication of "mere" fiction about the "quickly receding" past would be outweighed by gains in credibility and popular support for perestroika.

As history soon showed, that turned out to be wishful thinking. All the excitement generated by the USSR's publication of Orwell and other anti-Stalinist writers during the late 1980s notwithstanding, what the world witnessed was not a cultural revolution, but a very partial reclamation project.

What the *Literaturnaya gazeta* termed "the hall of crooked mirrors" into which *Nineteen Eighty-Four* "had fallen"—with the emphasis proudly placed on the past tense—was part of the sleight-of-hand of glasnost.

Indeed, it would not be until the late 1990s, after publication of an unexpurgated edition of *Nineteen Eighty-Four* in Russia, that the former USSR's "distorted" and "biased relationship to Orwell" changed fundamentally—and Russia's new cultural leaders and intellectuals could hold the fearsome mirror directly and unflinchingly up to themselves.

4

# Appreciating *Animal Farm*
# in the New Millennium

## I

Our first three scenes have witnessed capitalist travesty and communist tragicomedy. Or better: comic opera performed, as it were, with a libretto excerpted from *Nineteen Eighty-Four*. But rather neglected amid these ironic burlesques of American commerce and Soviet highcult occasioned by Orwell's last book is his previous one: the magnificent little beast fable of totalitarianism that launched him into fame and that he often called his "favorite" book, *Animal Farm*.

This scene spotlights the changing contexts and media of *Animal Farm*, especially how their sharp discontinuities since the collapse of the USSR in December 1991 have altered the production and reception of Orwell's fable. Our focus is on how differently Orwell's allegory is being encountered by new generations in the twenty-first century—that is, among those who are not even old enough to remember the existence of the Soviet Union. Extended consideration is devoted to a representative example of these changes and their implications: the remarkable new film adaptation of *Animal Farm* and how its technological marvels are transforming the young viewer's experience of Orwell's allegory.

# II

In October 1999, Turner Network Television broadcast its $24 million adaptation of Orwell's *Animal Farm*, co-produced by Robert Halmi Sr. and Hallmark Entertainment. The film is partly animated, with great British Shakespearean actors such as Patrick Stewart (Napoleon) and Peter Ustinov (Old Major) providing the animal voices.[1] Halmi, a refugee from Soviet-occupied Hungary during the early postwar era—he had spent World War II in Budapest under Nazi rule—said that he had intended to film *Animal Farm* for decades, but that the technology hadn't been available to do a sophisticated animated version. Jim Henson's Creature Shop, a cutting-edge voice-tech firm, helped provide the combination live-action and animated effects that the movie incorporates. Unfortunately, the new adaptation of *Animal Farm*—the first since the 1955 British version by the husband-wife team of John Halas and Joy Batcheler—aired as the news media were commemorating the fiftieth anniversary of *Nineteen Eighty-Four*. As a result, Orwell's Aesopian fable was lost in the long shadow of his anti-utopian nightmare.

It may take longer to watch Halmi's two-hour adaptation of *Animal Farm* than to read Orwell's little allegory of revolution and totalitarianism. Given the entertainment preferences in the age of the mass media, however, it is overwhelmingly likely that many people in the future—especially school-age youth—will encounter *Animal Farm* first, or perhaps exclusively, through this new video version. The new adaptation merges computer graphics, humans, animals, and what is termed in the animated film industry "animatronics"—animal robot "doubles" who possess human voices. While such high-tech puppetry and computer effects had already been used to stunning effect in *Babe* (1995) and *Babe: Pig in the City* (1998), Creature Shop takes them further in *Animal Farm*. These technological innovations make the new *Animal Farm* a breakthrough film.

Although the 1955 animated version of *Animal Farm* was followed by adaptations of the fable into a play (in 1964) and musical (in 1984), *Animal*

*Farm* remained—at least until now—best known in its literary version. Certainly this is a testimony to the beauty and power of Orwell's writing. But another reason, says Halmi, is that the Halas-Batcheler film couldn't have an impact dramatic enough to compete with readers' imaginations of the fable. Before animatronics, nothing substantially new on a technical (and imaginative) level could be done with *Animal Farm*.[2] Once animatronics became highly sophisticated, it seemed timely to the producers to re-film Orwell's parable. But as Halmi's long-term desire to produce *Animal Farm* suggests, he also had compelling personal—and political—reasons for aiming to bring Orwell's allegory to the big screen. That desire has its origins in Halmi's boyhood battle with East European communism. When Orwell published the British edition of *Animal Farm* in August 1945, Halmi was a young anticommunist resistance fighter battling Stalinism in his native Hungary.

"I was hungry . . . and surrounded by barbed wires and the so-called Iron Curtain," Halmi recalls. "We were completely isolated. You thought, 'Nobody knows about us, nobody knows what communism is, nobody knows what terror is.' And all of a sudden, *Animal Farm* was published and was smuggled into Hungary. It became my bible."[3] When Halmi was able to flee Hungary, he took Orwell's fable with him. "I have lived with this book for more than fifty years," he says.[4] Finally, by the mid-1990s, the science of movie-making caught up with Halmi's ambition to make pigs talk like commissars.[5]

# III

Then again, Halmi's reverence for *Animal Farm*—his "bible"—was apparently not so great as to keep him from taking considerable liberties in altering elements of characterization and plot.[6] Working closely with Halmi, screenwriters Alan Janes and Martyn Burke made numerous changes to Orwell's book.

Some of the alterations are minor. For instance, during Snowball and Napoleon's argument about building a windmill, Orwell doesn't include Napoleon urinating on the plans and Snowball responding: "You pig!" Other changes may have unexpected implications for the composition of the viewing audience. For example, Janes and Burke add a fleeting sex scene of Farmer Jones and the wife of another farmer in bed together. Minor though the change is—presumably, it is meant to suggest Jones's moral corruption—it might, as the TV critic for the *Los Angeles Times* lamented, deter parents from watching the adaptation with their ten-year-old children.

Still other revisions seek to update *Animal Farm* by cleverly linking it to topics such as animal rights and vivisection. For instance, Stalin's purges and show trials during 1936–38 are justified by the pigs as a violation of the "Crimes Against Animalism" code—an obvious allusion to the "crimes against the People" statutes of Stalin-era communist regimes. Unlike *Babe*, the charming fable about a gallant piglet that saves sheep and helps a kindly farmer win a prize—or its darker sequel, *Babe: Pig in the City*—the *Animal Farm* adaptation features numerous scenes of animal abuse and oppression, perpetrated not just by the humans but also the pigs. For instance, the film highlights barbarous torture scenes (including a grisly scene of an old hog being chopped up) and cruel indifference to animals' fates after their productive years (especially the powerful, tragic scene of aged Boxer, the noble yet gullible cart horse, being sent to the glue factory). The effect of these scenes is to promote an anti-vivisectionist animal rights agenda—something approaching PETA propaganda.

Janes and Burke have also added a narrator, a beautiful border collie named Jessie. Following Orwell's plot and characterization, the logical candidate for such a role would have been Benjamin the donkey, an intelligent skeptic and wry observer of events on *Animal Farm*, and the character often regarded as a stand-in for Orwell himself. But the adapters obviously sought an animal with which viewers would have a natural sympathy: a collie was an unsurprising and reasonable choice. Making Jessie the narrator gives the story a consistent, sympathetic voice.

Another successful decision was to move the story's timeline into the mid-1950s (Orwell ends the allegory with the 1943 Teheran Conference), which makes it possible to put a television in the barn, where it becomes a powerful propaganda device. Used by the pigs to distract the other animals, who instantly become mesmerized by its black-and-white images of pretty actresses and modern appliances, television is a more powerful opiate of the people than Marx ever dreamed of. Director John Stephenson uses vintage black-

and-white newsreel footage as an example of the pigs' propaganda films. Drugged by TV, the rank-and-file animals are content to follow the Seven Commandments of Animalism painted on the barn by Squealer (the pig who symbolizes *Pravda* and the Soviet news agency TASS).

I imagine that Orwell would have smiled with satisfaction at most of these changes. But it's also likely that he would have taken issue with the altered ending, a sort of epilogue that is meant to be more hopeful than Orwell's bitter final scene. (The 1955 Halas-Batcheler adaptation tried something similar: a barnyard rebellion to overthrow the tyranny of pig rule, possibly inspired by the failed uprising against the communist dictatorship in East Germany in June 1953 and doubtless also the ideological preferences of its financial backer and distributor, the CIA.)[7]

As Jessie remarks in a voice-over at the end of the film: "The walls have now fallen, the scars have now healed, and life goes on." These words give way to the strains of "Blueberry Hill," sung by Fats Domino. The farm's new owners are arriving: a man, a woman, and their children. Not drunkards like Jones, they look reassuringly bourgeois, upscale, and suburban. Halmi's revisionist postscript is evidently intended as an allusion to the fall of the Berlin Wall and the dissolution of the Soviet Union. But it undercuts the seriousness of the film and is at cross-purposes with the sense of urgency felt during the early Cold War era, when Stalinism was crushing democracy throughout Eastern Europe. Halmi's ending makes it seem instead as if the recent passage from communist tyranny to liberal democracy was as easy as walking up the driveway of the family farm.

"It's more about repression than Stalinism," director John Stephenson has remarked in defense of the altered ending. "You can see the characters in any organization, in any human group. They're typical of the human race." Stephenson added that *Animal Farm* "became an anti-dictatorship book. It applies to Kosovo today as much as it applied to Hungary then."

Certainly the satiric scope of Orwell's fable is universal—but it needs remembering that *Animal Farm* is also an allegory: its plot and characters have a specific correspondence to events in the USSR from 1917 to 1943. The adapters' commercially motivated "revisionism" is undeniably more innocent than the communist sort, but it is nonetheless worrisome. By altering Orwell's allegory into a general diatribe against "repression," the adapters rob Orwell's fable of its historical moorings and risk misleading viewers about the events that it satirizes—especially considering that younger viewers' (and even younger teachers') grasp of the historical events of the first half of the twentieth century may be more than a bit shaky.

Moreover, younger viewers may approach *Animal Farm* as if it were just a dress rehearsal for Orwell's themes in *Nineteen Eighty-Four*. But the fact is that, despite their similarity as "didactic fantasies," in the phrase of Alex Zwerdling,[8] *Animal Farm* and *Nineteen Eighty-Four* are notably different in their satirical techniques and targets. *Nineteen Eighty-Four* satirizes not just the Soviet Union and Stalinism but also elements of Nazi Germany, American capitalism, and the British welfare state. *Animal Farm*, on the other hand, is an allegory of the history of the Bolshevik Revolution and its aftermath, with numerous one-to-one correspondences between its key episodes and events in the USSR. But that totalitarian system collapsed more than a decade ago, making its history even more distant to a potential international viewing audience numbering in the hundreds of millions—including adolescents now encountering *Animal Farm* who were not even of school age when the Soviet Union dissolved in December 1991.[9] These facts necessitate a closer look at the fable's multivalent meaning, political significance, and historical context.

The misunderstandings of the new *Animal Farm* film are not so different from the misunderstandings that have haunted young readers' experience of the book, and a detailed examination of the latter may assist the millions of young viewers who will soon encounter *Animal Farm* on the screen (and perhaps never read the book). Having taught *Animal Farm* since the late 1970s both to high school and university students, I have noticed how Orwell's fable both engages and (inadvertently) misleads present-day readers. It is crucial *not* to approach *Animal Farm* merely as "great literature" that "transcends" its time and place—as one might with, say, some of the poetry of the great modernist writers. We need, therefore, to appreciate the specific historical and ideological conditions of World War II and the early postwar era, for they shaped both Orwell's conception of *Animal Farm* and how its original audience received it.

# IV

When George Orwell submitted *Animal Farm* in 1945 to Dial Press in New York, it was rejected with the explanation that "it was impossible to sell animal stories in the USA."[10] That anecdote is comical in hindsight, but the editors at Dial Press were not the only readers of *Animal Farm* to make this mistake. British readers did, too. Indeed, some British booksellers erroneously placed it in the "children's section" of their shops. (Orwell had to scurry around London to switch it to the "adult fiction" shelves.) Indeed, many early readers of Orwell's little masterpiece apparently did not realize that it was a brilliant work of political satire. They read the book much as did the young son of the art critic Herbert Read, one of Orwell's friends, who reported that his boy "insisted on my reading it, chapter by chapter . . . , and he enjoys it innocently as much as I enjoy it maliciously."[11]

It does seem absurd to the knowledgeable present-day reader that the literary public of the 1940s could have read *Animal Farm* "innocently." How could editors and publishers misjudge a sophisticated classic for a children's tale? How could they confuse an ingenious attack targeting the betrayal of revolution in general—and the Soviet Union in particular—for a simple animal story? I find that today's college students are liable to make the same error, and the cause of their confusion has to do with the language and form of *Animal Farm*. The fact is that *Animal Farm* works so beautifully on the literal level as an animal story that it lulls the unwary reader into staying on the surface, thereby misleading him or her into missing its underlying political and historical references. Ironically, then, it is a measure of *Animal Farm's* artistic excellence that it "fools" some readers into taking it for an animal story. The plain language, straightforward plot, and one-dimensional characters mask the complex subject matter and context. *Animal Farm* is simple on the surface—and quite subtle beneath it. As historically informed and artistically alert readers have long appreciated, *Animal Farm* is far more than an uncontroversial little children's book. A new generation of readers and viewers will need to keep the following basic points in mind, especially now that the geopolitical conditions that once sustained the pertinent historical and political frames of reference have largely dissolved with the dissolution of the Soviet Union itself.

First, *Animal Farm* is a political allegory of the history of the USSR—sometimes jokingly referred to as an "animallegory." Traditionally, an allegory is a symbolic tale that treats a spiritual subject under the guise of a worldly one, such as Langland's *Piers Plowman* and Bunyan's *Pilgrim's Progress*.

Second, *Animal Farm* is an allegory written in the form of a beast fable, in which the misadventures of animals expose human follies. Orwell draws on our cultural stereotypes of animals. Pigs have a reputation for selfishness and gluttony. Horses are slow-witted, strong, gentle, and loyal. Sheep are brainless, follow the flock, and have no individual initiative. Orwell's point of departure for the fable was a statement from Karl Marx's *Economic and Philosophical Manuscripts of 1844*: "The worker in his human functions no longer feels himself to be anything but animal. What is animal becomes human and what is human becomes animal."

So Orwell adapts the literary forms of the allegory and beast fable for his own purposes. "The business of making people conscious of what is happening outside their own small circle," he once wrote, "is one of the major problems of our time, and a new literary technique will have to be evolved to meet it."[12] Orwell's symbolic tale takes a political subject and treats it under the guise of an innocent animal story. But *Animal Farm* contains a stinging moral warning against the abuse of power.

Like most allegories, *Animal Farm* operates by framing one-to-one correspondences between the literal and symbolic levels. Its events and characters function as a simple story on the literal level. But they also operate on a symbolic level for readers who know the "code." In this case, the code is the history of Soviet communism. Orwell subtitled *Animal Farm* "a fairy story," but this was meant as an ironic joke: his beast fable was no mere "fairy story," but was happening, right then, in Stalin's Russia—and could happen anywhere.

Parts of Orwell's "code" are easy to "crack." For instance, the pigs represent the Communist Party. The pig leader Napoleon and his rival Snowball symbolize the dictator Stalin and the communist leader Leon Trotsky. Old Major is a composite of Karl Marx and Vladimir Ilyich Lenin, the major theorist and the key revolutionary leader of communism, respectively. "Beasts of England" is a parody of the *Internationale*, the Communist Party song. The rebellion in chapter 2 represents the Russian Revolution of October 1917. The battle of the Cowshed in chapter 4 depicts the subsequent civil war. Mr. Jones and the farmers are the loyalist Russians and foreign forces who tried but failed to dislodge the Bolsheviks, the revolutionaries led by Lenin. The animals' false confessions in chapter 7 represent the purge trials of the late 1930s. Frederick's stratagem to exchange banknotes for corn recalls Hitler's betrayal of the 1939 Nazi-Soviet pact in June 1941. The first demolition of the windmill, which Napoleon blames on his pig rival, Snowball, symbolizes the failure of the first Five-Year Plan, an industrial plan to coordinate the Soviet economy in the 1920s that did not bring prosperity. The second destruction of the windmill by Frederick's men corresponds to the Nazi invasion of Russia in 1941. The meeting of pigs and humans at the end of the story represents the November 1943 wartime conference in Teheran, which Stalin, Roosevelt, and Churchill attended.[13]

If a reader misses such allegorical correspondences, he or she may completely misread the book. In fact, *Animal Farm* functions as an allegory on four levels. On the immediate verbal level, it is a children's story about an animal rebellion on a farm. As an animal story, the work invites the reader to respond compassionately to the sufferings of vulnerable beasts. Indeed, Orwell once explained that a scene of a suffering horse (who later became the model for Boxer) inspired him to conceive *Animal Farm*:

> The actual details of the story did not come to me for some time until one day (I was then living in a small village) I saw a little boy, perhaps ten years old, driving a huge cart-horse along a narrow path whipping it whenever it tried to turn. It struck me that if only such animals became aware of their strength, we should have no power over them, and that men exploit animals in much the same way as the rich exploit the proletariat. I proceeded to analyze Marx's theory from the animals' point of view.[14]

Beyond an explicit, literal level, then, are three symbolic levels of meaning. First, as we have seen, *Animal Farm* is a historical satire of the Russian Revolution and the subsequent Soviet dictatorship. Second, *Animal Farm* is a political treatise that suggests larger lessons about power, tyranny, and revolution in general.[15] On this level, Orwell's book has a much broader historical and political message, one that is not limited to criticism of the Soviet Union. And third, *Animal Farm* is a fable. It carries a universal moral about the "animality" of human nature.[16] For instance, by the conclusion of *Animal Farm*, some of the pigs are walking upright and wearing human clothes: they are little different from corrupt human beings. The farm mirrors our human world, which is sometimes referred to as the "human circus" because the various types of human personalities can be compared to the character types of animals. Some humans are like pigs, others resemble sheep, still others can be compared to dogs, and so forth. On this level, Orwell's "fable" about human nature transcends both history and particular political events. We see how the fundamental characters of animals do not change. The animals behave consistently, in either a noble or selfish spirit, whether they are confined in the feudal, aristocratic, conservative farm run by Mr. Jones or the modern, progressive, radical "animal farm" ruled by Napoleon.

If the young son of Herbert Read thought that *Animal Farm* was just an animal story, the reaction of the son of the poet William Empson, one of Orwell's friends at the BBC, reflects another sort of misreading. Empson reported that his boy, a supporter of the Conservative Party, was "delighted" with *Animal Farm* and considered it "very strong Tory [Conservative] propaganda." Empson concluded his letter to Orwell about *Animal Farm*:

> I read it with great excitement. And then, thinking it over, and especially on showing it to other people, one realizes that the danger of this kind of perfection is that it means very different things to different readers. . . . I certainly don't mean that that is a fault in the allegory. . . . But I thought it worth warning you (while thanking you very heartily) that you must expect to be "misunderstood" on a large scale about this book; it is a form that inherently means more than the author means, when it is handled sufficiently well.[17]

Empson was right: Then and later, Orwell's book came to mean many different things to different people. And yet, even those who saw quite clearly the intended political message of *Animal Farm* rejected the book—and precisely for that reason. Indeed, its political incorrectness was the major reason why *Animal Farm* was rejected by two dozen British and American publishers before gaining acceptance for publication. (The scarcity of paper during wartime was a third, important reason for its continued rejection.) Given the wartime alliance among the Allies, some publishers deemed *Animal Farm* far too controversial. Four British editors rejected *Animal Farm* because they did not want to risk offending the Soviet Union by publishing such a harsh assault on its history. In the United States, numerous editors—perhaps as many as twenty, according to Peter Viereck—turned it down because they were Soviet sympathizers who considered Orwell's attack on the USSR unbalanced and exaggerated.[18]

But public opinion in Britain and America changed toward the USSR in 1945–46. As the need for wartime solidarity with the USSR came to an end, and as Stalin's armies aggressively occupied much of Eastern Europe, publishers became more willing to criticize the Soviets. "Uncle Joe" no longer seemed so benign.

Ironically, *Animal Farm* now seemed to be a prophetic book, one ahead of its time: Orwell seemed to have predicted the collapse of the Allied alliance. By unveiling the Soviet dictatorship as the new enemy of Western democracy, *Animal Farm* seemed to forecast the advent of the Cold War.

Another twist of ironic fate was at hand for *Animal Farm*. A work that, just months earlier, had been rejected by publishers as either an unmarketable "animal story" or a dangerous political book, now became a runaway bestseller.

# V

When a Chinese version of *Animal Farm* was staged in Beijing in November 2002, the play's director—who was worried that Communist Party officials might censor his production—was distraught to encounter a very different problem. "They don't get it," said the director, reporting that playgoers seemed to find it amusing and failed to grasp the political allegory—despite the fact that one of his pig protagonists is female and the wife of Napoleon (a veiled referent to Jiang Qing, the tyrannical spouse of Mao Zedong.) Some theatergoers said in exit interviews that they had never before heard of Orwell or his satirical fable.[19]

So here we have yet another example of the paradoxical, even contradictory responses that Orwell's brilliant fable evokes: *Animal Farm* emerged from and has generated political controversy—but it has also sometimes been naïvely misjudged as unpolitical—and American (or even Western) readers are not alone in their confusion. That fact should further remind us that, in order to better comprehend how and why such extremely opposed views of the book have arisen—and doubtless will continue to arise (or even increase) with the new film adaptation—readers will need to recall the historical and political context of Orwell's fable.

And let us not forget that Orwell himself judged *Animal Farm* to be his literary masterpiece. As he declared in his essay, "Why I Write," "*Animal Farm* was the first book in which I tried, with full consciousness of what I was doing, to fuse political purpose and artistic purpose into one whole."[20]

# II.

## Orwell's GDR?
## or Post-Mortems on the "Better Germany"

# 5

# In the Land of
# Little Brother

## I

George Orwell led me to Germany.

That's an odd thing to say, given that Orwell spent only a few weeks in Germany, as an *Observer* correspondent in occupied Germany at the close of World War II in April-May 1945.

But Orwell's German visit—and especially his daily contact with Nazi propaganda during his wartime stint as a BBC broadcaster (1941–43)—left its imprint on the language and atmosphere of *Nineteen Eighty-Four.* That's why his work has resonated powerfully for successive generations of German readers.

And that's how the "Orwell connection" drew me, ultimately, to Germany. It was in the context of what one historian has called the Germans' "fascination" with *Nineteen Eighty-Four* that I began to explore German history. My encounter with Orwell's work a quarter-century ago had established my first visceral connection to postwar socialism, anti-totalitarianism, and European cultural politics—and it led me to write two books about the educational system of the onetime German Democratic Republic (GDR).[1] Hailed by German socialists as *das bessere Deutschland* (the "better Germany"), the GDR was otherwise known simply as East Germany, the communist state that passed into oblivion on October 3, 1990, when it united with the eleven states of West Germany and entered the Federal Republic of Germany (FRG).

Indeed, it was precisely the convergences between the worlds of *Nineteen Eighty-Four* and divided Germany that originally drew me to study Germany's cultural politics. "Little brother," an East German acquaintance of mine whimsically called his former homeland—a clever reference not just to Oceania's dictator but to the official GDR paeans to the USSR as "Our Great Socialist *Bruderland.*"

For years, it was the Orwellian flavor of GDR life—its Newspeak, its Party-line rectifications, its ideological belief that "all animals are equal, but some [Party] animals are more equal than others," and above all its mutable past that was belched from versificators and sucked down memory holes—that intrigued me. One chapter of my first book on Orwell dealt with the postwar West German reception of *Nineteen Eighty-Four*—where Orwell is the best-selling English-language writer of the century. I also wrote a piece on *Nineteen Eighty-Four* as "prophecy and warning" for a Leipzig journal (courageously accepted, the editor proudly reminded me on our first meeting, even before the fall of the Berlin Wall).

In the course of my research during the 1980s, I became electrified by my conversations with several middle-aged eastern Europeans and East Germans who told me how they had procured copies of *Nineteen Eighty-Four* in the 1960s—in *samizdat*, since reading the novel was illegal. Devouring the book overnight, they passed it on through the dissident underground—knowing they faced imprisonment if caught with it. East German acquaintances described the eerie experience of already having known Orwell's catchphrases through western as well as GDR news sources—not just *der Grosse Bruder*, but also *Zweidenken* and *Doppelzüngigkeit* (doublethink), *die Gedankenpolizei* (Thought Police), *Gedankenverbrechen* (thoughtcrime), *Neusprech* (Newspeak), *Krieg ist Friede, Freiheit bedeutet Sklaverei, Unwissenheit ist Stärke* (War Is Peace, Freedom Is Slavery, Ignorance Is Strength). These East Germans recalled their astonishment that an Englishman who had never lived under a dictatorship could describe with such accuracy the regime of terror that they had experienced as young people in rebellion against the state. For them, *Nineteen Eighty-Four* crossed the line from dystopian fiction to living nightmare.

None of this is entirely surprising. For German history and *Nineteen Eighty-Four* share more than a casual relationship; indeed the association is bizarre and schizophrenic. In West Germany, Orwell stood for years as an English prose model for Gymnasium students and as an intellectual hero for liberal writers such as Heinrich Boll and Günter Grass. But even as *Nineteen Eighty-Four* topped *Der Spiegel's* bestseller list for almost two years running during 1982–84, Klaus Höpcke, the Deputy Culture Minister of the GDR, was declaring in the Communist Party's leading theoretical organ that *Nineteen Eighty-Four* addressed "the characteristic features of capitalist reality . . . , the multinational firms and their bloodhounds." Höpcke's reading of the novel— which had been banned with the rest of Orwell's oeuvre since East Germany's creation in October 1949—put Party functionaries, as we have seen, in a curious position. Much like Winston Smith, they were falsifying history even as they discussed a book about the falsification of history—indeed, as they discussed an officially banned book that GDR citizens could not admit they had read.

During the early postwar era, when the separate states of partitioned Germany came to embody the divisions between the capitalist West and communist East along with their opposing ideologies, Germany occupied the front line of the bipolar Cold War. Attacked in East Germany as anti-Stalinist propaganda, and promoted in West Germany as anti-Stalinist warning, *Nineteen Eighty-Four* came to represent for many Germans a horrifying prophecy not only of what the Reich might have been—but of what the GDR, as a Soviet satellite, had actually become.

# II

By 1990, it was no longer enough for me just to read about the GDR's Communist Party, the SED (*Sozialistische Einheitspartei*, Socialist Unity Party). I wanted to experience it—or at least its demise—firsthand. The Orwell connection led me to spend 26 months during the 1990s in the "New Germany" and to visit eastern Germany's schools, universities, and cultural institutions. And I wanted to ask: What did East German students learn? What were they now unlearning? For some aspects of their *Umerziehung*, or *Un-erziehung*, struck me as special forms of doublethink, which entails "holding two contradictory beliefs in one's mind simultaneously, and accepting both of them." The Party hack—the "doubleplusgood duckspeaker"—knows in which direction the Party wishes his views to be altered, writes Orwell, and thus "knows he is playing tricks with reality." But "by exercise of doublethink," adds Orwell, "he also satisfies himself that reality is not violated."

So I wanted to know: How Orwellian was, and is, eastern German life? How are eastern Germans confronting the waves of new revelations about their own Nazi and Stalinist collaborations? And is the ongoing political re-education of eastern Germans—into (among other transformations) good consumers—just another form of thought control?

Again and again in our interviews, my East German dissident acquaintances had given me a starting point for the answers: All of them affirmed that the communist campaign to win minds began on the "cultural front," i.e., my own profession of teaching. The offensive commenced in the schools. Youth and education formed the two pillars of the GDR utopia. As the old SED slogans trumpeted:

> *Wer die Jugend hat, hat die Zukunft!*
> (Who has the youth, has the future!)

> *Man muss die Menschen nur gebührend schulen, dann werden sie schon richtig leben!*
> (You need only to school people properly—then they'll live right!)

Some of my East German acquaintances re-enacted, often with mock-serious voices and gestures, the ceaseless, ritualistic SED sloganeering of the GDR's Communist Party (SED). Their descriptions of their own GDR school days—especially when leavened with vivid accounts of Nazi catchwords and youth activities—eerily evoked for me the climate of *Nineteen Eighty-Four*. Indeed SED Newspeak—or what might have been termed *Ostspeak* (East-speak)—was ubiquitous in the former GDR. The Party had a slogan for everything, because so-called DIAMAT (dialectical materialism) aimed to be a

*"Where a comrade is, there is the Party— that is the best argument!" This official banner of the SED (East German Communist Party) appeared on a building in the eastern German city of Eisenach in April 1983.*

comprehensive Marxist-Leninist *Weltanschauung* that explained everything— a claim reflected in the title of the standard book gift for GDR youth of the 1950s: *Weltall, Erde, Mensch* (Cosmos, Earth, Human Being).

Indeed, for East German youth above all, SED Ostspeak became the public mother tongue. In school and through the national media, the SED droned and drummed and dinned Party duckspeak into schoolchildren and even preschoolers. Following Stalin, SED leaders built their collectivist chimera on an ideological campaign based on thought control. *"Sturmt die Festung Wissenschaft!"* ran the old Party slogan. "Storm the citadel of learning!" Marshal Stalin himself had issued the marching orders, declaring educational institutions "the citadel of learning" that "we must capture at any price. This citadel must be taken by our youth, if they wish to take the place of the old guard." The Soviets called the campaign *vospitanie* (moral-social development); the East Germans termed it *weltanschauliche Erziehung* (education for a world outlook). Whatever the name, the intent was the same: creating the new socialist *Mensch*. Ideology and character-building were the content, civic training was the method.

It was too late to convert most of the old-timers, the SED agreed. But certainly the youth could be persuaded of the validity and inevitability of communism, even if demonstration of its superiority entailed a dialectical sleight-of-hand, what Orwell in *The Road to Wigan Pier* called "that pea-and-thimble trick with those three mysterious entities: thesis, antithesis, synthesis." The Kremlin had long known how to play DIAMAT. "Marxism is omnipotent," Lenin proclaimed, "because it is true!" Stalin advanced the corollary: "Marxism is true, because it is omnipotent!" Countless SED leaders, quacking DIAMAT logic, affirmed both propositions and bannered the triumphant conclusion in GDR schools for decades: *"Der Sozialismus siegt!"* "Socialism is winning!"

The children could be "persuaded." Stalin himself, lionized in SED meetings as "the world's greatest teacher and scholar," had promised: "Give me four years to teach the children, and the seed I have planted will never be uprooted!" Comrade Josef Vissarionovich, of course, was himself extirpated from Soviet and GDR life soon after Khrushchev denounced his big brotherly "cult of personality" at the Twentieth Congress of the Communist Party of the USSR in 1956. But Stalin's seed found fertile soil in the progeny of Party pedagogues. Through school and youth programs, post-Stalinist GDR and Soviet bureaucrats tirelessly propagandized—or re-educated—the young. For to remake humanity, to form the "new socialist human being," demanded seizure of the "citadel of learning."

# III

There are two citadels to be captured, however, just as there are two sorts of eastern German un-learning. The first is the citadel of the knowable and ascertainable. Its seizure entails the unlearning of facts and dates, of sacrosanct dogmas and doctrines, the knowledge of what was and what is. This is unlearning as faith-stealing. Reality becomes an ideological shell game whereby State propagandists replace one citadel with another, so that only a spectral citadel remains: the Ministry of Truth. Now the command economy of the mind prevails: You unlearn and relearn to hold two contradictory ideas in mind at once. And believe both—on command. Classic Orwellian doublethink: $2 + 2 = 5$.

Ignorance Is Strength!

But there is also unlearning to dream, to wonder about what yet might be. This second fortress of the self is the citadel of the imaginable. You unlearn to hope, to aspire to a different and radically better future. You undergo the de-illusioning that spirals downward into disillusion—and ultimately into cynicism or nihilism.

How Orwellian was, and is, eastern German life? The Orwellian dimension of eastern German life since 1989 has consisted not just in the incessant, relentless, systematic unlearning of Party lies and the "rectification" of historical falsehoods, but in dream killing, in the unlearning of utopian possibilities. As one elderly woman in Weimar, daughter of an SS soldier and herself an SED member, cried to me at the close of a six-hour conversation in 1990: "Now? Now I believe in nothing! Nothing and nobody! Except my family. Church, state, Party, nation—they've no meaning for me. . . . They [the Nazis and SED] robbed me of my innocence, cheated me of my youth, duped me of my ideals."

We in capitalist America have never had to unlearn our ideals, the ideals of liberal democracy, in so radical a fashion. So we sometimes forget that, for hundreds of millions of people, communism once was—and for many millions still remains—a dream of justice and equality. "A spectre is haunting Europe—the spectre of Communism," wrote Marx and Engels in *The Communist Manifesto*, and for postwar Americans that apparition became the totalitarian terror of *Nineteen Eighty-Four*. "Better dead than Red," we told ourselves through wave after wave of the "Red Scare." "The Iron Curtain," "the Wall," "the Evil Empire": decade after decade, "communism" has meant to us the abolition of freedoms, the confiscation of property, the overthrow of governments, and revolutionary violence. We often fail to appreciate that, for the citizens of many countries, "communism" has long signified a utopian dream, not a hellish nightmare.

Or in the words of the old SED hymn, intoned at countless official GDR functions, *"Die Partei hat immer recht"* ("The Party is always right"):

> [I]t was a dream that gave it birth
> Not a dream that will dissolve in mist by day
> But one that was also Lenin's:
> "Thunder! Strike! But also dream!"

Our songs are quaked from anger
From beautiful words, careful tones . . .
We have lived every syllable
Every note is written with blood. . . .

Since 1989, eastern Germans have been learning to "think like westerners," especially Americans, and to equate Leninist dreams with Orwellian nightmares. Several generations of eastern Germans—and their counterparts throughout the European continent—share the existential despair of my acquaintance from Weimar, a melancholy not limited to a handful of disaffected intellectuals, but rather a mass phenomenon.

This widespread experience, especially as it relates to the imagined world of *Nineteen Eighty-Four*, was the theme of a university course I once regularly taught in the history of utopian thinking. Titled "The Quest for Community," it traced a dream—or chimera?—whose pursuit has cast a long shadow across the twentieth century. Now, as did their parents a half-century ago in the wake of the collapsed Nazi "utopia," a new generation of Germans is mercilessly unlearning to dream about the best of all possible worlds, and even to trust in ideals at all. For ideals can be perverted, idealists can go too far.

Idealism is the utopiate of the apparatchik.

# IV

Throughout the communist world, the promise of collectivist utopia eventually gave way to the reality of Orwellian anti-utopia. The Stalinist reaction to the horrific Nazi utopia led to a communist police state itself not so different from the empire of Oceania in *Nineteen Eighty-Four*. And the lessons of anti-utopian thinking have penetrated deeply into eastern German minds. Today, capitalism seems to be teaching *Ossis* (eastern Germans), however belatedly, that you must reject utopianism in toto as dangerous and deluded idealism. You must face the hard limits of what human nature and the here-and-now make possible. You must make the best of the actual choices presented by reality, rather than pursue a communitarian dream.

"All history," wrote Orwell in *Nineteen Eighty-Four*, "was a palimpsest, scraped clean and reinscribed exactly as often as was necessary." The rewriting of history *à la* Orwell's *Nineteen Eighty-Four* is one of the few constants in modern German education. From the majesty to the disaster of Prussian monarchy, from the wisdom to the folly of Weimar republican democracy, from the glory to the horror of National Socialism, and from the greatness to the abomination of "Red" communism, German lessons are swiftly learned and "unlearned."

Now eastern Germans are unlearning socialism and communism. Now they are unlearning the virtues of centralized planning and the vices of world capitalism, and learning the wonders of the marketplace and the joys of competitiveness. Now, among the "young revolutionaries" turned young consumers, socialist faith is proving just as obsolete as GDR products; now, it is D-marks (or "euros") über Karl Marx.

The unlearning proceeds apace. Not that most GDR adults had grand illusions, at least by the late 1980s, about the virtues of the much-heralded *Erste Deutsche Arbeiter-und-Bauernstaat* (First German Workers' and Peasants' State). But many of the children did—and so did some of the educators themselves, who created and distributed the propaganda in which they partly believed. Moreover, as one Party functionary in Leipzig told me, even the skeptics had believed more than they had thought they had: "Sure, I knew that not much work got done. And I knew the estimates of GDR emigration. But I had no idea that the Party was so corrupt, and that the system was so moribund and decrepit. I had only a vague idea of the yawning gap between the propaganda and the truth."

No generation of Germans has possessed more advantages than the present one: no war from which to recover, no dictatorship to endure, no hyper-inflation. Yet many eastern Germans feel less like proud victors in a peaceful revolution—free at last to rejoin their long-lost family members in the West—than they do gullible victims faced with occupation by a smug, alien power. Many eastern Germans feel deprived of everything they knew. Now, it is all untrue; now they're radical skeptics or revolutionary nihilists. As one teenage FDJ member in Berlin, in his final year of high school, told me in 1990, just weeks after the fall of the Berlin Wall: "Everything we learned was a lie! And now—now?!—we're going to get the TRUTH?! C'mon! Gimme a break!"

*"Die Partei, die Partei / Die hat immer recht!"* went the old song: "The Party, the Party / It's always right!"

That teen's cry of despair came with the melting away of the seemingly rock-solid communist past. But the despair endures today. As a March 2003 story in the *New York Times* was headlined: "Young Germans Ask: Thanks For What?" The story interviewed eastern German teens who freely vented their disillusion with the post-communist present—especially with capitalist "Amerika"; they were given to drawing sardonic comparisons between Hitler and George W. Bush and holding anti-war protest signs with messages like "Bomb Texas—They Have Oil Too!" Nor did the teens spare the GDR and its own political past from censure. The story added that a "fondly comic view of East Germany is now prevalent in popular culture. The latest box office hit is 'Goodbye, Lenin,' a bittersweet comedy about a loyal son trying to recreate an East German life for his dying mother, as her society crumbles under a flood of western goods and Deutschmarks."[2]

# V

Yes, the unlearning proceeds apace—and so too does the political vertigo. And yes, many eastern Germans still feel deprived of everything they knew—and now they also know this: they will never feel and know with that old certainty again. For they believed the old song: *Die Parte* indeed *was* "always right"—and nothing will ever replace it.

> It gave us everything
> Sun and wind
> And was never miserly.
> And what it was
> Was Life
> And what we are
> We are through it.
>
> It never abandoned us.
> When the world almost froze over
> We stayed warm.

This Mother of the Masses
Fed us and cradled us
In her mighty arm.
The Party, the Party,
It's always right!

If the Party "was Life" and no longer *is*, what then? When the Mother of the Masses ups and leaves, when the world does in fact freeze over? What happens when it comes to this? The notion that you can know anything is undermined, that you can trust in anything is subverted, that you can believe in or hope for anything is crushed. At that moment of shattering revelation, Orwellian unpersonhood and Nietzschean nihilism pass into Kafkaesque despair.

Until something or someone comes along to fill the vacuum. Then 2 + 2 = 5, if Big—or Little—Brother says so.

# 6

# I Was a Teenage
# Thought Criminal,
# or Little Brotherly Love

*"Are you guilty?" said Winston.*
*"Of course I'm guilty," cried Parsons.... "You don't*
*think the Party would arrest an innocent man, do*
*you? Thoughtcrime is a dreadful thing, old man."*
—*Nineteen Eighty-Four*

*It was forbidden to import printed materials of any*
*kind from the West by any method. But who observes*
*every such edict on forbidden matter his entire life?*
—Baldur Haase, *Orwells DDR*

# I

My friend Wolfgang Strauss, a retired professor of British and American literature and linguistics who had taught at the universities of Leipzig and Jena in East Germany, told me about an incident from the 1950s, in which the mere possession of Orwell's work cost a young East German his freedom:

> Comparisons between the vision of George Orwell and the former
> East Germany are very compelling to me. I always begin my lectures
> on Orwell by reading from some declassified documents compiled by
> the DDR's secret police. They tell the story of a young man who was

sentenced in the 1950s to three years in jail because he obtained *1984.* . . . That was the entirety of his "crime." This "crime" was officially termed: "Illegal importation and distribution of writings hostile to the regime." That wording was the terror that the East German government felt about this *true* socialist! . . . I always conclude my seminars on Orwell with excerpts from this unjust case. The students of today are always very moved. Invariably they remark: "Thank God, we are glad to be so young. We have been spared the ordeal of living through that terrible time."[1]

Fortunately, the imprisoned student has lived to tell his tale. He published his horrifying story in November 1997, calling his book *Orwells DDR: Briefe, die ins Zuchthaus führten* (Orwell's GDR: Letters that Led to Jail). Professor Strauss informed me about *Orwells DDR*; he praised it highly and mailed me a copy upon its publication.

The book, by Baldur Haase, 64, makes for painful, if eye-opening, reading. It certainly confirms that the East German authorities played hardball against all "deviationists," whether young or old, during the cultural Cold War.

Haase's memoir, like Winston Smith's story in *Nineteen Eighty-Four*, is about an arrest and a trial: indeed it portrays a show trial for teenage thoughtcrime in which the DDR, or *Deutsche Demokratische Republik*, made a mockery of democratic practices. As we shall see, the Orwellian character of the GDR "justice system" was so extreme in Haase's ordeal that *Orwells DDR* could well have stood for "Deutsche Doublethinking Republik"—and Haase with justice could have subtitled his book "Little Brotherly Love."

# II

*A day never passed when spies and saboteurs . . . were not unmasked by the Thought Police.*
*—Nineteen Eighty-Four*

The story of young Baldur Haase in *Orwells DDR* is harrowing and cruel, yet simple. Haase was eighteen years old and living at home in the Leninstrasse in Unterwellenbrunn, a village near Leipzig. He was a Catholic. He had just finished his apprenticeship as a printer and planned to work in a printing shop.

Soon—all too soon—he would.

Born in 1939 in the Sudetenlend (today the Czech Republic), Haase fled with his family at the close of the war. (The Sudetenland had been forcibly annexed by Hitler in 1938 and was returned to Czechoslovakia in 1945.) The Haase family then settled in the Soviet Occupation Zone. As a schoolboy, Haase's favorite subjects were German, geography, and history. He had pen pals throughout the world. After graduating from high school in 1958, he became an apprentice printer. Already in 1957 he had caught the attention of the *Stasi* because of his extensive correspondence with young people in the free world. In 1958, the *Stasi* initiated what was known as an "unofficial postal check."

During the week of Easter 1958, Haase attended a working-class youth congress in the East German city of Erfurt. The gala event was presided over by Communist Party chief Walter Ulbricht and included representatives from West Germany. There Haase met a West German youth, Rainer Marggraf from Duisburg, and befriended him. A few weeks later, the young West German sent him a food package, within which was sandwiched Orwell's *Nineteen Eighty-Four*. Haase devoured the book and then hid it. He strongly identified with Winston Smith and began surreptitiously to keep a diary. In it he recorded his feelings about the GDR as a police state and included some jokes about, and criticisms of, Ulbricht. Later he wrote:

> I found the book exciting, and I compared the fictional state of Oceania with my own DDR.
>
> In our country there was also a Party boss, who had been named The Dictator by RIAS, the West Berlin radio station. There were countless jokes around about our Big Brother, der Spitzbart [the goatee, a.k.a. Walter Ulbricht], whose official portraits also hung in hallways, schools, universities, waiting rooms, pubs. We too in the DDR had a single political Party, and there was an official song that it was "always right."
>
> I had to think of Orwell, who had written: "Whatever the Party holds as truth is truth. It is impossible to perceive reality otherwise than through the eyes of the Party." And the DDR also had a secret

*SED chief Walter Ulbricht stands in the* Stalinallee *in front of the Stalin monument before it was officially dedicated at the World Youth Festival on 4 August 1951.*

police similar to Orwell's Thought Police.

The more intensely I preoccupied myself with Orwell's book, the more I realized that it was no utopian novel, but a state that really existed, only under a different name, the name of the DDR.[2]

With this recognition, eighteen-year-old Baldur Haase secretly (and unbeknownst to him) joined the ranks of countless Soviet and East European dissidents. As Grigorii Pomerants, the Soviet dissident philosopher-intellectual, expressed it: "People read *Nineteen Eighty-Four* for the first time and they discovered that Orwell, who got his education at Eton and on the streets of colonial Burma, understood the soul, or soullessness, of our society better than anyone else."

The little drama of Baldur Haase's education via Orwell—and, shortly, re-education via Big Brother—was now approaching its climax.

One day in January 1958, there was a knock on his door. The plainclothes men were cordial, even friendly: The SSD—secret police—had come to arrest him. Soon Haase learned why: he had been denounced for obtaining "obscene and traitorous literature." Not only had he read "this filth" himself, but he had also "poisoned" other East Germans by discussing it. He was "an enemy of the People"—or as Haase characterizes himself in *Orwells DDR*: a *Gedankenverbrecher* (thought criminal). It was for the protection of "the People," and ultimately his own protection, that he was arrested. Or so explained the GDR state interrogator in charge of his case.

Haase's interrogator refused to disclose his name. Haase privately gave him the nickname O'Brien. "Orwell's book is not a novel, it is anti-socialist propaganda," O'Brien declared to Haase during the opening interrogation. The interrogator soon "persuaded" Haase through warnings of dire consequences and promises of leniency to write a detailed confession.

Haase elaborated on O'Brien's charges against Orwell and himself in his twenty-page written "confession." Haase later recalled the summarized contents about his enthusiasm for the seditious novel: "'Big Brother' is similar in his face to Stalin. He reminded me of Walter Ulbricht, whose picture was hanging everywhere." O'Brien congratulated Haase on his articulate, thorough job. "An excellent report," he joked with mild mockery. "The judge will have no trouble with this document."

O'Brien was right. At the close of the brief trial, the judge read aloud the verdict: "You are convicted of obtaining Western smut and criminal literature. It is obscene, criminal western literature of the worst kind. It is traitorous propaganda. The German Institute for Contemporary Literature in [East] Berlin reports that the content of the book is not only dangerous to our state, but is enemy literature that promotes hatred against the USSR and all socialist states."

Hasse was convicted of the crime of "endangering the state through heresy" and for "collecting forbidden documents." The judge went on to cite a July 1958 report from the German Institute for Contemporary Literature that Orwell is "the most hated writer in the Soviet Union and the socialist states." The report added that *Nineteen Eighty-Four* was third on the GDR's "index" of most widely disseminated books by West German propagandists.

# III

Haase received a jail term of three years and three months. Fortunately, wrote Haase later, "My enemy diary was impossible for them to discover. It lay under a wooden plank in the field at home. I began to record entries in June [1958], right after I had read Orwell's novel." But Haase had not hidden his diary because he was particularly cautious or prudent. After all, he had left *Nineteen Eighty-Four* lying around. Rather, young Haase hid it because he wanted to imitate Winston Smith, who also hid his diary.

It was little consolation to Baldur Haase that Winston ultimately fared much worse that he did. In Winston's case, the Thought Police discovered the diary, and he was sentenced to twenty-five years. But Haase admits that it was fortunate that the state did not find his diary, which had simply been deposited in a hole near a tree in his backyard. (He retrieved it upon his release from jail.) For the diary disclosed thoughtcrimes worse than mere possession of *Nineteen-Eighty Four*. In his diary, Haase had, in effect, written "Down with Big Brother!" He had caricatured with a pencil, "Big Brother, Walter Ulbricht," and had recorded thirteen jokes about him. Haase certainly would have received an additional sentence if all this had been discovered. "A political joke equals one year" was the popular rumor.

Haase entered the Waldheim prison in Saxony (previously the home of a notorious jail for political prisoners) in April 1959. His two years in jail as Convicted Criminal 546/59 were not an easy time for young Haase. The quiet lad acquired the mocking sobriquet "professor" because he was introverted and known to be an avid reader. Haase was also the youngest inmate, which drew some older prisoners to jest that, having already turned to a life of crime in his teens, he must be "a very bad case." Still other inmates mocked him for having the same name as Baldur Schirach, the leader of the Hitler youth and later Gauleiter of Vienna.

But ironically, here in Waldheim Haase got his first professional job: he started working in the prison print shop. He began to print propaganda brochures. One of them was titled "BGS" (*Bundesgrenzschutz*, federal border protection)—the GDR acronym for lauding East German border guards and for branding West Germany as a rapacious capitalist land of "bandits, gangsters, and robbers." (In official Ostspeak, a BGS man, says Haase, was a West German border soldier, "a murderer.")

Exactly two years to the day after his incarceration—April 14, 1961—Haase was released. He was ashamed and spoke about his "crime" to no one. Neighbors and co-workers often heard about it, but he didn't discuss it. He briefly considered emigrating to West Germany—the Berlin Wall had not yet been erected. But he rejected it, fearful that if he were caught trying to commit *Republikflucht* (escape from the Republic), his sentence would be much worse than that he received for reading *Nineteen Eighty-Four*.

And so Haase remained in East Germany and remained silent. Not until his book was published did he speak publicly about his unjust arrest, trial, and imprisonment. Even after German reunification in October 1990, he remained puzzled as to how the *Stasi* had known in 1958 of his "dangerous" communications with a West German correspondent. He had always surmised that somebody had spied on him and denounced him.

But who? For years, he had suspected two East German friends—or perhaps Rainer Marggraf, the West German youth who had mailed him *Nineteen Eighty-Four*.

Not until 1993 did Haase find out the horrible truth: it was his ex-brother-in-law—a tragicomic example of "Little Brotherly Love" in the GDR.[3] The tale was all there in the *Stasi* documents that he had received from Berlin, faithfully recorded by a Thought Police agent. And this tale within the tale of Baldur Haase was also simple, even unexceptional, an almost typical story of family betrayal—what Winston's wife Katherine would doubtless have labeled as "our duty to the Party"—that probably repeated itself thousands of times during the history of the GDR.[4]

This is how Haase fell into the *Stasi*'s hands: On 19 June, 1958, he celebrated his nineteenth birthday at home with his entire family. In attendance were his recently married older sister and her husband. As the family sat around the birthday cake in a festive mood, an ebullient young Haase innocently and excitedly told them about his new friendship with a West German who had invited him to visit West Germany and even travel to Brussels.

On hearing this piece of news, Haase's brother-in-law Wolfgang did not delay. Under the cover name "Otto Oelmann," he reported everything the following morning to the *Stasi*. From then on, the state telescreen was on Haase. The *Stasi* tracked him for nine months and spotted his thoughtcrimes.

And so Haase's fate resembled not just Winston's but also Parsons's—indeed Parsons's fate twice over: he was not only convicted of thoughtcrime like Parsons, but also betrayed by a family member:

> "Who denounced you?" said Winston.
>
> "It was my little daughter," said Parsons. . . . "She listened at the keyhole, heard what I was saying, and tripped off to the patrols the very next day."

The rest of Haase's tale is quickly related. He reconsidered an escape into the West but was frustrated by the erection of the Berlin Wall in August 1961. After diligent service in his modest job as a cultural affairs bureaucrat in a small provincial office, Haase was rewarded in 1969 with an opportunity to organize local cultural events. He was sent to a three-year course of study at the Johannes Becher Institute for Literature in Leipzig, which was named after the late Minister of Culture and celebrated state poet. Thereafter, until the fall of the Berlin Wall in 1989, he was a staff member at the cultural institute in Jena.[5]

Haase thus became, in his words, "a little servant of the state, just like Winston Smith at the Ministry of Truth, though even more unimportant than him." Unlike Winston, Haase was not even a member of the Outer Party, let alone the Inner Party. He was nothing more than a "tiny cog" in the bureaucracy of the Ministry of Truth, a humble propagandist and non-Party functionary in "Orwell's GDR."[6]

# IV

In November 2002, Herr Haase wrote me from his home in Jena to inform me about the forthcoming expanded second edition of *Orwells DDR*. He stressed that he intended in his revised edition to highlight "the theme of the effect of literature on a reader, that is my identification with the protagonist, Winston Smith." Haase added: "I was similarly re-educated in jail as was Winston Smith in Room 101. I became a loyal 'subject' of the dictatorship, even a servant of the state." He proudly added that he had become a serious student of Orwell's work. He had even discovered that, in the leading encyclopedias of Germany, Brockhaus and Bertelsmann, Orwell was listed as born on 27 January, the error of which he had recently informed the editors.

Herr Haase also emphasized that readers of *Orwells DDR* have shown strong interest in Haase's own life. He had conducted dozens of readings and lectures, above all in *Gymnasien*. "I continually receive invitations to speak about George Orwell and the persecution of his literary works by the autocrats of the SED dictatorship. Today's seventeen-to-eighteen-year-olds are astounded that such persecutions and punishments occurred in the GDR because of this world-renowned book." Haase was gratified that copies of his book were ordered from the United States and Canada. Even the Harvard University library had ordered a copy. "I was astonished and also a bit proud that the book captured international interest."

Herr Haase also alerted me to his web site, which is named Antsta (short for "Anti-*Stasi*") and opens with the question: "Because of Orwell, you were put in a GDR jail?" Haase answers as follows: "The SED dictatorship condemned Orwell as an enemy of socialism. . . . *Animal Farm* and *Nineteen Eighty-Four* were put on a secret index by SED bosses and the *Stasi*. Whoever risked reading them was in danger of being arrested and sentenced for 'heresy and endangering the state.' Jail: that's how one dealt with modern world literature in the GDR, the Land of Reading."

On another page of the site, referring to himself in the third person, Herr Haase expresses his identification with Orwell even more openly, taking Orwell as his model of the courageous, critical leftist: "Just as his favorite author, George Orwell issued a warning against every kind of dictatorship and totalitarianism, he [Haase] has taken it for his task to train others in the work of political education and the understanding of democracy. . . ." Haase's web site adds that he is especially alarmed about the increasing tendency to downplay the evil of the SED state as a "moderate dictatorship" and to deny its violations of human rights. Haase says proudly that he "dares to challenge Nobel Prize winner Günter Grass," who champions these views yet who "never had to see the inside of a *Stasi* cell and experience a GDR jail." Haase again identifies himself with Orwell:

> Some people found it outrageous that a still relatively unknown writer [Orwell] came and broke a taboo of putting Stalin and Hitler in the same category. Orwell was, however, not a man who observed the taboos of the times. He was one of the few for whom the betterment of society was more important than personal welfare. Nonetheless, he stayed throughout his lifetime faithful to his basic socialist convictions and was not—as the SED dictatorship sought to brand him—a sworn enemy of socialism. Orwell was a warning voice against totalitarianism of every kind. That the wounded dogs in the communist dictatorship barked is understandable.

In a recent letter, Herr Haase told me that he and several colleagues are busily at work planning an international colloquium in Berlin "on the occasion of the 100th birthday of George Orwell." He also related that he had found that other citizens of the former GDR had committed the thoughtcrime of reading Orwell, too—and had paid for it with years of their youth. One acquaintance had also been sentenced to prison (three years) in the 1970s. His crime? Copying passages from *Animal Farm* and passing them out to people.

Herr Haase concluded his letter on that sober note: "So I'm not the only citizen of the former DDR to whom such things have happened!"

Such was life in the self-proclaimed Land of Reading, the Land of Little Brother.

7

# Politics and the
# German Language

*It was expected that Newspeak would have finally superseded Oldspeak by about the year 2010. Meanwhile it gained ground steadily. . . .*
*—Nineteen Eighty-Four*

## I

In 1991, I lectured at Leipzig University on Orwell and *Nineteen Eighty-Four*. The parallels between *Nineteen Eighty-Four* and the police states of Nazi Germany and Stalinist Russia are obvious and well known, and I myself had already written about them. But in a post-lecture discussion, I listened as Leipzig students—not all of whom had read *Nineteen Eighty-Four*—drew detailed analogies between Orwell's Oceania and the GDR. "Big Brother's little twin!" one student called the former GDR. Indeed, the GDR and *Nineteen Eighty-Four* entered the world together in 1949, another noted; several remarked, contemptuously, that the closest approximation to stultifying Oceania in Eastern Europe turned out to be their own tiny land located on the Elbe.

Warming to their task, the students elaborated: the Party in *Nineteen Eighty-Four* was the SED; the Thought Police was the *Stasi*; Goldstein and his Brotherhood were the GDR dissidents; the child Spies (*Späher*, "scouts") were the JP (*Junge Pioniere*, Young Pioneers) and FDJ (*Freie Deutsche Jugend*, Free

German Youth); and Newspeak was the Party mumbo-jumbo (*Parteirotwelsch*) at SED meetings. Even Orwell's Two-Minute Hates and Hate Week had their analogues in Party slogans, youth rallies, and school programs. "*Tragt den Hass in jedes Herz!*" ("Carry Hatred in Your Heart!") ran one slogan, which could often be heard during the GDR's mandatory "anti-fascist" "defense education" sessions, including school rifle practice and military drills for fifteen-year-olds. And on and on and on.

Especially in its early years, the GDR propaganda was ubiquitous and ceaseless, as if agitprop functionaries were self-consciously modeling their work on the blaring slogans of Orwell's *Nineteen Eighty-Four,* particularly "Ignorance Is Strength!": Hence the official Party commands to GDR citizens to do what is Right, indeed even to think Right:

> You only need to educate people properly—then they'll live right!

> The Party, the Party! It's always right!

GDR propaganda testified to the Party's faith in the famous slogan of the master himself. As Lenin had trumpeted:

> Trust is good, but control is better!

But it was not just in its aggressively idealistic infancy—or merely during the Stalinist era of the pre-Wall period before August 1961—that the GDR state propaganda uncannily echoed Oceania's Newspeak. East German acquaintances of mine emphasized that such official government Ostspeak endured throughout the entire life of the GDR.

What changed in the late 1980s, however, was that *das Volk* began to fight the Party propaganda by reinvigorating the German language through rhyme, alliteration, puns, double entendres—indeed, via all other available resources. No longer was the communication of unorthodox GDR political preferences limited to amusing anecdotes, secret derogatory nicknames like "Ulbie," insultingly familiar endearments like "Our Erich," or to a plethora of hilarious jokes and hushed japes that one feared to relate outside a trusted circle.

The result was a newly energized, often deliciously clever and memorable— and public—*Volksprache.*

Even before 1989, such defiant language had emerged half-publicly in alternative and music circles as a new, aggressive *Szenesprache* ("scene lingo"). By the early 1980s, German youth slang such as "*Scheissspiesserladen*" ("shitty philistine joint") and "*Null Bock*" ("no way" or "I don't wanna") filled the song lyrics of bands like Rosa Extra. The new-wave band Pankow became the star bad-boy group of the decade, with hits like "*Komm aus'm Arsch*" ("Out of the Ass") and the album *Hans Makes Good*, the story of "Hans Nihilist," roaring the rage of a generation.

By the fall of 1989, a linguistic explosion could be contained by Honecker and the Party no longer. A powerful, authentic language of The People rose up from the bureaucratic Dead, a demotic discourse, a language of the streets—and it not only swept away Party Ostspeak, but ultimately the Party and the Orwellian GDR, the German Doublethinking Republic.

# II

*Language is the most important and the most powerful weapon in the hands of a state that has decided to transform human beings.*

—Nineteen Eighty-Four

*It is clear that the decline of a language must ultimately have political and economic causes. . . . [T]he present political chaos is connected with the decay of language. . . .*

—Orwell, "Politics and the
English Language"

"Old Erich" himself was the first to go—on 18 October, to be precise. Egon Krenz, Honecker's longtime heir apparent, now took over. A former FDJ chief (1975–83) who handed over control of the organization only at the ripe age of 46, Krenz bore the mocking sobriquet *der Berufsjugendliche* (the professional youth), which now became a public moniker. In classic apparatchik style, Krenz maneuvered to win all three of Honecker's offices: General Sec-

*This brochure introduced the GDR's first major reconstruction program, launched in 1951, to the general public. The title reads: "Our Five-Year Plan of Peaceful Reconstruction."*

retary of the SED, Prime Minister, and Chairman of the Council of State. While insisting that the SED would remain the only political party in the GDR, Krenz also undertook tentative measures to introduce glasnost. But now Gorbachev's 7 October warning to Honecker—delivered during the official celebration of the GDR's fortieth anniversary—proved all too true: "He who comes too late will be punished by History."

It was decidedly too late. Dismissed by reform leaders as a rubbery *Wendehals* (wryneck, turncoat or quick-change artist), the man who had flown to Beijing to congratulate Deng Xiaoping after the Tiananmen Square massacre lasted less than two months in office. Krenz lamely relaxed restrictions on travel abroad to 30 days; *das Volk* hooted. He lifted the ban on numerous formerly "anti-socialist" publications (including *Animal Farm* and *Nineteen Eighty-Four*); *das Volk* scoffed. He secured Central Committee approval for freedom of assembly and association; *das Volk* jeered.

Ever bolder, the marchers referred to the ZK (*Zentralkommitee*, Central Committee) as *Zirkus Krenz* (Krenz's circus) and dubbed the new General Secretary himself "Krenz Xiaoping." Indeed, the ridicule of Krenz's name, background, and even physical appearance (especially his toothy grin) was ubiquitous, proclaimed on protest placards and in street chants in an astoundingly witty, unbuttoned German that only weeks earlier would have brought certain arrest. Some examples:

Reforms, yes, but *unbeKRENZt* (not limited)!

*Blumen statt Krenze!*
(Flowers instead of garland wreaths [*Kranze*]!)

Away with the *Krenz*truppen! (border or "Krenz" troops)

*Demokratie ohne Krenzen!*
(Democracy without limits [*Grenzen*]!)

*China Lob und Wahlbetrug*
  *Egon Krenz, es ist genug*!
(Praising China and rigging the elections
  Egon Krenz, we've had enough!)

From Egon's arithmetic book: 100 − 20 = 98.85
  (on the falsified May 1989 elections)

Support our Egon in the next election: 105%!

Grandmother, why do you have such big teeth?

Egon, first do something! Then smile!

More brave and brusque, more brassy and brazen and barefaced the street chants became with each passing day, as the protesters continued to march. Indeed these historic weeks of mid-October 1989 represented the first semantic crescendo of what would soon become known as the "Unbloody Revolution"—and the first moment in which the revolutionary *Volksprache* became the national *lingua franca*. It also signified another first: the first thing that East Germans took back from the Party duckspeakers and doublespeakers was the German language in all its freshness and feistiness—as Egon Krenz could confirm by listening to the shouting in any city in the nation.

*Zirkus Krenz*: the performance is over!

Egon, remember Erich and Walter

Go before your *Greisenalter* (old age)!

Enough of the Ego(n)centric!

eGOn!

Egon—BEGONE!

He went. After only nine weeks in power, *Zirkus Krenz* closed down. Egon followed Erich and made a quick exit from the stage.

# III

*The fight against bad English is not frivolous and is*
*not the exclusive concern of professional writers.*
—Orwell, "Politics and the
English Language"

"The People have the Word," an old Party slogan had falsely proclaimed. But by the opening days of November 1989, with Krenz and his minions on the defensive, the Word (play) about to set them free could be heard in every town and village in the country. As the streets of every GDR town and city swarmed each night with thousands of protesters marching against the communist regime, the (East) German language threw off its Orwellian fetters completely and began to flex itself with a clarity, simplicity, and purity of expression that Orwell's own essays advocated and exemplified.

The month of November witnessed not only the fall of the Berlin Wall; it also saw the doughty, dauntless linguistic Revolution of the Streets cascade to a second peak of power and pertness. The popular civic outrage—at travel restrictions, at the Party, at the GDR police state—spilled over and expressed itself with new articulateness. The angry street *Deutsch* fueled the populist fury.

The biggest issue for ordinary GDR citizens before the Wall's collapse was still travel. "What illness is worse than AIDS in the GDR?" they joked. "The Buda-pest!" And indeed, the Hungarian fever was now epidemic.

By the first week of November 1989, tens of thousands of GDR citizens were heading for Hungary or Czechoslovakia in hopes of gaining passage to the West; others were chanting "*Wir bleiben hier!*" ("We're staying!") as they escalated their demands for freedom of travel. "*Ohne Visa bis nach Pisa!*" ("Travel to Pisa without a visa!"). "*Mit dem Fahrrad durch Europa / Aber nicht als alter Opa!*" ("A European bike tour / but not when I'm an old Granddad!").

Until now, the street chanters had focused on their civil rights and had inadvertently adopted a version of the old Stalinist "cult of personality" by limiting their fiercest attacks to the Party leaders. But all that now changed. Now, with the late-November revelations of the luxurious lifestyles that the SED *Bonzen* in Wandlitz had enjoyed, the Party—not just Honecker, Krenz, and the Politburo, but the SED itself—became the target of protesters' wrath.

The chorus of protests reached a third, stentorian *fortissimo,* becoming ever more fearless and relentless:

*SED—das tut weh*! (that hurts!)

*SED—Geh*! (Go!)

*SED—Sicheres Ende GDR*! (A certain end for the GDR!)

*SED—Nee*! (No!)

*SED—Ade*! (Bye-bye!)

*SED, gib acht,*
  *Das Volk ist die Macht*!
  (SED, pay heed,
  The People are the power!)

*S wie Sauwirtschaft, E wie Egoismus, D wie Diebstahl = SED!*
  (S as in a disgusting economy, E as in egoism, D as in theft
  = SED!)

*40 Jahre Lug und Trug*
  *SED—es ist genug*!
  (40 years of lying and deception
  SED—that's enough!)

Our Volk needs the SED like a fish needs a bicycle!

And soon it was not just the corrupt SED but Marxism itself that would be run over by the locomotive of History. "Privileged Ones of all countries, remove yourselves!" the protesters proclaimed. They were fed up not just with the SED but with Ingsoc—or rather Gersoc—in all its forms and acronyms. And so when the SED dissolved at the year's close and a new party—the PDS (Party of Democratic Socialism) was reconstituted in its wake by the SED faithful, the East German *Volk* would have none of it. The demonstrations and chants continued:

*SED—stalinistisch, egoistisch, diskriminierend;*
*PDS—perspektivlos, demokratiefeindlich, stasifreundlich*

(SED—stalinist, egoistic, discriminatory;
PDS—hopeless, hostile to democracy, friendly to the *Stasi*)

*PDS—Pleite des Sozialismus, Partei der Stalinisten, Pack deine Sachen!*
(PDS—Bankruptcy of socialism, Party of Stalinists, Get out!)

*PDS—Parasiten, Diktatoren, Stalinisten!*

The fittingly pathetic *dénouement* came in December with the appearance of Erich Mielke, longtime head of the hated *Stasi*. As he fended off castigation and catcalls, Mielke exclaimed in a plaintive speech before the new GDR Volkskammer (People's Assembly), "But I love you all!"

It was decidedly too late: Little Brother's belated valentine from the Ministry of Love went unrequited.[1]

# IV

> *Political language—and with variations this is true of all political parties, from Conservatives to Anarchists—is designed to make lies sound truthful and murder respectable. . . .*
>
> —Orwell, "Politics and the English Language"

With the opening of the Wall on 9 November 1989—which in turn led to the collapse of the communist regime in the succeeding months and to German reunification in October 1990—the protests and demonstrations against communism ceased. The sloganeering and street chants faded away.

And yet, although a key target of the East German *Volk* had been the Orwellian dimension of official GDR jargon, which of course disappeared with the extinction of the GDR government, a new form of doublespeak seemed to arise immediately from its ashes—proving again not only the phoenix-like tenacity of bureaucratese, but also that the cancer of Orwellian semantics feeds on all political hosts, indeed knows no governmental or ideological bounds.

Of course, bureaucratese and political euphemism had hardly been absent from Teutonic speech across the border—as a casual glance at the statements of West German government officials at any time in the postwar era would easily confirm. Indeed, quite apart from the subterfuge of politicians, German *Vorschriften* (regulations, red tape) have been long renowned for their obscurity, obfuscation, and obtuseness.

But the German language of the post-unification era developed a distinctive creativity that seemed to draw symbiotic sustenance from the genius and audacity of the GDR *Volksprache* of 1989. Yes, it was almost as if FRG government, corporate, and even extremist sectarian leaders—not to mention the German public—had learned to camouflage and animate their doublespeaking rhetoric by taking language lessons from the GDR protesters.

Perhaps the biggest political problem in reunified Germany during the 1990s was the reappearance of neo-Nazi activity and the explosive rise of violence against foreigners. Predictably, the German language soon spawned an Orwellian vocabulary that gave frightening voice to this xenophobia. Indeed, within a year after German unification, German slang had become rife with ugly neologisms. To combat the linguistic contagion, the GDS (Society for the German Language)—a watchdog group devoted to exposing German Newspeak—inaugurated an "Unword of the Year" prize in 1991.[2] The award aims to "call attention to thoughtless, often inhumane, and cynical language use in which the requirements of social propriety and human relationship are especially clearly missing"—and it represents the German counterpart to the Doublespeak Award, which American educators introduced in the 1970s.[3]

Here are the award-winning German unwords for the 1990s:

1991: *auslanderfrei* ("foreigner-free")

1992: *ethnische Säuberung* ("ethnic cleansing")

1993: *Überfremdung* ("excessive foreignization")

1994: *Peanuts* ("Peanuts": a remark by former German bank
    president Hilmar Kopper in downplaying the seriousness

posed by the bankruptcy of a German investment firm, which would cost the public 50 million marks)

1995: *Diatenanpassung* ("budgetary adjustment": a phrase that referred to the raising of their own expense accounts by representatives in the German Bundestag)

1996: *Rentnerschwemme* ("hordes of retirees")

1997: *Wohlstandsmüll* ("affluent rubbish": a statement by the former president of Nestle's, Helmut Maucher, about citizens unwilling or unable to work)

1998: *sozialverträgliches Fruehableben* ("socially contracted early demise")

1999: "collateral damage" (The English phrase, rather than the German word—*Randschaden*—was generally used by government spokesmen and the German press.)

This list warrants further comment, for these unwords reflect issues in German society that continue to arouse heated emotions and political debate. The 1991 Unword winner, *ausländerfrei* ("foreigner-free")—as in the neo-Nazi street chant: "keep Germany *ausländerfrei!*"—remains in circulation in certain right-wing circles today. The next two winners, *ethnische Säuberung* (ethnic cleansing) and *Überfremdung* (becoming "over-foreign"), vied with other political euphemisms in referring to Germans' outrage with mass immigration, such as *multikriminelle Gesellschaft* (multi-criminal society) and *integrationsunfähig* (unable to integrate). The neologisms continued to have anti-foreigner or anti-immigration overtones: for example, 1997's *Wohlstandsmüll*, which referred to "affluent rubbish," that is, native (and especially immigrant) scroungers who milked the system, and 1998's runner-up, *Osterweiterung*, which expressed anger at the idea of expanding the EU to include poorer eastern European countries. All of these unwords reflected Germany's national anxiety over the upheavals that came in the wake of reunification and the transformations occurring in German society that would lead to the constitutional change in 1999 mandating new, looser criteria for German citizenship. Several of the unwords also served to express popular resistance to top-down, government-sponsored initiatives.

But some observers have argued that the Unword awards are administered by a "left-wing Thought Police."[4] For instance, when novelist Martin Walser received the German Booksellers Peace Prize in 1998, his acceptance speech became the object of the Unword jury's scrutiny. Walser unleashed a furious controversy among intellectuals when he deplored the "moral club" that the German media had used to beat on anyone who did not accommodate their politically correct views about the Holocaust.[5] That phrase gained Walser—a prose stylist of the first rank—the dubious honor of the 1998 Unword prize. According to the Unword jury, Walser himself used a "moral club" against the media, whereby he veiled his honest intentions and damaged the integrity of the German language. But a columnist in the *Frankfurter Allgemeine Zeitung* spoke for many observers when he argued that the Unword jury "gods" condemned conservative "sinners" according to precepts of political correctness. "The jury gods are themselves liable to swing the Unword club against sinners who fail to heed their edicts."[6] Other critics derided the Unword selections on nonpolitical grounds. Mocking the annual Unword awards in 2002, the women's magazine, *Bunte*, declared its own unword winner: "Unword." The magazine deplored "arrogant schoolmasters" who presume to outlaw certain expressions as "unwords" and asked defiantly: "Who needs that?"[7]

Other newly popular terms of doublespeak in the early 1990s reflected the condition of the struggling eastern German economy and the East-West tensions that had intensified in suddenly reunified Germany. The leading Unword nominees included *Personalentsorgung* (personnel disposal, a.k.a. job firing), and *Warteschleife* (holding pattern, a phrase used to describe the period before a scheduled layoff took effect). During this employment twilight zone, workers were officially on *Kurzarbeit Null* (zero part-time), which meant that their shifts had been "reduced" to nothing. Such workers were not included in eastern *un*employment statistics; they were officially "*under*employed." They were usually still required to show up to work to draw their wages. Bonn soft-pedaled high unemployment and social upheaval in the east, preferring to stress the region's progress toward *schlanke Produktion* (lean production). Westerners who went east to work received the standard western salary *plus* a bonus. ("Bush money," resentful easterners dubbed it, perceiving that Bonn regarded the east as "bush" country.) This meant that, for instance, western teachers were earning more than three times the salaries of their eastern colleagues (roughly $2,000 per month vs. $655 per month). Thus western Germans did indeed seem to many easterners like viceroys in the "Wild East." Inevitably, the situation provoked waves of western defensiveness and superciliousness alternating with eastern anger and resentment.

Feeling as if they were being treated as second-class citizens, many eastern Germans did not refer to their region by the official phrase, "new federal states of the FRG," but by the insulting word *Anschlussländer* (annexed states). The term recalled the Nazi euphemism for its shotgun occupation of Austria and other German-speaking areas in the 1930s—and thus implied that the West German government bore resemblance to the Third Reich, both in its actions and in its legalese. The comparison between Bonn's politicians and Hitler's henchmen was clear.

And that comparison not only reflected easterners' anger and anxiety about the course of reunification, it also showed their attunement to new forms of western Newspeak—or what some wags called *Neudeutsch* after reunification. No, this was not Gerspeak: the *Ossi* coinages were a defiant and vibrant *response* to official Gerspeak from Bonn, reflecting the awareness of easterners that a form of Newspeak had again sprung to life in the German language—indeed, that corrupted language was not limited to East German communism. And though *Neudeutsch* was never so brutal as Ostspeak, it was arguably far more insidious and narcotizing than the tired phrases and awkward euphemisms of the SED.

So it was fortunate that skeptical East Germans did not find it easy to relinquish their penchant for unmasking linguistic subterfuge. Once you see it, you are liable to see it even in its most subtle guise, and you will be wary about mouthing or even accepting jargon whenever you encounter it. For such unmasking or decoding is not just a skill, it is also a discipline. Moreover, once you learn to see something, you must be forcibly retrained—or reeducated—*not* to see it, as the concept of doublethink in *Nineteen Eighty-Four* demonstrates.

So a paradoxical development arose after reunification during the early 1990s: many eastern Germans became even more indignant toward the new, less virulent species of Newspeak that arose after reunification than they had been (until late 1989) toward the Ostspeak of the SED.

Thus, eastern Germans countered Bonn's *Neudeutsch* with punning, self-mocking neologisms that reflected eastern fears of devolution. Two such terms were *Verrostung* (rusting out) and *Verzonug* ("becoming the Zone"). The latter was a reference to backward, impoverished eastern Germany during 1945–49 under the Soviet occupation army, when it was known as "the Zone." (West Germans had mocked it by that name for years afterward during the Cold War.) The allusion not only represented a self-deprecating form of easterners' black humor, but also reflected their anxiety that the post-reunification east might degenerate into an atavistic condition much like that which prevailed in the reparation-torn Soviet occupation zone.[8] As that fear deepened, both the populist neologisms and the government Newspeak proliferated. Antagonized by what they considered a new politics of injustice, vocal eastern critics saw Comrade *Wessi* as little better than Comrade Stalin. Indeed, it seemed like the communist epoch all over again: Big Brother was back.

Not surprisingly, the tensions between *Ossis* and *Wessis* generated a politics of envy even among easterners themselves, with the beneficiaries and victims of the new system keenly resentful toward each other. Have-not *Ossis* attacked fellow easterners who were succeeding in the new system; one term for them was OM (*ostdeutscher Mitläufer*, eastern German fellow traveler), which referred to eastern "collaborators" with the *Wessis*. OM was a pun on the IM (*inoffizieler Mitarbeiter*), or the state's "unofficial colleagues," in the official GDR euphemism—in other words, *Stasi* collaborators. (Unsurprisingly, a new coinage emerged to account for the flood of revelations: the verb "*outen*"—to out. Formerly pertaining, as in the Anglophone world, only to the practice of revealing someone's homosexual orientation without his or her consent, it was now expanded to include the disclosure of someone's former *Stasi* collaboration.)

Many eastern Germans compared their land to an occupied country that had lost its rights. Indeed, they were also quick to note with derision that the western German architects of *Abwicklung* ("wrapping up" or "winding down") avoided more direct, colloquial terms for their brazen "annexation" and colonial domination of the east. *Abwicklung* was the euphemism used for the dismantling of GDR institutions and the laying off of thousands of eastern German employees, rather than *Auflösung* (dissolution, closing down) or *Kündigung* (firing, laying off).

Coined in early 1990 in sharp reaction to Bonn's reunification policy, *Abwicklung* arose before the inauguration of the Unword prize—otherwise it seems likely to have won. Indeed, the word *Abwicklung* received such bad press in the east that in mid-1991 the *Abwicklung* department of the *Treuhandanstalt*, which was in charge of selling off old GDR state firms, decided a change was needed. The department initiated a public campaign—complete with DM 1,000 reward—to rename the department with a "more fortunate term." A more pleasant euphemism was indeed found among the 1,600 entries: "Department of *Rekonstruktion*."

And so down the Orwellian memory hole went *Abwicklung*, too. It was officially dismantled: *abgewickelt*.[9]

# V

> *In our time, political speech and writing are largely the defense of the indefensible.*
>
> —Orwell, "Politics and the English Language"

Recent years have witnessed German unwords reach a new height of cleverness and controversy. Let us review some standouts of the last five years in greater detail:

1998: The Unword of the Year—or "Un-phrase," since it is indeed a mouthful—was "socially contracted early demise." The term reflected the politics of socialized medicine and national health care in Germany, but the choice occasioned controversy, since some observers thought that Karsten Vilmar, the president of the Federal Chamber of Physicians, had used the expression humorously or ironically in December 1998. He criticized the cost-cutting plan for health care sponsored by the federal government as follows: "Patients will [under the proposed plan] need to be content with less service. We must think over whether we can maintain our quality of patient care or whether we must promote the socially contracted early demise of our patients." Critics of the Unword jury defended Vilmar, explaining that he was speaking in jest and was not at all calling for the killing of patients.

"It depends on the degree of public visibility a speaker possesses," replied the linguistic scholar Horst Dieter Shlosser of the University of Frankfurt, jury chair for the Unword of the Year awards.[10] Schlosser maintained that one has to be helpless or prone to victimization in order to be "allowed to be ironic." Shlosser said that when a humorous formulation is used by a public figure, it tips into "naked cynicism." But "Vilmar isn't any kind of underdog who goes against the powerful," Shlosser argued. "Rather, Vilmar himself is the boss of a powerful pressure group. He's not a cabaret performer. He's the official representative of physicians."

Other unword candidates for 1998 reflected the cynical politics and economics of euphemism. A cardinal instance was "human capital." Coined by Albrecht Schmidt, the head of the Bavarian Consortsium of Banks, it asserted that if policymakers properly calculated the cost-benefit ratios they would strengthen the German economy by offering less education and encouraging earlier teenage labor. According to the Unword jurors, Albrecht's term served to "reduce human beings merely to their business value," an example of the "pure materialism that was once the distinguishing characteristic of real existing socialism in the GDR, where the worth of human beings was also calculated."

1999: When the war in Kosovo began, a NATO speaker referred in a Brussels press conference to "collateral damage," borrowing military language to avoid mentioning civilian victims of the war. The English expression was only rarely translated into German: it simply entered the German language in its English version. It was therefore doubly euphemistic. Not only did it veil itself in impersonal military jargon; given the obscurity of translationese—as an "Englishism"—it was especially hard for non-native speakers to understand. Thus the term awakened objections not just from watchdogs of political euphemism but also from German language purists, all of which led to its becoming the 1999 unword. According to the unword jurors, "'collateral damages' obscures and veils the killing of innocent people through NATO attacks":

> Given its impressive-sounding resonance and difficulty to understand, it distracts from the horrible reality of these casualties and attempts to render war harmless. The expression implies that war victims are an insignificant side effect. Properly translated into German, it means "side

damages" or "marginal damages" (*Randschaden*) —and one would never speak of civilian victims of a war in such plain German. It would not be possible politically or socially.

The Unword jury declared that "collateral damages" is "part of a manifold attempt to cast the invasive Western assaults in the Balkans war in a friendlier light." Until last year, "collateral damages" had still not entered any German dictionary. But the newest edition of Duden, the official Webster's of Germany, contains this definition: "Bad damages that occur in the course of a military action, which are not intended and that are not directly connected with the goal of the action, but which are, however, accepted as a consequence."[11]

2000: "National liberation zone" (*nationale Befreiungszone*) was the first post-'90s Unword. This cynical expression referred to regions in eastern Germany, where "through terroristic attacks, foreigners and minorities were expelled and residents were intimidated," according to the Unword jury. The jury added that the expression (which was not used for the first time in 2000, but gained wide recognition that year) is "doubly cynical" because it characterizes an extreme, violent sect in expansive, even heroic terms as "national," and because it calls the persecution of people their "liberation."[12]

2001: The next Unword of the Year was "divine warrior" (*göttlicher Krieger*), a heroic characterization for Taliban fighters and al-Qaeda terrorists. The term reflected a lack of "critical distance by the media towards pseudo-religious claims for warmaking by criminals who claim for themselves the name of God," according to the Unword jurors.[13] The jury said this term was not acceptable because "no belief in a god regardless of the religion can justify a war or terroristic attacks." Also proposed was the statement of Chancellor Gerhard Schroeder after September 11 expressing "unlimited solidarity" with the U.S.—a declaration he soon regretted and revised. But the jury established that the Schroeder nomination was not a linguistic criticism but "a pure political criticism." (The jury's ruling on the Schroeder statement has been cited as evidence by some observers that the Unword jury is not biased in favor of the German Left.) The jurors added, however, that Schroeder's formulation showed that "solidarity is already an empty word when it is used with the adjective 'unlimited.'"[14]

# VI

*In prose, the worst thing one can do with words is to surrender to them.*

—Orwell, "Politics and the
English Language"

*The purpose of Newspeak was not only to provide a medium of expression for the world-view and mental habits proper to the devotees of Ingsoc, but to make all other modes of thought impossible. . . . The intention was to make speech, and especially speech on any subject not ideologically neutral, as nearly as possible independent of consciousness.*

—*Nineteen Eighty-Four*

The entry of unwords such as "collateral damage" unchanged from English into German—with their foreignness masking their euphemistic meaning—is worrisome to many Germans. "Are we soon going to be speaking Denglish or Germeng?" asked the linguist Rudolf Hoberg in the collection *Die Deutsche Sprache an der Jahrtausendwende* (The German Language at the Millennium). Reflecting many Germans' fears of "linguistic decline," Berlin professor Peter Schlobinski spoke of the danger of a "mishmash language" dominated by English.[15]

And so, ironically, our story of "Politics and the German Language" comes to turn partly on politics and the English language. Perhaps this is fitting: what goes around comes around. For Orwell based Newspeak and *Nineteen Eighty-Four* itself partly on Nazi rhetoric and the Nazi state, whose expressions (such as "Nazi" for National Socialist) inspired Newspeak terms (such as Ingsoc for "English Socialism"). Orwell saw Nazi Deutsch narrowing thought via linguistic sound bytes, and he understood that the same was occurring in English. Orwell the BBC broadcaster saw that politics and the German language is inevitably related to politics and the English language; the perils of political language that he identified in his most famous essay are common to all languages—and all languages are interconnected.[16]

Despite such interconnections, the situation raises a large and difficult question pertaining to what might be termed comparative political linguistics: Do present-day Germans possess a heightened sensitivity to ideological forms of linguistic abuse as a result of their decades of exposure to debased language, first to Nazi rhetoric and then to Stalinist and SED jargon? Because of Germany's so-called "double burden," that is, because it was the sole nation to experience both fascist and communist dictatorships in the twentieth century, Germans have arguably lived in an atmosphere more pervaded by linguistic deception and manipulation than has any other people.

On this view, it certainly seems possible that Germans today perceive and use political language in a manner different from citizens who have dwelt only in democracies, such as the Americans, British, and French. For instance, whereas the French have focused historically on maintaining the purity of their language, the Germans have been more deeply interested in preserving the political integrity of their tongue from ideological perversion. Theirs is not an aesthetic concern, but a political one: Germans could not, as it were, "afford" linguistic formalism. The French have fretted more about the colonization and the McDonaldization of their language, but most Germans—the linguists' alarms about a "mishmash language" such as Denglish notwithstanding—have worried much more about the totalitarian domination of their minds and souls. And many Germans are well aware that, as Orwell witnessed, the German language itself became complicit with Nazism—that Nazi Deutsch not only reflected but also shaped Nazism.[17]

Indeed, perhaps the Germans' experience of linguistic perversion via Nazism (and Stalinism) accounts for why *Nineteen Eighty-Four* has been more popular in Germany than in any other nation in the non-Anglophone world. Because the Germans have more experience with variants of Newspeak than any other people, they are liable to insist more uncompromisingly on language that is not defiled by politics. Younger generations of Germans are undeniably quite sensitive to *Neudeutsch*. And yet it is also true that decades of exposure to deformed language may also, especially among the elderly who grew up in such an environment, continue to desensitize or stunt their awareness of language abuse.

It may also be said that, of all the nations that experienced fascist or communist dictatorships, Germany possessed the best-educated populace and the richest literary tradition. If this is true, then German intellectuals and writers above all should have recoiled at the corruptions of language that these ideologies imposed. Because of the distinguished literary tradition in German classicism and Romanticism that was being undermined, it was more obvious, say, to the average eastern German than to the typical Russian peasant, that an egregious abuse was being committed. None of this means that Germans, including German intellectuals, did in fact object *en masse* to Nazi and Stalinist *Neudeutsch*, but it does suggest that the doublethinking necessary to disable a German mind was greater than in most countries, precisely because of the level of education that the Germans possessed. This corresponds to the difference that Orwell mentions in *Nineteen Eighty-Four* between Oceania's proles, who require no propaganda to remain docile, and the Party members, who need constant propagandizing because they themselves are propagandists. If they are to remain sharp, effective state instruments, Party orthodoxy must be continuously reinforced in them. If Winston Smith at the Ministry of Truth is to remain a useful tool, he must be re-rendered virtually unconscious on a daily basis. By contrast, a prole needs only the crudest propaganda—to be surfeited on Hate films or the novels of the Minitrue fiction department.

In this respect, the GDS and the Unword jury have reflected Orwell's own conception of power and its perils. Orwell was not so fearful of coinages from below that gave vent to populist anger or frustration. Rather, he was anxious about the manipulation of language by those in power who were capable of controlling public thought by narrowing or obfuscating language. "If there is hope, it lies in the proles," muses Winston. He might have added: "If there is hopelessness, it owes to the powerful."

The GDS and the Unword jury are attacking a phenomenon not so different than what the East German *Volk* fought with their street demonstrations, chants, and placards. When their targets are just, the Unword jurors serve as edifying linguistic vigilantes, a therapeutic Thought Police seeking to quell political abuse while it is still at the level of language and before it manifests more problematically in public policy.

# 8

# Unwords and Unfreedom
# in the Citadel of Unlearning

> *You know the Party slogan: "Freedom Is Slavery."*
> *Has it ever occurred to you that it is reversible? Sla-*
> *very is freedom. Alone—free—the human being is*
> *always defeated. It must be so, because every human*
> *being is doomed to die, which is the greatest of all*
> *failures. But if he can make complete, utter submis-*
> *sion, if he can escape from his identity, if he can merge*
> *himself in the Party so that he is the Party, then he is*
> *all-powerful and immortal.*
>
> —O'Brien to Winston Smith,
> *Nineteen Eighty-Four*

## I

Much of my time in the GDR and post-reunification eastern Germany was spent in the company of educators and students. Given my interest in Orwell, our conversation often turned to the Orwellian dimensions of GDR education, especially the policies and materials of the GDR Ministry of Education, or what an eastern German friend jokingly referred to as "Minied."

Education, and especially participation in the communist youth organizations, was the path to a good career in the GDR, and the Ministry of Education represented the path to power in the SED and the GDR government.

Every SED elder knew that Erich Honecker himself served as the first head (1946–55) of the sole state youth organization, the Free German Youth (FDJ). And that, on succeeding Walter Ulbricht as Politburo head in 1971, Honecker had brought dozens of old FDJ cronies into powerful government positions. And that he now supervised his old beat closely with his wife Margot, Minister of People's Education since 1963. And that he had chosen Egon Krenz, his successor at the FDJ, as his heir apparent. The central role of education in the GDR could not be clearer: virtually from the creation of the Soviet zone of occupation in 1945 to the GDR's end in 1989, Erich, Margot, and their ward Egon personally attended to the running of the youth organizations and the schools. Nothing in the education system would be left to chance; it was a family-run operation.

That lesson was communicated clearly to me during my 1990 visit to the Friedrich Schiller high school in Weimar just as the GDR was heading into oblivion and German reunification was at hand. A history teacher handed me an official manual from Panorama, the GDR press office. The title alone implied a confident answer to its question: "Students and Studies in the GDR: How Does the GDR Solve the Problems of Higher Education?" The teacher flipped past the chapters headed "Universities of the People" and "Students Without Worries" to stop at page 26, "How Free Are Students in the GDR?"

> The freedom of GDR students is inherent in their complete certainty that they will not be made use of for the profit and power interests of big capital. It is inherent in the fact that they need have no fear of unemployment. It is inherent in the fact that they have unlimited opportunities to gain scientific knowledge, to make the Socialist mode of thinking and acting their own in the shortest possible time. And all of this, not as a goal in itself, but in order that the students can thus fully participate in the shaping of the Socialist social order. . . .

After this reminder of the revolutionary forbearance "inherent" in the socialist faith, the section closes with a quotation falsely attributed to Engels (who had been citing Hegel) that—given its Orwellian application in the GDR—represented a classic example of doublethink. My acquaintance read it aloud: "*Freiheit ist die Einsicht in die Notwendigkeit*" ("Freedom is the recognition of necessity").

"Freedom Is Slavery!" I thought. But the teacher drew the moral himself. "That sums it up," he told me. "You want to know about my *Freiraum* [free space] in teaching? There was no such 'freedom.' What was 'freedom' to us? A word. The Free German Youth were not free. The German Democratic Republic was not democratic. The People's Ministry for Education, the People's Police—and a thousand other 'People's' agencies—never served the People."

He pulled another official booklet from what he jokingly called his *Giftschrank* (poison shelf), the word formerly used in the GDR for library stacks holding proscribed books. It was titled "Education in a Socialist Country: The GDR's Education Policy." We turned to page 36: "The aim of our education is a self-confident socialist personality committed to socialism and creatively active in many fields together with fellow citizens. This aim determines instruction in all subjects and school activities, but can only be accomplished if school and life form an entity." The booklet gives a running list of postwar examples of the perfect dialectical unity practiced by the socialist school and the youth organizations:

> Great events of international importance always set off activities on the part of pupils in the GDR. . . . Young Pioneers and members of the FDJ supported the struggle of the Algerian people against French colonialism by collecting exercise books, pencils, and toys. They expressed their solidarity with the brave people of Vietnam in their struggle against U.S. imperialism by collecting money and signatures. . . . The GDR's young people extend their solidarity to the people of Chile. . . .

The booklet concludes with the ringing words:

> Educators will look for even better ways to implement our programs, to constantly improve conditions of instruction, and to realize ever better the available potential for the all-around development of socialist personalities. The communist future will make itself felt more strongly in present-day educational developments, because, as Margot Honecker stated in her contribution to the discussion of the Ninth Party Congress, "We have always looked on education as the preparation of young people for their active participation in shaping the new society."

Or as the old Party slogan of the early postwar years proclaimed: Our new life must be different!

Along this road toward "the new society," SED educators somehow forgot the insights of the Party's oft-quoted grandfather, Marx's colleague Wilhelm Liebknecht, the founder of the German Social Democratic Party, which was the nineteenth-century socialist predecessor to the postwar Marxist-Leninist SED. They forgot Liebknecht's warning to his Social Democratic colleagues in a celebrated speech in 1872 that the "unfree state" turns education into propaganda.

> "Like the school, like the state" goes an ideological proverb. "Like the state, like the school." This would be the genuine translation and trans-position in the sense of *Realpolitik*. The school is the mightiest instru-ment for liberation, and the school is the mightiest instrument for en-slavement, depending on the nature and the purpose of the state. In the free state, it is a means for liberation; in the unfree state, the school is a means of enslavement. *Bildung macht frei*—education makes you free.

Liebknecht concluded with a warning that would one day apply to Ingsoc—and to "Gersoc": "To expect the unfree state to educate its people would be equivalent to expecting it to commit suicide."[1]

# II

> *The problem, that is to say, is educational. It is a problem of continuously moulding the consciousness both of the directing group and of the larger execu-tive group that lies immediately below it.*
> —*Nineteen Eighty-Four*

"If you want to understand us, go to the schools," a retired East German teacher wrote me from Erfurt in 1990. "The key to understanding the GDR lies in grasping the functioning of the educational system. No area of East German society more decisively formed the 'socialist citizen' than education.

And nowhere will the rise and fall of the GDR be more sharply and poignantly revealed to you than in the relation between the school and the state."

She was right.

For the GDR lived and finally died by the old Party slogan: "Who has the youth, has the future." The slogan was often attributed to Martin Luther, but it was made famous by Wilhelm Liebknecht. At the turn of the century, in late Imperial Germany, the statement served as a battle cry for radicals seeking to win young workers to their banner; decades later, the SED adopted it as the official motto of its youth organizations and derived state policies from it. And with good reason: Liebknecht was right. As the communists knew, the fate of a nation depends on the education of its people.

And so education—with its complex interplay of Marxist-Leninist theory and praxis—became the key institution in the GDR. East German education, a.k.a. "Minied," with its extraordinary ideological rigidity, existed primarily to legitimize socialism as a worldwide movement and to validate its historical destiny to replace capitalism. And in this goal it was more fervent than even the Kremlin, disseminating neo-Stalinist ideology in almost its pure theoretical form. For East Germany had its own special educational problems.

First, the GDR educational system was, necessarily, more overtly ideological than the educational systems of its socialist *Brüderländer*, since it took as its mission the task of wiping out not just tendencies toward capitalism but also National Socialism—all the while officially pretending (once again, in classic doublethink fashion) that nobody left in East Germany had a Nazi past. (Early postwar GDR school readers contain story after story about not trusting one's grandparents—code for "possible Nazis"—a not-so-subtle example of GDR education policy in action.) Educators in other socialist nations were largely spared the kinds of ideological acrobatics that were the stuff of basic Minied training in the German Doublethinking Republic.

Second, East Germany was more rigidly Stalinist than even the former USSR, at least by the 1970s and '80s, because the regime always felt it necessary to distinguish itself drastically from still-"imperialist" West Germany. Except for ideological differences, there was no reason for there to be a GDR: unlike other Eastern European countries, the five states of East Germany had never previously been brought together as any historical or administrative unit and had no common traditions. They were purely a creation of World War II and Stalin himself. So the educators promoted a purer "Marxism-Leninism" than did educators anywhere else.

Third, as I suggested at the outset of this chapter, education was the way to the top in East Germany, even more than it was in other communist countries. To head the major GDR youth organization, the FDJ, was to have virtually the same level of power (if not the prestige) of the Secretary of State in the U.S. In other communist nations, ministries directly linked to force—the army or the secret police or even the ministry of the interior—were the avenues to power. Those ministries were vitally important in the GDR. But education was the most likely place from which to build one's Party career—largely because of the early career success of Erich Honecker. As we have seen, for almost forty years, Honecker and his wife Margot personally ruled the education ministry and youth organizations. By 1989, more than half the Politburo members were former Ministry of Education officials (old pals of Honecker's), and his own chosen successor, Egon Krenz, had been FDJ chief during the 1970s and early '80s.

During this latter period, the GDR educational system became *more*, not less, rigid and doctrinaire. Consider, for instance, the youth reformatory at Torgau, a city located on the Elbe River northeast of Leipzig best known for the meeting of victorious U.S. and Soviet troops in 1945. For me, the stunning news reports about the Torgau Reform School evoked scenes of Room 101—or even an Oceania "joycamp" (forced labor camp). It featured the torture of children, prettified as "reform."

The Torgau Reform School became infamous when reports surfaced in 1992 about its pre-1989 practices of treating wayward children as enemies of the state. Established in 1964 on the direct orders of Margot Honecker—one of her first official acts as the new Education Minister—the Torgau Reform School has been called "Margot's Concentration Camp" or the "Children's Concentration Camp" in the German press. Conditions were far harsher than in adult jails; human rights abuses of the inmates were legion. Wardens locked up children for days in dank, dark cells. Teens were ordered outside in sub-zero temperatures "for exercise." Youths were confined to grim Dickensian workshops for hours on end, making lamps for Warsaw Pact submarines. All windows had bars; German shepherds patrolled the high walls outside. Some inmates swallowed paint, ate light bulbs, and burned their beds in desperate suicide attempts to escape the school—invariably without success. The goal, of course, was that of Room 101: *Umerziehung* (re-education). (Today, Frau Honecker—known as "The Witch" to many eastern Germans—is safe and free with her daughter's family in Chile.)

Despite Willy Brandt's policy of *Ostpolitik* (inter-German détente) in the 1970s, and despite Mikhail Gorbachev's rise to power in the USSR in the 1980s, the GDR maintained many harsh youth policies right up to the end. And despite détente and perestroika—or rather because of them—East Germany (and GDR education in particular) became even more stringent and orthodox in its Marxism-Leninism. The reason was *Abgrenzung* (cutting off, delimiting), the policy pursued by the GDR since 1972 to distinguish itself from West Germany. No other communist state faced a comparable problem of legitimacy or identity; no other risked losing millions of its citizens to a rival neighbor. Finding it ever more difficult to define itself and defend its system against the obvious economic superiority of West Germany, the GDR redoubled its promulgation of propaganda in the schools.

# III

*The two aims of the Party are to conquer the whole surface of the earth and to extinguish once and for all the possibility of independent thought.*
—*Nineteen Eighty-Four*

The imperative mood was well chosen by the SED: "Our new life MUST be different." A climate of obligation, necessity, and compulsion enveloped the training maneuvers drilled in its educational institutions, which Stalin himself had called the "citadels of learning." It was an environment that provoked Martin Buber to declare: "The real struggle is not between East and West, or communism and capitalism, but between education and propaganda. Education means teaching people to see the reality around them, to understand it for themselves. Propaganda is exactly the opposite. It tells the people: 'You will think like this, as we want you to think.'"

*"With Stalin Is Peace." This poster, colored in red and featuring three red hammer-and-sickle flags of the Soviet Union, including the Red Star of the Soviet army, announced the thirty-fourth anniversary of "the Great October Revolution" in 1951. (According to the old calendar of czarist Russia, the revolution occurred on 25 October 1917. When the Soviet Union adopted the Gregorian calendar in 1918, the "October" Revolution was thereafter celebrated on 7 November.)*

"Give me four years to teach the children," said Stalin, "and the seed I have sown will never be uprooted." Thus did Stalin, echoing the behaviorist Ivan Pavlov, one of the forefathers of Marxist-Leninist educational psychology, announce his pedagogical equivalent of a Five-Year Plan. To Stalin, writers were "the engineers of human souls," teachers were the mechanics, and children were the raw material to be molded in the image and likeness of scientific socialism. As numerous socialist realist novels preached: "You make socialists like you made steel: hard."

The GDR, of course, gave Stalin forty years. But the "children of the Republic" finally came in from the desert to quench their thirst for Liberty. Still, SED-style Stalinism—or GDR "Stasinism," as my western German friends dismissively termed their neighboring police state—did indeed sink deep roots into GDR hearts and minds. Its hold validated the Stalinist conviction that the "citadel of learning" warranted "capture at any price."

Stalin operated by two old Russian proverbs about the German: "A good fellow maybe, but better kept under foot," and "Much may be made of the German if he be caught young." The citadels of learning became citadels of political re-education. The GDR school perpetually spewed propaganda, equating resistance to communism with unreconstructed Nazism and thereby setting young against old in every family. Beginning with the ideological indoctrination of pre-school children, and continuing through elementary and high-school education, GDR inculcation of communism was relentless.

Through kiddie magazines, youth organizations, and required extracurricular activities, students were directed toward their certain future: members of the socialist work force. In the wake of the Revolution of 1989, educators and students were the largest, most articulate, and most traumatized segment of the population to be affected by the political upheaval. After conducting interviews over a period of eight years with dozens of them, as well as with former students and parents of students in eastern Germany, I became convinced that the deepest roots of GDR society were indeed located in the institution that molded the youth of its citizens, and that the most searching questions about the region's past and future were to be found there.

And how could such relentless propagandizing not have imprinted itself deeply on the generations of East Germans to pass through GDR schools since 1945? Just as high school is closer to the core of the American experience than anything else in our national life, so too did the same hold true for the GDR. Only more so, since there was practically nothing outside school for young people apart from Party-sponsored youth organizations such as the FDJ. And as I discovered not long after the fall of the Berlin Wall in a conversation with an eleventh-grade student at the Friedrich Schiller high school in Weimar, that organization's name—*Freie Deutsche Jugend* (Free German Youth)—was another piece of pure Ostspeak:

"What percentage of your classmates belonged to the FDJ?"

"Everybody in the class. . . . You pretty much had to join. You had no choice."

"What happened if you didn't join?"

"Hard to predict. I always figured it was better to be safe. Why take the risk? You could lose the chance to go to university, or to study your chosen subject, or to get a good apprenticeship. Your parents might get in trouble, or you'd get a bad assignment in the People's Army, or a host of other things. . . ."

Yes, it was "better to be safe"—better to be an Orwellian "goodthinker" who would duckspeak "*goodthink*—meaning, very roughly, 'orthodoxy,'" as the Newspeak Dictionary in the Appendix to *Nineteen Eighty-Four* defines it.

And yes, it was as if the Free German Youth took a page for its Ostspeak dictionary from Orwell. For as he wrote in the Appendix to *Nineteen Eighty-Four*: "In the case of the word *free*, words which had once borne a heretical meaning were sometimes retained for the sake of convenience, but only with the undesirable meanings purged out of them."

# IV

*The entire group of people broke into a deep, slow, rhythmical chant of "B-B. . . !" . . . a heavy, murmurous sound, somehow curiously savage. . . . It was a refrain that was often heard in moments of overwhelming emotion. . . . [I]t was an act of self–hypnosis, a deliberate drowning of consciousness by means of rhythmic noise.*

—on the Two-Minute Hate outpourings in
*Nineteen Eighty-Four*

*The denial of reality . . . is the special feature of Ingsoc and its rival systems of thought.*
—*Nineteen Eighty-Four*

"The deliberate drowning of consciousness," "the denial of reality": Yes, "the rival systems of thought" to communism know them too—as eastern Germans quickly discovered after the "anti-fascist Wall of Protection"—in official Ostspeak—had fallen.

"Drugs, porn, violence, and homelessness—that's what's coming to our schools and streets, mark my words," a German teacher in the Friedrich Schiller high school warned me during my 1990 visit. We argued together, cordially, about the pluses and minuses of reunification for the next generation. Unlike his colleague, the history teacher, he did not rush to condemn the SED. Like many teachers, he had been a "convinced communist" in earlier days. From the *Giftschrank* in the storage room next to the teachers' lounge he fetched yet another official booklet, "General Education in the GDR." We turned to the question-and-answer section on page 23. The question, which the booklet brightly answers, was exactly the one I had just posed to the history teacher:

Q: Can one say that "youth problems" do not exist in the GDR?
A: Yes, with certain reservations one can say that, because in the GDR such grave problems as unemployment, with all its detrimental consequences to the harmonious development of young people, do not exist. Youth in this country does not know the merciless competition for

apprenticeships, study places and jobs, which young people in many other countries confront. There is no "drug scene" here and juvenile delinquency is at an extremely low level compared to Western countries. . . . The overwhelming majority of young people feel really at home in socialist society.

"False—" said the German teacher, as if it were a true/false test, pressing his finger to the final sentence and then waving the booklet at me remonstratively, "—but not altogether false, not by a long shot."

Drugs, porn, violence, homelessness. Yes, they have become commonplace in the east, just as they have in western Germany and throughout the capitalist West—or what was once called (derisively on the Left, quite sincerely by Orwell) "the free world." In that respect, my German colleague won our argument. Indeed the eastern passage to capitalism is turning out to be neither so smooth nor so programmatic as implied by a two-panel cartoon ad promoting *Business Week* in the immediate aftermath of reunification. The ad contrasted the forbidding "before" picture of a portly, unkempt Marx as radical agitator with the smiling "after" visage of a slimmed-down, clean-shaven, three-piece-suited Karl as networking entrepreneur.

But is not the Pandora's box of such social evils perhaps the inevitable accompaniment of capitalism—and of freedom itself? For individual freedom is not authentic, existential freedom unless it can be indulged and abused—unless the capacity for self-determination can even be turned into a means of self-enslavement.

As we have seen, Wilhelm Liebknecht, the founder of the German Social Democrats, had admonished his fellow socialists that "the unfree state" turns education "into a means of enslavement." But there is a world of difference—the difference distinguishing the "free world" from a "slave state"—between the genuine personal liberty to choose one's fate and a state tyranny that virtually outlaws the exercise of basic civil liberties.

However much the consumerist, prolefeed mentality of so-called "advanced" capitalism narrows individual liberty, however Orwellmaniacal the tendencies inherent in technological progress and the untrammeled "free" market, what East Germans repeatedly told me was this:

There is a world of difference between free choice and state dictate.

# V

*We cannot outline the future of socialism. What so-cialism will look like when it takes its final form we do not know and cannot say.*

—Lenin

*If you shut up the truth and bury it under ground, it will but grow, and gather to itself such explosive power that, on the day it bursts through, it will blow up everything in its way.*

—Zola, *J'Accuse!*

You were free in the GDR to conform, to obey, to yield. You had liberty so long as you took no liberties. GDR pedagogy meant the inculcation of ideology and information, not the development of persons. "Our new life MUST be different!"

Education was not an existential, I-Thou relationship, as Buber had urged. Education was not cultivation but implantation. Rearing little Party members, it was "a pedagogy absent a pupil." It is not just that it wasn't "child-centered"; it was child-absent. Or as the old German aphorism has it: "*Freiheit ist von Gott, Freiheiten vom Teufel*" ("Liberty is from God, liberties from the Devil"). The pupils at the Friedrich Schiller high school would have done far better to heed the words of Schiller himself: "*Das Gesetz hat noch keinen grossen Mann gebildet, aber die Freiheit brutet Kolosse und Extremitaten aus*" ("Never yet has law formed a great man; 'tis liberty that forges giants and heroes").

Freedom requires room to expand—but that wasn't possible in the GDR, "that fenced-in playground that was my land," as the East German novelist Christoph Hein once wrote. Few GDR citizens took liberties beyond the playground square. Their emancipation was an Orwellian proclamation, not a fact.

Such a state of affairs was defensible in the dialectical doublethinking wonderland of Marxist-Leninist theory, for freedom had always been suspect in revolutionary catechesis. Lenin himself called liberty "a bourgeois dream." "It is true," he said cynically, "that liberty is precious—so precious that it must be rationed." In *State and Revolution* (1918), which was directed against the "opportunism" of Marxist opponents such as Rosa Luxemburg and Karl Kautsky, Lenin developed his doctrine of "democratic centralism," according to which the "social" liberty of the individual was identified with party-mindedness and state collectivism. Under this formula, bourgeois "individualism" was a form of social pathology—"Freedom Is Slavery!" In SED Ostspeak, to be "for society" was to be "for oneself." "While the state exists," wrote Lenin in *State and Revolution*, "there can be no [traditional concept of] freedom. Where there is freedom, there will be no state."

It is yet another delicious irony that, in the fullness of revolutionary History, the GDR fulfilled Lenin's prediction to the letter. So long as the GDR existed, there was no freedom; almost as soon as truth burst out—as if with an apocalyptic Zolaesque cry of "*J'Accuse!*"—the state "withered away." The GDR had reached, as it were, Lenin's "higher" phase of communism. For Lenin had argued that, as long as reward is proportional to worker output, a "lower" form of communism prevails in which the state is still needed. When reward becomes proportional to worker need, the state will dissolve naturally.

After forty-four years of communist rationing, *das Volk* "needed" liberty. The avenging dialectic finally turned on the SED itself; 1989 became the year of Marxism in the streets. East Germans heeded at last the words of Lenin's most outspoken German antagonist, their own Rosa Luxemburg, who wrote in her 1919 study of the Russian Revolution: "*Freiheit ist immer nur Freiheit des anders Denkenden*" ("Freedom is freedom only if it also applies for the one who thinks differently").

For decades, citing that passage in SED meetings was forbidden. Honoring her in the breach, the SED had instead named dozens of schools and streets after Rosa Luxemburg.

Her name had become—like freedom—only a word.

Or an Unword.

# 9

# Portrait of a Defiant DIAMATnik

## I

*The command of the totalitarians was "Thou shalt."*
—from Emmanuel Goldstein's book in
*Nineteen Eighty-Four*

Robert Havemann (1910–82) has long stood before me as one of the unsung heroes of the GDR—and of present-day Germany. If younger Baldur Haase had a walk-on role *à la* Winston Smith as a GDR dissident and thereafter remained in the wings, Havemann took the high stage in a headline role—indeed as the leading man among the small troupe of GDR dissidents—for the last two decades of his own life. Havemann understood the difference between the character of Orwell and the Orwellian character of the GDR. The respect for truth, the belief in the sanctity of the individual personality, the emphasis on clear language and truthful history, the conviction that reason and logic are essential instruments in the comprehension of reality—these are the values that Havemann perceived in Orwell's work, and they are also the values that Havemann ultimately came to embrace in his struggle to turn the GDR into a nation more humane and more ethical, indeed into the "better Germany." As this scene makes clear, Havemann's fight with GDR officialdom to cast off the shackles of Party goodthink and to maintain his intellectual freedom illuminate both the nature of GDR communist orthodoxy during the 1960s and also the general plight of East European dissidents throughout the postwar era. And Havemann's fate also illustrates the extraordinary difficulty such a dissident encountered in outspokenly voicing unpopular truths—of being an Orwell in an Orwellian state.

# II

*Socialism can create freedoms that are only hopes and dreams in bourgeois society: the freedom of the individual from all material dependence on other people. In capitalism humans can only liberate themselves from material dependence insofar as they make others dependent on them. In socialism, material freedom and independence of the individual are based on the fact that he is dependent on the whole of socialist society.*
—Havemann, *Fragen Antworten Fragen*

Robert Havemann grew up near Berlin as the son of a conservative nationalist teacher in Weimar Germany, which by the early 1930s was suffering the highest unemployment rate in the industrial world, with almost a quarter of the male population out of work. The economic conditions generated despair and bolstered the attraction of, and support for, radical political ideologies such as fascism and communism. In mid-1932, worried about the marching Brownshirts and fearful that the National Socialists would come to power, the 22-year-old Havemann joined the resistance group New Beginning, which had been secretly formed before Hitler's rise to power in January 1933 to combat a possible Nazi dictatorship. At the same time, Havemann also became a member of the KPD (the prewar German Communist Party).

Havemann had completed his doctorate in physical chemistry in 1932 and had started working at the Kaiser Wilhelm Institute for Physical Chemistry and Electrochemistry in Berlin. Not long after Hitler's takeover, Havemann lost his position. During the mid-1930s he worked odd jobs and performed underground activities for the KPD (which had been outlawed by the Nazis) and various resistance groups. In 1938, the leading members of New Beginning were arrested by the Gestapo; thirty of them were executed. But Havemann's resistance work remained undetected and his allegiance to the Communist Party remained strong.

Rehired by the Kaiser Wilhelm Institute for the war effort, Havemann worked during World War II as a physical chemist by day and organizer of resistance activities by night. He co-founded the resistance group known as the European Union and conducted rescue missions for Jews and the politically persecuted. In 1943, Havemann and three others were arrested by the Gestapo on charges of treason and sentenced to death. His three co-conspirators were executed in May 1944. But friends persuaded Reich authorities that Havemann's scientific expertise was indispensable to the war effort, and so Havemann's execution date was delayed. He was instead jailed in Brandenburg Prison outside Berlin, with a special laboratory set up for him near the cell of the young Erich Honecker. Even in prison, Havemann remained unbowed and undaunted in his anti-fascist efforts: while imprisoned, he organized a new resistance group and even secretly printed an illegal newspaper written by the inmates.

Havemann was liberated in 1945 by the Russians, and returned—once again—to the Kaiser Wilhelm Institute (now located in American-occupied West Berlin), where he was promoted to director by American authorities. He joined the East German Communist Party immediately after its founding in early 1946. Two years later, he was removed from his position—once again—for political reasons, when he denounced the American nuclear weapons program, marched in anti-American demonstrations, and made pro-Soviet statements to the press.

# III

*The principle of "Unfreedom as Necessity" has today*
*no kind of social and political justification but rather*
*constitutes—so long as it still prevails in any of the*
*socialist nations—the most significant inhibition of*
*the development of socialism and also simultaneously*
*mars the international status and credibility of*
*socialism. What therefore has become a necessity in*
*socialism as never before is freedom.*
—Havemann, *Fragen Antworten Fragen*

Before and after the founding of the GDR, Havemann stood loyal to the "better Germany." In the early years of the GDR, he became a *Volkskammer* (People's Chamber) representative (1949–63), a Cultural League member, and recipient of the second-class National Prize and the Fatherland Merit Medal in Silver.

His summary dismissal by the Americans had only made him a more loyal Party man and impassioned Cold Warrior—on the Soviet side. As a professor at Humboldt, in East Berlin, he urged West Berliners to boycott the Marshall Plan, persuaded qualified colleagues to fulfill their national duty by contributing to the GDR atomic program, and lionized Stalin in the *Tägliche Rundschau* as "the greatest scientist of our time." He defended the Soviet suppression of the GDR workers' rebellion on 17 June 1953—the first mass uprising against Soviet authority in the postwar era—and was a vocal advocate of the harsh punishments meted out to the rebels by Walter Ulbricht, SED chief and Stalin's handpicked dictator. (In fact, Havemann was one of the government spokesmen who had defended Ulbricht in a speech to the workers in the streets on June 16—and one of those who had been shouted down.)

Until 1956, Havemann remained an unwavering Party loyalist. But in the wake of the shock occasioned by Khrushchev's "secret speech" in February 1956 (which exposed Stalin's crimes) and the Hungarian uprising and failed revolution in October of that same year, Havemann lost his faith in the Party's omniscience. No longer could he unflinchingly chant the old workers' song at

*These banners from the Fourth (1954), Fifth (1958), and Sixth (1963) SED Party Congresses illustrate the process of "de-Stalinization" that occurred after Stalin's death in 1953. The Fourth Party Congress still acknowledged four "fathers" (Marx, Engels, Lenin, Stalin). The Fifth, in sharp reaction to all cults of personality, retreated to the symbol of the worker's arm. By the time of the Sixth Party Congress, international communism had settled on the troika of Marx, Engels, and Lenin.*

Party meetings: "Brothers, onward towards the sun! Onwards towards freedom!" No longer was he willing to abide by the old Party hymn: "The Party, the Party / It's always right!" No longer would he duckspeak the official dictates of the GDR and its Big *Bruderland*.

So it was predictable that, when the official campaign against revisionism began in January 1957 at the Thirtieth Meeting of the Central Committee of the SED, Havemann was not spared. Leading philosophers such as Ernst Bloch and Wolfgang Harich were condemned as "deviationists" and "revisionists" in philosophy, and Havemann was targeted in the natural sciences. All three men were guilty—in the Party jargon of the day—of objectivism, cosmopolitanism, and social democratism. But Havemann had a powerful protector: the USSR. Prominent Soviet leaders in Moscow still appreciated that Havemann had outspokenly defended the development of the postwar USSR atomic program and had taken a public and unambiguous pro-Soviet position in the emerging Cold War—even at the cost of a (temporary) career setback.

Then, in the late 1950s, a zephyr of revisionism blew in from the east—from the USSR—an after-effect of de-Stalinization and the excitement caused by Sputnik's launch in 1957. The change made elite physicists such as

Havemann especially valuable; and it led to a thaw in the SED's stance toward him. In 1960, the so-called "technical-scientific revolution" introduced by cybernetics was being promoted in the USSR and throughout Eastern Europe, an innovation that gave impetus to fresh thinking by leading Soviet-bloc scientists. Because he had served the Soviet Union with distinction, and because his benefactors had not forgotten him, Havemann was in a favorable—if not fully secure—position to criticize the SED hierarchy. Thus emboldened by seeming ferment, Havemann went public with his critical new ideas, taking full advantage of GDR leaders' fear of silencing a scientist in excellent standing with "our Russian friends."

Beginning in January 1962, and continuing for more than two years, Havemann delivered a popular series of lectures to students (and secret-police spies) at Humboldt University. By this point in his life, the fifty-two-year-old Havemann was a professor of physical chemistry at Humboldt and director of the Berlin Institute for Physical Chemistry—in other words, a respected scientist as well as a Party member for nearly three decades. Unlike most Party leaders, he was highly esteemed by non-Party scientists and by the younger technical elite in industry. His lectures drew lively discussion, and auditors attended from as far away as Jena and Leipzig.

In these lectures, Havemann argued that Soviet and SED philosophers (dubbed "DIAMATniks" by GDR students, after dialectical materialism) were clinging to positions of "vulgar materialism" and "mechanistic materialism." These were philosophical positions, said Havemann, that already decades ago had "resulted in the discrediting of DIAMAT among scientists of the world." To prevent ossification into dogma, Havemann maintained, Marxism-Leninism had to take account of modern developments in the natural sciences. Orthodoxy could only hurt the basic sciences, whose research and development required freedom of inquiry. Marxism-Leninism had no subject matter of its own; the dialectic was a method, and progress in its application depended on the results of other sciences.

Surely Havemann would have eventually landed in hot water had he merely persisted in this type of philosophical critique. But far more dangerously, he broadened his subject matter from cybernetics to life—and extended his argument toward its inevitable conclusion: a questioning of the SED's authority. Havemann warned against ideological orthodoxies of all sorts, ridiculing

Party ideologists as the "Central Administration for Eternal Truths." "You can command human beings and prescribe to them a great deal," Havemann declared, "but you can't prescribe to them what they should think." In essays such as "Freedom as Necessity," Havemann noted that state socialism had taken Hegel's famous phrase and transformed it completely as follows:

> Freedom (of the state) requires insight into the necessity of unfreedom (of the individual).
>
> Unfreedom as necessity! . . . So you go with your friendly Party man to the Brandenburg Gate and show him the Berlin Wall, the "Anti-Fascist Wall of Protection"! . . . Able-bodied people and our youth are not permitted to travel to the West. Everyone knows why: Because they would flee there and stay, in massive numbers, just as they did before 13 August 1961, the date of the erection of the Wall.
>
> But whoever says that in public is tried for denouncing the state and will be jailed for some years. The mistrust between the state and its citizens is extremely deep on both sides and it is justified. In the so-called elections, more than 99 percent of voters vote for the single list. There are no opposing candidates. If the state believed this vote of confidence from its citizens, it would tear down the Wall. But the state knows that this 99 percent vote only occurs because the citizens do not trust their state. That's why the Wall remains and is even further perfected. The Wall is the material form of state mistrust and therefore the irrefutable argument for the continuation of the general mistrust of its citizens toward their state.

Havemann concluded: "Unfreedom as necessity! . . . The People have complete insight into the necessity of their unfreedom. The result is a newer, higher form of freedom."[1] Havemann had now come to reject dialectical doublethinking as well as the state-ordained "necessity" of unfreedom. To him such "higher" insights had come to mean, "Freedom Is Slavery."

The professor was speaking from personal experience, experience that would only be reinforced in the decades to come.

# IV

*The German Nazis and the Russian Communists
came very close to us in their methods, but they never
had the courage to recognize their own motives. They
pretended, perhaps they even believed, that they had
seized power unwillingly and for a limited time, and
that just round the corner lay a paradise like that.*
—from Emmanuel Goldstein's book in
*Nineteen Eighty-Four*

No, Havemann was not blind to the Orwellian character of "Stalinist pseudo-socialism" in the GDR. He nonetheless remained a Marxist, albeit a "revisionist" like Leslek Kolakowski and Adam Schaff in Poland, Eduard Goldstücker in Czechoslovakia, Ernst Fischer in Austria, and Roger Garaudy in France, all of whom Havemann quoted and admired. Havemann continued to believe, as Sartre expressed it in his *Critique of Dialectical Reason* (1960), that Marxism was the "horizon" toward which the modern world and all other philosophies were heading.

Despite his fierce criticisms of the SED—even including comparisons between it and the National Socialists—Havemann remained true to his vision of the GDR as the "better Germany," and lived as if it were so. In the years that followed, Havemann's moral courage and his spectacular defiance of GDR authorities were extraordinary. West German friends worked behind the scenes with GDR friends to smuggle out and publish his lectures, which became bestsellers in West Germany as *Dialektik ohne Dogma* (Dialectics without Dogma, 1964) and *Fragen Antworten Fragen* (Questions Answers Questions, 1970). In *Dialektik ohne Dogma*, Havemann explained his change of heart toward the SED in words that testify to the onetime power of the Marxist dream to capture even the strongest mind—and of the internal battle of wills that must ensue to oust the Thought Police agents after "they get inside you." Coming from a man of such great integrity and fortitude, and illustrating a heroic, unceasing commitment to the process of "working through" the ex-communist's burden of God-that-failed disillusionment, Havemann's statement is a stirring declaration of hope. This compelling autobiographical passage marks the culminating moment in the book and warrants quoting in full:

> If one changes his opinions on important questions, it isn't enough to set forth the new views and criticize the old ones. One must inquire as to why one thought differently before, why one today thinks differently. . . . One must lay the change in one's thinking before others in all openness. Whoever seeks to give the impression that he never erred is behaving dishonestly and deserves no credit.
>
> Before what held force for me was the principle: Truth is "partisan." I held every thought that wasn't "Marxist" to be threatening and false. Naturally I wasn't so arrogant as to judge whether certain opinions merited the characterization "Marxist" according to my own thinking. That decision was a matter for the Party. I was reared to unconditional modesty toward the collective wisdom of the Party. I believed: *Die Partei hat immer recht.* . . .
>
> Before I was of the opinion that one could recognize a good comrade by how fast he could understand new insights of the Party and publicly campaign for them. The bad, uncertain comrades, on the other hand, were recognizable by their immodest superiority, whereby they objected and asked completely pointless questions, which one had best not even answer. The worst cowards of all, however—who already stood with one foot in the camp of the class enemy—were the unfortunates who risked criticizing the leading comrades of the Party, indeed criticizing even the leading comrade. . . .
>
> Year after year I believed myself to be a good Marxist. Precisely because I believed that, I wasn't. Today I don't believe it any more. I am in doubt, restless. I am trying to think through everything. . . .
>
> Before [1956], [criticism of] the Party leadership was taboo for me. The Party had the right to censure and to suppress all opinions that it didn't share. Today I know that all of us, outside and inside the Party, have the right and the duty to form an independent judgment, as I have explained in my lectures.

Havemann's lectures criticized dialectical materialist dogma with temerity. Ultimately, however, they represented only another doomed attempt—like the attempts of outspoken East German thinkers of the 1940s and '50s such as Anton Ackermann, Wolfgang Leonhard, Wolfgang Harich, Ernst Bloch, and numerous others—to mark out a "third way" between SED Stalinism and western capitalism. "A spectre is haunting Europe," Havemann announced hopefully, echoing the classic lines in *The Communist Manifesto*, "the spectre of humanistic socialism, the spectre of the third way."

# V

*The first thing for you to understand is that in this place there are no martyrdoms. . . . In the twentieth century, there were the totalitarians, as they were called. There were the German Nazis and the Russian Communists. The Russians persecuted heresy more cruelly than the Inquisition had done. And they imagined that they had learned from the mistakes of the past; they knew, at any rate, that one must not make martyrs.*

—O'Brien to Winston in Room 101,
*Nineteen Eighty-Four*

Havemann's call for a third way raised the full fury of the DIAMATniks and SED Thought Police against him. "Why should we permit this Socrates—he is not as smart as Socrates!—to despoil our children?" demanded Hanna Wolf, director of the SED Party College in Berlin. *Forum*, the newspaper of the FDJ, tried to humiliate Havemann and discredit his criticisms by publishing a long list of his previous professions of faith in the regime, to which Havemann sent a simple, one-sentence reply: "Yes, I was wrong—that's why I was a Stalinist and became an anti-Stalinist."

Like his predecessors, Havemann was branded a heretic and a revisionist for defying the "eternal truth" of the Party leadership's infallibility—a thoughtcrime all the worse in Havemann's case because he had formerly been a privileged Inner Party member of the GDR *nomenklatura*, not an insignificant Outer Party functionary like Winston Smith—let alone a mere prole like young Baldur Haase.

But Havemann was now unwilling to toe the Party line and stifle the truth. He criticized the SED in a prominent December 1965 article in *Der Spiegel*, the leading news magazine in West Germany. He suggested in *Der Spiegel* both that the GDR establish opposition parties and that West Germany re-admit a reformed KPD (the prewar Communist Party that had been banished in West Germany since the mid-1950s) as moves toward possible re-unification.

So the "Central Administration for Eternal Truths" treated Havemann as not just the GDR's philosophical gadfly, but also as its freethinking scientific heretic. He had warned in his lectures of 1963–64 against the Party's approach to dissenters becoming a "papist Inquisition toward Galileo"—and thereafter the Italian communist newspaper *Unita* admiringly compared Havemann himself to a freethinking, Marxist Galileo. Other prominent Marxists in France and throughout Eastern Europe agreed. Havemann advocated "ideological coexistence" with the West, which he defined as "engagement with what others think" and as "presuppos[ing] freedom." "Reactionary regimes," Havemann declaimed to his students, "have striven at all times in history to keep the People ignorant."

"The Party," replied Horst Sindermann of the SED Central Committee, "can't leave rotten eggs lying in the nest." Havemann lost his post as director of the Berlin Institute for Physical Chemistry in March 1964 for insisting on freedom of information and expression. He was expelled from the SED in October 1964 and was dismissed in April 1966 from the GDR Academy of Sciences because of "continued damage and an outlook foreign to the Party." ("Under the cover of criticizing 'inadequacies' [in Marxism-Leninism]," explained the Party's official ideologist Kurt Hager, "Havemann wants to disseminate, in organized fashion, skepticism.") Soon Havemann's only remaining income was a small pension that the state awarded to all recognized resistance fighters and anti-fascists.

No protest in the universities ensued. The intellectuals and students, let alone the general population, raised barely a whimper against the dismissal and silencing of Havemann, who had become the unyielding witness of the post-Wall era, the Orwell-like conscience of his generation.[2]

# VI

*Life without freedom only becomes bearable to man*
*when he ceases to feel this lack of freedom.*
—Havemann, *Fragen Antworten Fragen*

Looking back from 1990 on her GDR university days in the mid-1960s, East German dissident Freya Klier spoke of her generation's experience of dogmatic "scientific socialism" as the core curriculum of a GDR education, confirming Havemann's critique and suggesting how—in the same way that Havemann himself had once coped—she and her classmates unwittingly fitted themselves to their Procrustean Stalinist beds. In her study of GDR education, which was titled *Lug Vateland* (Lying Fatherland), Klier describes an Orwellian system of thought control:

> Everyone who began his studies after 1961, and stayed the course, left the university damaged. . . . "Scientific communism" lasted for all of us at least three years and was not a matter of a creative engagement, but of the SED's cramming its power-preserving, self-dignifying doctrines [into us]. All of us prettified and rationalized this, in order to keep our scholarships and because we didn't know anything else. The horizon of our thinking was systematically shrunken during these years.

Or as Havemann had put it himself in *Fragen Antworten Fragen*: "Orwell describes the mentally sick behavior in his novel *Nineteen Eighty-Four*. The task of the Ministry of Truth is not to produce a definite consciousness but to extinguish consciousness."

Today some otherwise admiring eastern German leftists—who should know better—blame Havemann for preventing the emergence of a reformed SED. For instance, a historian and friend of mine at Humboldt University once conceded to me that Havemann evolved from the Stalinist mouthpiece of June 1953 to a courageous activist. Yet he "lost himself in 'third-way' dreams," insisted my friend, though he reluctantly granted that Havemann stands in hindsight as "the best GDR socialist of them all."

Havemann never sought asylum in the West, even though he was kept under virtual house arrest for the last decade of his life. He lived just long enough to witness the first stirrings of protest against the hated SED regime, stirrings that would lead seven Octobers later to mass demonstrations throughout East Germany and to its unexpected collapse within just a few months more. But Havemann did not survive to see the outcome he had helped set in motion—he remained a socialist Moses, dying before he could witness the regime of unfreedom swept away.

# VII

*Who has the youth, has the future.*
—Wilhelm Liebknecht

Throughout the 1990s, as part of my research on the New Germany, I visited and taught history and social studies classes in eastern German high schools. One October day in a Weimar Gymnasium in 1994, my students were reading Bertolt Brecht's *Galileo*, a searing indictment of religious dogma and the Church during the Inquisition. I asked the class if any passage in the play recalled to them the man who had explicitly warned that the SED's repression of dissidents reminded him of the Inquisition's treatment of the real-life Galileo.

The class stared blankly; nobody knew what I was talking about.

I explained that I was referring to Robert Havemann, the GDR's leading dissident of the 1960s and '70s, a leading scientist—like Galileo—who spoke out against the repression of truth and who ultimately set in motion the Revolution of 1989.

Silence. Nobody knew who Havemann was.

Then a girl meekly raised her hand, murmuring that she *had* heard of Havemann, but she didn't know exactly who he was, or what he had done. *Ach, ja!* Now she remembered: Havemann had been in the news recently: Gregor Gysi, the head of the PDS (the successor party to the SED) had been Havemann's lawyer during the late 1970s and '80s, and *Stasi* documents just obtained and released by Havemann's widow showed that Gysi had reported their confidential lawyer-client conversations to the *Stasi*.

"The citadel of learning," Stalin had declared, was worthy of "capture at any price."

The price turned out to be very high indeed for eastern Germans, most especially for intellectuals, educators and students—as the Orwellian fate of Robert Havemann attests.

# 10

# Amid the Rubble of
# "Orwell's Reich"

*All fixed, fast-frozen relations, with their train of
ancient and venerable prejudices and opinions, are
swept away. . . . All that is solid melts into air, all
that is holy is profaned, and men at last are forced to
face . . . the real conditions of their lives and their
relations to one another.*

—Marx and Engels,
*The Communist Manifesto*

## I

My first trip to Leipzig occurred just weeks after German reunification in
December 1990, long after the national euphoria over the fall of the Berlin
Wall had degenerated into mutual East-West recriminations and as the eastern German economy was itself in fiscal free fall toward total collapse. The
Leipzig weather reflected the social climate. And so on a cold, drizzling,
smoggy Leipzig afternoon, I sat in a dingy second-story cafe a few blocks
from the Karl-Marx Universität, chatting with a few students as I waited for
a young academic colleague to arrive.

I was shocked by how utterly dark and dilapidated the entire region of
eastern Germany seemed to be; it was like the setting of a grittily naturalistic

movie set in ravaged war-torn Germany, or even a cheerless Cold War spy thriller from the 1950s. I had boarded a train from Meissen to Leipzig—a mere fifty miles—that had taken eight hours. "You could run faster," a student joked to me, aware that I was a marathoner. He wasn't far wrong. Getting to campus that morning, I had jogged through the streets and passed the city streetcar, which moved just a tad more slowly than the train. In both cases, I was told that the rail and trolley lines were so antiquated and decrepit that speeds exceeding a horse trot would shatter them.

"It's like a scene from the early postwar era, after the Allied bombings," I had remarked on visiting the Frauenkirche in Dresden. The beautiful church was still in disrepair, forty-five years after the devastation of February 1945.

"Yes, the *Trümmerliteratur* (rubble literature) has regained its relevance," one student replied to me. Indeed the postwar stories—about the bombed-out cities in which children sift through debris and *Trümmfrauen* (rubble women) work to clear the main streets—invited depressing comparison with the chaos rapidly enveloping the entire eastern region.

"Orwell's Reich," quipped another student. He had attended my university lecture on Orwell the previous day. To him and his friends, the deteriorating, now-defunct German Democratic Republic (GDR) bore apt comparison with the mass devastation and economic shortage in Orwell's Oceania.

Now Jürgen, a *wissenschaftlicher Assistent* (lecturer) in political science at the university, enters. Two students have told me a little bit about him. "He's no Robert Havemann," says one, alluding to my admiring reference to Havemann in yesterday's lecture.

The students banter with him and disperse as he sits down. But Jürgen is in no mood for small talk. He is somber: he has come to tell me about his life as a Party activist and organizer at the University. I can barely contain my excitement. I wonder: Is this what it might have been like to talk to Winston Smith after the fall of Oceania?

# II

Our appointment will be brief, Jürgen reminds me. He is here "on business."

So I begin directly: What was it like to be a junior faculty member and longtime Communist Party functionary under the Honecker regime?

"I had a place secured, a paved road before me," came the answer, as if from a great distance. "You—you've spent your whole life competing. We haven't. My career track was clear—*Dozent*, then Professor, then *Ordinarius*. In time, if I were reasonably productive, it would have all been there. Now, no university in Germany will have me. Probably I'll have to emigrate. That's the only way to escape everyone forever asking me what I did in the Party and why I did it."

Authorities have just announced that several departments—among them law, political science, journalism, and Marxism Leninism (M-L), will soon be shut down; Jürgen expects to be released in six months. He has spent the last ten years at the Karl-Marx Universität, the oldest university in eastern Germany and widely regarded as the second-leading GDR university after Humboldt University in East Berlin. Talk has been buzzing that Humboldt could soon be closed down altogether, since united Berlin doesn't need a rival to the Free University (FU)—and since old Cold Warriors at the FU have hardly forgotten being driven from Humboldt in the late '40s. Such a scenario would leave the Karl-Marx Universität the top university in the east.[1]

But Jürgen's thoughts are elsewhere. Academic politics holds little interest for him now; it all seems curiously irrelevant. His mind is preoccupied with *Abwicklung*. Eastern German students deride it as another "Unwort" (Unword), an example of official (western) German Newspeak. *Abwicklung*—as we saw in chapter 7—is a euphemism used in Bonn government policy statements for the dismantling of GDR institutions and the laying off of thousands of eastern German employees. The Leipzig students with whom I've spoken seem to consider it the epitome of western-style bureaucratese and the Orwellian vocabulary of FRG capitalism.

*Abwicklung* is the order of the day in Leipzig, a city of 560,000, the second largest in eastern Germany. Those who served the Karl-Marx Universität in "ideologically burdened" departments, or who held Party offices, or who had contact with the *Stasi*, will probably not retain their positions. Jürgen admits that, even if he were to undergo an ideological *Überprüfung* (screening), he would "start with those three counts against me anyway." Fifty out of 100 academic staff members in history have already been sacked. Word has it that faculty screenings in Saxony will be particularly close, he says. Given the election victory of the Christian Democrats a few weeks ago, law-and-order, anticommunist conservatives will be in charge.

In protest against the *Abwicklung* of academic departments, leaders of the student body, which numbers 13,000, have blockaded the university and are organizing demonstrations. Last week students occupied the main buildings on campus; a dozen went on hunger strike, others have boycotted classes in some "protected" departments. But Jürgen says that these protests will change nothing. The die has been cast, and "ideologically burdened" faculty—or even entire departments (such as philosophy) that served as mouthpieces for the state philosophy of M-L—are already history. Or better: "History."

# III

I watch Jürgen nervously flick the ashes of cigarette after cigarette, his palms wet and his wiry frame coiled over our little table. Like Jürgen, my thoughts are also elsewhere—but not on the politics of *Abwicklung*. Rather, I feel as if I'm present at a private reading of our generation's *God That Failed*, that powerful collection of postwar memoirs of several leading ex-communist intellectuals of the 1930s and '40s. And more. As an English Ph.D., a scholar of George Orwell's work, and a teacher of courses in the history of utopianism, I feel also the frisson of uneasy recognition: Here was a man of my own generation, a student of his state's philosophy and literature, a onetime idealist who had spent his entire life desperately clinging to utopian illusions.

Who was he now?

Even as we talked, the senior faculty at the university were drafting a motion concerning their collective identity, themselves preoccupied by the same overwhelming question. They were voting, unanimously, that the university return to its old name—to the hallowed name by which it had been known for more than half a millennium (before the communists renamed it in 1952): Leipzig University.

More than anything else, it was Jürgen's understated, almost deliberately self-deflationary delivery that made his words so powerful. Yet I now realize that it was I, more than he, who invested our three hours together with such dramatic significance: after all, he had been living in the aftermath of the spontaneous demonstrations against his Party by *das Volk*—the "Leipzig Miracle" of October 1989—for more than a year. But this was my first extended visit to an erstwhile communist country, my first real encounter with all that I had read. Though I was familiar with the painful history of the socialist movement, I had learned it largely through books. And so each living encounter brought on for me the visceral experience of déjà vu. *Nineteen Eighty-Four* and the GDR—and *The God That Failed*—all appeared in 1949. Had history stopped there? The repressed emotions, the incremental concessions, the everyday compromises: Was this the 1990s or the 1940s?

Through my mind ran Marx and Engels's famous sentence in *The Communist Manifesto* about the course of revolutions: "Venerable prejudices and opinions are swept away. All that is solid melts into air, all that is holy is profaned, and men at last are forced to face … the real conditions of their lives and their relations to one another." And here was Jürgen, a good Marxist functionary, baring to me the story of his withering-away life.

This wasn't what Marx had meant, was it?

# IV

None of this is to say that Jürgen made any claims to having had an unusual connection with the Party. No, he was typical of his cohort of Party functionaries.

Yes, *that* was just it: he was typical.

Son of two Party members, Jürgen, like 98 percent of GDR children, attended the GDR's standard polytechnical elementary (POS) and secondary (EOS) schools and entered the Young Pioneers—a socialist version of the Cub Scouts and Brownies—in first grade. Proudly donning his blue neckerchief on special Pioneer Days such as the national birthday of the Pioneers (December 13), he was the model communist boy scout. "*Immer bereit!*" ("Always prepared!"). Jürgen recalls that the Pioneer motto encompassed several kinds of commitment: "always prepared" to study; "always prepared" for peace, friendship, and solidarity; "always prepared" for productive socialist labor; and so on. Little Jürgen could recite by heart the twelve Pioneer Laws ("1. Young Pioneers respect people. 2. Young Pioneers show respect for other nations.

*Like father, like son: (top) the Hitler Youth March in 1933 in Chemnitz; (below) the Free German Youth parade in 1950 in Berlin.*

. . ."). After school, he participated in a variety of Pioneer activities; the Pioneers sponsored "work groups" for chess, mathematics, singing, and various sports. The groups taught the child to think "collectively" and to think about the value of work outside the sphere of required schooling.

In fourth grade, Jürgen joined the Thälmann Pioneers, receiving his red neckerchief as he pledged to live up to the ideals and example of Ernst Thälmann. He was a "Timur Helper"—like the Soviet child-hero from the socialist-realist novel, *Timur and His Troop.* Jürgen ran errands for retirees in his neighborhood and assisted them with household chores.

And though he wasn't much of an athlete, Jürgen went to several summer camps, each one of them named after a famous German or East-bloc socialist, in which he often sat around the campfire and sang folk and political songs. Every Wednesday afternoon, he attended Thälmann Pioneer meetings; at one memorable meeting, he was elected to the office of "scribe"; his task was to keep records in the "group book." By the age of eleven, Jürgen regularly helped organize the festivities for major national celebrations, such as the fiftieth anniversary, in 1967, of the Great October Revolution.

After his socialist "youth confirmation" ceremony (the so-called *Jugendweihe*) and his entry into the post-Pioneer organization (the Free German Youth, or FDJ) while in eighth grade in 1970, Jürgen held three different offices in his FDJ class: secretary, then deputy, and finally culture functionary. His responsibilities included supervising the FDJ membership and organizing FDJ outings to museums. In school, he became the regular class representative to the Russian Olympiad; he excelled at Russian grammar, sang Russian folk and Soviet *Komsomol* songs with gusto, and could answer the FDJ equivalent of Trivial Pursuit questions such as "What is the main department store in Moscow?" Since sixth grade, he had written faithfully to a Russian pen pal; later he sometimes would go with his mother to "German-Soviet Friendship" (DSF) evenings, where he would talk to soldiers and their families in Russian.

"I enjoyed my years in school," Jürgen says with a smile. "I don't know whether I was a 'convinced socialist.' For the most part, I didn't associate school, or even Pioneer activities, with politics. Very little was directly political, actually. The group activities fostered togetherness and 'collective thinking.' You thought of the welfare of the group.

"Of course, the older you got, the more you realized what was politically acceptable to mention in public. Even my mother, who had little good to say about West Germany, always watched the ARD and ZDF channels on TV— and she would tell me never to say in school that we watched it. I would never say, 'Did you see that great movie on ZDF last night?' And neither did my other classmates. You just didn't mention it. . . . Still, I never felt under any pressure to participate in the Pioneers or the Russian Olympiads—writing and language and music were always my pleasures."

# V

Politics entered his life unmistakably, Jürgen says, with his entry into the FDJ and his matriculation to the Ernst Schneller EOS in Meissen, which was named after an old communist resistance fighter against the Nazis. The two summer camps that he attended during his school years were less like Boy Scout outings than army camps, featuring military exercises and training in the use of small firearms. All but one of the twenty-five students in his high school graduating class were FDJ members; seven of them were "politically oriented"; three applied to the Party for candidate membership even before graduation. Whereas the elementary school teachers, especially in the early grades, had been little concerned with ideology, Jürgen says, many EOS teachers were *rote Socken* (red socks, i.e., Party loyalists). Although his mother knew many of them through her Party circles, Jürgen never felt he could confide personal difficulties to them about family or politics; they were never *Vertrauensleute* (trusted persons).

"Almost all my EOS teachers were in the Party," Jürgen says. "Most of them were competent academically, but often they were limited by the curriculum. For instance, you could choose art or music in the EOS. I chose art because the teacher was intelligent and friendly. But she had to teach mostly Soviet art and socialist realism, and even when we briefly discussed ancient art, it was through an image of 'socialist antiquity.'

"Other teachers had less subtle minds and more overt agendas. My eleventh-grade civics teacher specialized in *Feindbilder* [enemy images] of the West, and you received grades based on your political convictions. Sometimes he would have us watch a laughable TV show such as [Karl-Eduard von] Schnitzler's *Schwarzer Kanal* [Black Channel], which purported to analyze western events but was the most blatant, pathetic GDR propaganda—West Germans called him 'the Red Goebbels.' Nobody would ever sit through it if it weren't required—people joked that a 'Schni' was the unit of time it took to switch channels if you inadvertently saw his face on TV.

"Anyway, the civics teacher treated the weekly revelations of Schnitzler—or 'von' Schnitzler, I should say, and the aristocratic background of this 'worker's spokesman' elicited even more jeers—as if they were straight from Lenin's tomb. The civics teacher was an old army officer, the reddest of the *rote Socken*, tolerating no deviations from the textbook's line whatsoever. NATO was bad, the Warsaw Pact was good. The Prague Spring was bad, the Wall was good. Bad Americans came through the Brandenburg Gate in August 1961, and courageous officers from our NVA (National People's Army)—such as our civics teacher!—stood their ground, fended off the invasion, and in cooperation with loyal workers erected the Wall to prevent future assaults. For the most part, we believed what the history books said—without ever really listening to the civics teacher or acquiring a *Feindbild* of the U.S. or the West. It was all just dead history to us, never talked about outside class except on some official occasion.

"Curiously enough, though, I liked the old civics teacher—you knew where you stood with him. 'You are the socialists, the elite, the future leaders of

society! Behave like it!' he would thunder. Once he even asked me to apply to become an army officer! But I had no interest in that. All in all, I preferred him to the careerists, such as my twelfth-grade civics and geography teacher—he was a real hypocrite! 'C'mon, tell me what you really think!' he'd say. 'We can all speak freely here!' And then—I say this in hindsight—he would report on any deviations to the Party officials at the school, which kept a file on political troublemakers and potential adult 'subversives.' It was clear to me even then that his every action was angled to become school principal or for some kind of promotion—and eventually he did become a school principal somewhere."

Even before Jürgen scored a 1, 2—an A plus—on the *Abitur*, his high school leavetaking exam, it was clear to Jürgen's family and teachers that he would go on to university. His parents were college-level teachers; higher education was in the family. Undecided between *Germanistik* and philosophy, he chose philosophy when a friend of his mother, a professor of philosophy in Halle, persuaded her that his future was brightest in that subject. Jürgen joined his parents in the Party after gaining his *Abitur* at 19. His mother, a radical and idealist with both feet planted firmly in the air, has been left hanging there. Among the first to be fired, she had been a senior M-L lecturer at a technical college in Karl-Marx Stadt, now also returned to its former name, Chemnitz. Jürgen's father, whom she divorced when Jürgen was 10, taught M-L in a Halle college that has also recently been nicely "wrapped up": *abgewickelt*.

"My mother is an economist who knows only Marxist economics—and it's been canceled by History," Jürgen jokes. He takes a deep drag of his cigarette and tosses his head back. "It's too late for her to do an *Umschulung* [retraining], or to begin over. Likewise with my father. Their lives are over.

"At eighteen, I still believed in socialism, I believed in its ideals," Jürgen says. "That's probably because my mother believed in it so passionately—my mother, a true believer, but also one of the few truly intelligent socialists I've ever known. But at least as big a part of me entered the Party for careerist reasons. Maybe 30 percent of us entered for the ideals—maybe 30. Seventy percent entered for the career advantages. After entering, maybe 10 percent stayed believers—maximum. My mother was one of the rare ones—the Idealistic Materialist! But most of us stayed for the advantages—it was simply much, much easier to make it up the ladder.

"By nineteen I was already disillusioned—more by the timidity than by the lies," Jürgen goes on. "You knew what you couldn't say, you policed yourself. You never even thought outside those categories. Like *Nineteen Eighty-Four*. What, surprised? Yes, I've read Orwell. *Doppelzüngigkeit* [doublethinking]—that's exactly what it was, though we called it dialectics.

"It wasn't that the university was less open than the EOS. Just the reverse. We had a number of fairly free discussions in M-L about the future of socialism, even on controversial topics, such as whether the 'Law of History' meant that religion was dying out. No, it was that by now you had lost your innocence. Even the FDJ officials at the university would joke about FDJ activities—'OK, people,' they'd say, 'let's get this over with.' You'd have a half-hour meeting about some upcoming event, about which nobody cared, yet which let the FDJ official report to the Party that we met. Then we'd all go out for beers."

# VI

Jürgen's most difficult decision had come at the age of thirty when the Party offered him the three-year post of FDJ secretary at the university. He would be in charge of organizing youth meetings, evaluating students for Party membership, and keeping tabs on FDJ members.

"I never wanted to do it—I'm not really a political person. I refused, but they said, 'You'll do it, or no *Assistent*—let alone *Ordinariat*.' Finally, at my parents' urging, I gave in. I wanted the security, and I thought I could just go along and make things work.

"It proved to be nothing but a headache. Ridiculous. Old men telling young people what they 'really' wanted! For instance, in preparation for the GDR's fortieth anniversary last October 7, [Egon] Krenz tells [FDJ chief Hartmut] Lange and the Berlin director of the FDJ to organize a youth festival. The Berlin director tells the district leaders, and I get the word: 'Bring your best people.' But—of course—nobody wants to go. And I have to pressure and plead with them—all the while pretending that it's an 'honor' to be 'invited' to the Fortieth Anniversary Celebration. A bureaucratic nightmare—all *Doppelzüngigkeit*. Of course I knew I was living a lie—but by then it had been fifteen years."

I ask Jürgen if, in his position, he had much contact with the *Stasi*. Folding his hands, Jürgen gazes out the window. "Not much," he answers. His eyes are fixed on the traffic below. "Once in a great while they would come around, just asking for information. We'd chat—I always considered it just a part of my duties—and of my duty as a socialist. Don't you feel that way about the CIA? . . . No? Well, I never knew anything very private or damaging about anyone. And I never again heard about whatever the agents were inquiring about—they never got back to you."

Tentatively, I inquire about Jürgen's specific contact with *Stasi* agents—for that is the blackest mark one can have in reunified Germany. Under the planned *Überprüfung* (screening) that will (under the aegis of western German examination boards) be conducted according to ideological as well as professional criteria, a *Stasi* connection will constitute grounds for automatic dismissal from the university—and perhaps even condemn one to joblessness or emigration.

Jürgen turns around toward me. His voice is steady. He replies casually, "I'd rather not discuss that subject any further. What other questions do you have?"

Could you, in your position, ever criticize the Party?

"That was the one small advantage. Sometimes, if you couched it in the right terms and avoided making it a public criticism, yes. Then sometimes the higher-ups would listen—because now you too represented the Party. 'We must do this,' I might say—and I had a bit of leverage on the inside. But it was very little, really. It was a delusion to think we could ever reform the Party from within. And we knew the rule: Never criticize publicly, not even at a Party meeting. . . . Sure, the youth leaders were always questioning, always expressing reservations—but the older people would always be 'explaining' to us that X or Y had to be seen dialectically. And brilliant dialecticians they were!

"But I respected very few of them. They too were careerists, afraid to speak their minds. Yet—to stand up at a meeting and criticize Honecker directly?! Never. Your career would have been over with that very sentence. And anyway, what would it have accomplished? It would have been crazy. And far worse to leave the Party once you had joined than never to have joined at all. It was like the Mafia: once you were in, you were in for life. One or two senior profs did leave before 1988—when it first became possible to leave and survive—but you had to be outstanding to do that.

"People began to leave in 1988—no earlier. The young people welcomed Gorbachev, but the old people controlled the Party and wouldn't listen. They thought things would just go on forever as they always had. The Party defections came in droplets and then in waves. In 1988, two or three people at the University. In early '89, maybe twenty. In the summer of '89, 200—by then, it was becoming too late to penalize faculty, because too many were leaving. And by November, leaving didn't mean anything anymore."

Jürgen admits that he stayed in the Party until January 1990. "Until 11:59," he says ruefully. He had still believed it might be possible to build a reformed Communist Party with a mass following.

"October 10, 1989—the day of the first big demonstration here [when 50,000 Leipzigers marched peacefully through the streets]—we had a Party meeting scheduled. We canceled it just as the march was beginning—to save our lives! Funny, unlike many Party members, I was curious and rather supportive of the marchers. It even crossed my mind to join them—but everyone in the Party knew that observers were keeping tabs on the demonstrators, and that was enough to deter us. . . .

"To us, it still seemed possible then to reform socialism. Even after the citizens' committee occupied the local *Stasi* headquarters [in December] and began calling officially for the ouster of the Party. As late as January of this year, we were having Party meetings—as if we could abolish the SED and claim the People's support—just like that! As if a name change [to PDS, Party of Democratic Socialism] were enough! . . . We were completely out of touch with reality. It was all a delusion—I was living in a *Schlaraffenland* [fool's paradise]."

But Jürgen says he was as surprised as anyone else about the revelations that began surfacing in late November 1989 about the corruption of the SED leadership. He'd had no idea of the full story—it had been kept within a tight little circle. However timid and hard line he knew them to be, he'd had no idea that former Party and *Stasi* leaders had diverted hundreds of millions of marks to foreign bank accounts, had embezzled tens of millions for ski lodges and vacation villas. The stories during those winter months had filled him with anguish about the Party. Yet still he had stayed. . . .

Jürgen glances out the window again. The light is failing.

But he does not move. He does not rise from his seat.

Yes, still he had stayed. Some part of him, beneath all the careerism and *Doppelzüngigkeit*, still had believed in the collectivist god, still had trusted in the socialist *Schlaraffenland*.

# VII

Stepping out into the rain, I remember Arthur Koestler's parting reflection in *The God That Failed*: The end does not justify the means; the means determine the end.

Walking back in the twilight to the university, I run into an acquaintance in the German department there, Reinhard, a man slightly older than Jürgen. An *Assistent* who had withdrawn from the Party in July 1989 after the SED's public support for the Tiananmen Square massacres, Reinhard had been one of the very few Leipzig faculty who had been on the streets in early October '89 to protest.

We talk as I accompany Reinhard toward his office. I mention my impressions of my conversation with Jürgen, whom Reinhard knows slightly. Seating himself in his cramped office, whose centerpiece is a huge metal desk piled high with books and papers, Reinhard says that he too has read Orwell and Koestler. Everyone in eastern Germany knows Orwell's *Nineteen Eighty-*

*Four*, Reinhard claims, but he's more interested, for the moment, to discuss with me the work of Orwell's friend and anti-Stalinist "comrade," the "Hungarian anti-fascist" Koestler. Reinhard mentions Koestler's *Sonnenfinsternis* (*Darkness at Noon*), the brilliant anti-Stalinist novel about the Soviet show trials and the totalitarian mentality, in which Rubashov, an Old Bolshevik defendant, abases himself, confesses to treasonous crimes he never committed, and accepts execution out of loyalty to his youthful communist ideals—his last act of devotion to the Party.

He himself has known Rubashovs, Reinhard says, nodding glumly. Koestler's psychological understanding of Rubashov and the logic of Party loyalty is acute, he says, though Stalin obtained his confessions by good old-fashioned torture, not via some mysterious process of self-incriminating confessions. We talk about Koestler's membership in the Communist Party (KPD) of the 1930s and the anguish and remorse that he felt when he realized that the Party was a fraud and a charade. In an existential sense, Rubashov *was* guilty, says Reinhard; his real crime was that he was willing to serve the Party until the end. Like Winston Smith in *Nineteen Eighty-Four*, Rubashov was as corrupt as the system that produced him.

We muse together on the Stalin cult, on the mass hallucination of those years, on the Party mentality. Then, suddenly, Reinhard swivels his chair and rolls over to a cluttered bookcase. Eyeing an old copy of *Neues Deutschland* stuffed between some books, he yanks it out. It is dated January 1989. With mock ceremony, Reinhard reaches into his inside coat pocket, pulls out a leather case, and with professorial fastidiousness, dons his glasses. He turns to me and smiles.

"As an exercise," he says impishly, "let's count the references to Honecker."

We go through the front page of the paper together. Total: seventeen.

"Definitely on the low side, I'd say," Reinhard pronounces. He shakes his head. Honecker was a long way from Stalin, he says. But how did he go along until July 1989 with such a system as that?

"Youthful ideals," I reply.

Reinhard does not respond. Instead he says: "If you had read [West German publisher Axel] Springer's *Bild-Zeitung* over the last four decades"—a mass cult rag amounting to a cross between our *National Enquirer* and *USA Today*—"you'd probably have gotten a more accurate picture of Germany than from *Neues Deutschland* or *Junge Welt.*"

The comparison stops me short, transporting me back again to the American literary scene: it is the early 1980s, and General Jaruzelski has just suppressed Poland's Solidarity movement. Susan Sontag comments in a Town Hall speech in New York that a *Reader's Digest* subscriber of the 1950s and '60s would have been better informed about the realities of communism than a *New Statesman* or *Nation* subscriber. A stunning claim! Sontag's observation—a mea culpa for her trip to Hanoi, her fear of criticism from radicals, her sentimental attachment to socialist pieties, her own moral blindness—triggered a firestorm of protest from the Anglo-American Left. But its kernel of truth seemed to me undeniable. Why hadn't the democratic Left listened more closely to the waves of foreign émigrés, the Cassandras from Koestler through Kundera and Kosinski, who had proclaimed the horrors of Stalinism? Why had leading liberal-Left magazines largely closed their ears—and their pages—to such voices?

Is there a Lesson—or Unlesson—in it all? Sontag drew one from from the crackdown on Solidarity: communism is the most devious collectivism, a high-flown, "dialectical" fascism—"fascism with a human face," as she called it.

But is that it? Or is that just a new revisionism? Clearly, the émigrés had been speaking an important truth, if not the whole truth. And the American Left had been living a lie—and with much less pressure to conform than SED members. Yet somehow this assessment seems to glide over the agonizing, visceral tug-of-war inside the souls of those like Koestler whose life stories appeared in *The God That Failed*, the years of love-hate through which most Party heretics—and believers—suffered.

How were you able to summon the strength to leave the Party? I ask Reinhard.

A long sigh. Reinhard tells me about his reaction to the Tiananmen Square propaganda in the GDR. Removing his glasses, he says he does not want to falsify his past.

"It was the vulgarity of it all," he says finally. "It was all so stupid—when you could see on West German TV what was really happening. . . . If they had presented it intelligently, the Party line might have been plausible. The stupidity of it all! As if Hitler and fascism were still the enemy! All presented so black and white! Like almost everything else, nothing they said corresponded to the complicated realities of the West—it was so dumb, so one-sided, so extreme. Your own TV set refuted it every night—as did your own relatives every visit. I just couldn't go on condoning the system, I had to do something. So I got out. I feared for my job, but I got out."

Reinhard pauses. He gazes absently out the window. It is dark outside.

Turning toward me, Reinhard looks at me intently, and then smiles.

"As my old grandfather used to say to us, there's just one thing wrong with socialism: *Es funkioniert nicht* [It doesn't work]."

We chuckle together. Still, I want something more than, or different from, such talk. But I don't know what to say.

Reinhard goes on talking, now explaining why he supports the Social Democrats. He says he voted for the Social Democrats in the recent election; he couldn't imagine supporting the reconstituted SED (Communist Party), the PDS (Party of Democratic Socialism)—and certainly can't imagine actually *joining* this new incarnation of "the Party."

I remark that numerous students at the university seem, however, to be showing renewed interest in socialism, including the PDS. Could "the Party" one day rise again from the ruins? I ask. Did the god—or merely the Faithless—fail?

Reinhard looks out the window. Night has fallen. He turns back toward me. He nods, and then shakes his head.

"Yes, already one hears it everywhere—'That never happened under socialism. . . .' Socialism is a beautiful dream. Within five or ten years, it will only become more powerful in the east again. As the dissatisfactions with capitalism mount, as the victims of competition become bitter, people will speak again of its vision of equality and social justice and brotherhood. . . . Ah, it is a beautiful dream—and one which can never work. But it will never die."

# 11

# Of Laughter, Forgetting, and Memory Holes

## I

On a warm October afternoon in Leipzig, I am walking with a half-dozen university students from Karl-Marx Universität—now, in 1991, again called Leipzig University. Across the street is the Leipzig railway station—before the war, it was the biggest in Europe—and the Gewandhaus, where the Leipzig orchestra plays. Kurt Masur, who helped negotiate with police to hold their fire against Leipzig protesters before the city's first mass demonstration—two years ago come October 9—is still conducting at the Gewandhaus.

We take seats on two concrete benches in the shadow of the monumental plastic sculpture *"Aufbruch"* ("Awakening"), a legacy of socialist realism that depicts a group of people struggling to move forward, as if awakening to political consciousness. Our discussion centers on themes that arose today during my university lecture on Orwell and *Nineteen Eighty-Four.* Across the courtyard from the grotesque socialist realist sculpture stands a much older sculpture: a towering statue of Leibniz. The wise old Leipzig professor represents the classical spirit of the Enlightenment. Just a few yards beyond Leibniz is the sacred spot where began the already historic marches and the "We are The People" chants that brought down the SED regime and East Germany itself only two Octobers ago.

Since the fall of the Berlin Wall, Leipzig has been known as the *Heldenstadt* (city of heroes), as the faded bumper stickers on a few cars remind me. But the word has become tinged with irony. Though the city is in the middle of a construction boom, the Leipzig students are the first to tell you that the greedy machinations of new eastern German entrepreneurs and western German carpetbaggers, along with politically compromising revelations about leading dissidents in the *Stasi* files, have badly tarnished the city's heroic image.

Our conversation turns to a few remarks of mine from my university lecture on Orwell, which several of the students had attended. I had mentioned that Milan Simecka, the Czech translator of *Nineteen Eighty-Four*, spent two years in prison in the 1970s for translating Orwell. That was after the Soviet army crushed the so-called Prague Spring—the period of "socialism with a human face" briefly inaugurated by Aleksandr Dubcek in 1968—in the pre-Gorbachev and pre-*glasnost* days.

My reference to Simecka provokes the students to bring up a much better-known dissident, Milan Kundera. The students mention Kundera's *Book of Laughter and Forgetting*, which several of them have just read in an introductory seminar in Slavic literature. Kundera's novel consists of a series of scenes in which time is measured back and forth from the Prague Spring. I've read Kundera's novel too. I'd even considered assigning it in my undergraduate course on utopian literature, one of whose units pivots around Orwell's critique of Wellsian utopianism in *The Road to Wigan Pier* and his anti-utopian vision in *Nineteen Eighty-Four*. The students and I trade observations on Kundera and Orwell. Like Orwell's dystopia, *The Book of Laughter and Forgetting* centers on artifacts of writing: for Winston, a diary and the love note from Julia; for Kundera's female protagonist, Tamina, a diary, notes, and lost correspondence. They remark on how much Kundera owes to Orwell—and argue that he goes beyond Orwell. I resist that claim—though I've come since then to understand what they meant and to agree with them. Kundera addresses the political frontally, like Orwell, but he also fuses the personal and political. He achieves what Orwell accomplished in *Animal Farm* yet failed to do with complete success in *Nineteen Eighty-Four*: to turn political writing into an art. But Kundera's interests are more existential than ideological. Whereas Orwell emphasizes the social and the naturalistic within the realistic tradition of the novel, Kundera explores the impact of power on the existential angst of the post-atomic person. But he handles the horrors of collectivization and depersonalization with a lighter touch, reflecting our jaded acquiescence to them—and also the fact that new developments of technology have led to delicate new forms of thought control and linguistic contamination.

*The Book of Laughter and Forgetting* is also, like *Nineteen Eighty-Four*, about the theme of rewriting history. But Kundera approaches this in transpolitical terms. For instance, the male protagonist, Mirek, attempts to preserve the true history of Czechoslovakia after August 1968 by keeping a diary and preserving correspondence. Meanwhile he also imitates the very regime he is struggling against in his personal life by trying to make his former love, Zdena—whom he now regards as unattractive and beneath him—disappear from his life. But Mirek's personal history is hard to erase: "She refused to be crossed out." The only real difference between Mirek and his hated state machine is that the communist regime finds it easier to rectify Czech history. Kundera draws the analogy emphatically in the novel: "Mirek is as much a rewriter of history as the Communist Party, all political parties, all nations, all men."

We agreed that Orwell does examine how totalitarianism depersonalizes relationships, rewrites history, and decides what truth is—both what is to be remembered and what is to be forgotten. But Kundera does it from the inside as well as the outside, showing that every person rewrites his or her history.

I remark to the students that Orwell might regard Kundera's novel as trivializing politics by addressing the struggle between capitalist and communist values via biting irony, sardonic passivity, and absurdist humor. But they do not find Kundera a cynical quietist at all.

"He's hilarious," says one student to me.

"I couldn't stop laughing," adds another.

The students cite the speech by Husak, "the president of forgetting," who tells Czech children that "they are the future." The students laugh at this piece of engineered forgetting. They tell me that "my Orwell" would doubtless consider Kundera "a bit of a formalist"—exactly what their old M-L professors would have pronounced. Then the students excitedly speak about the macabre opening scene in *The Book of Laughter and Forgetting* that describes how, after a Czech Party leader was charged with treason and hanged in 1948, the communist propaganda apparatus airbrushed his face out of a ceremonial photograph.

"What an example of the Orwellian rewriting of history!" exclaims still another student. I'm struck by the opinion of the students about the significance of humor in Kundera's work. I reply that Orwell was himself a lot funnier than many critiques recognize. Kundera highlights humor in order to give his work the flavor of ordinary existence. He is interested in creating a novel real to life and peopled by real characters. Part of the difference, of course, is that Orwell is writing in the midst of reports about the Gulag and in the aftermath of the Holocaust, whereas Kundera is writing within a decade of the collapse of East European communism, long after de-Stalinization and after the communist citizenry had forfeited its ideals about the system.

Two students suggest that I speak with their Slavic professor, who, although an eastern German, may have keen insight into all this.

The conversation veers to other topics during the next half hour. But the students' observations stay with me. Much later it occurs to me: Kundera's novel isn't just about forgetting, it's about *laughter*. Perhaps I'm too concerned with Kundera's forgetting and not enough with his laughter! Both Kundera and Orwell depict the rewriting of history, but Orwell does it mostly in a very serious vein. Kundera portrays what it is like to live in that system, whereas Orwell is simply concerned to portray the system. Both depict wondrously alive characters, but Orwell's "character" is Oceania—and it is multifaceted and vital. It is larger than life, "oceanic": yes, one could even praise Orwell's choice of name.

But Oceania is not funny (though its childish sadism—torture via rats in Room 101—is certainly bathetic). By contrast, laughter is central to Kundera's work because it is a human emotion that enters in response to the system and involves living and coping with it. But the system itself has no humor: Big Brother is a cool abstraction. And Kundera did have to live with this system for forty years. Orwell never did, and so he approaches it as a horrifying idea that he hopes will never be realized in Britain. Kundera and Orwell are really depicting different "characters" within similar fictional worlds. Moreover, especially for the insiders—the Winston Smiths who were Party members and ultimately victims of the system—Orwell's book *is* an accurate portrait. But Kundera better captures ordinary life under the system, especially in its later years, when citizens simply tried to avoid bureaucratic hassles and remain inconspicuous. Kundera captures the absurdity of their ordinary experience.

And so I realized my own forgetting. I, an American intellectual historian, a scholar of utopian thinking, a literary-cultural critic of socialism had grasped half—but only half—of the world in which Kundera lived.

The students' observations stay with me, and I make arrangements through one of them to meet both their Slavic professor and another younger colleague in the Slavic department the following afternoon.

# II

It's a warm day in the smoggy city center. Heike and I sit near the spot where her students and I conversed. I tell her that I am writing a book about the GDR educational and cultural apparatus.[1] She remarks that my topic is "significant and very serious—not at all an 'academic' topic for us East Germans." She is keenly interested yet somehow distant, preoccupied. Heike repeats that my research will have "great personal significance for us easterners." She adds that I may find it easier to conduct the research: "You are a foreigner, whereas our distrust of *Wessis* is very high."

Heike is tense; she gazes fixedly down at the ground, her hands clasped tightly in front of her. The conversation turns to the "personal" dimension of my "serious" topic—and to Heike's quarter-century in the SED as a student and then professor here at the university.

She is subdued, pensive—yet surprisingly forthcoming. Yes, I realize, it may indeed be easier for her to talk about her communist past with "a foreigner" whom she will probably not meet again.

"*Nie wieder*," Heike keeps repeating. "Never again."

Never would she join the reconstituted SED, now called the PDS. Never again would she join any party or movement, of whatever political stripe. Politics holds no interest for her. Her experience in the SED has disillusioned her toward—or, as she says, "inoculated" her against—party and ideological appeals. Permanently.

"I have learned my lesson," Heike says.

Heike, 46, a *wissenschaftliche Assistentin* (lecturer) in Slavic literature at Leipzig University, speaks in soft German—entirely free of Americanisms, unlike the speech of most West Germans—about her decades in the Party. Pale yet animated, her face is vital with expression, if lined with years; like many eastern German women, she wears no makeup.

She pauses again. Her voice is subdued and distant. "Nobody among us was a hero." Heike pauses. And then:

"'Police files are our only claim to immortality.'"

I flinch.

Heike says it is a line from *The Book of Laughter and Forgetting*, which she read in the early '80s. I mention that I've spoken to her students about it. She says she's always wanted to teach it, but before 1990 the novel—available in the GDR in Czech only—remained under lock and key in the library, strictly off limits to all except GDR Slavic scholars.

"You had to have courage, and I didn't," she says simply. "You had to be a hero, and I wasn't."

Heike goes on to tell me at length about her husband, a recently terminated Marxist-Leninist philosophy professor, and about her own years as a professor and Party member. She speaks about a procession of silent, daily, near-invisible compromises that she made for reasons of career and family—the stuff of a Kundera novel. As she spoke, I could not help but wonder whether I would have acted any differently in her place.

I look again at the *Aufbruch* sculpture, then at the hundreds of students scurrying between buildings to catch their next classes. The scene resembles any urban American campus. How different were Heike's small, incremental concessions from my own? Her careerism? Her rationalizations? For me, an American literary historian and critic of European socialism, meeting Heike has meant an uncomfortable, provocative brush with *erlebte Geschichte* (lived history). And something more. Heike's soul-searching reminds me of Irving Howe's old joke: Marxism has died, only to be reborn in U.S. English departments. Do our literary Marxists know people like Heike? I'm none too sure. I suspect that Heike knows something that they—that I myself—ought not to forget. Hers is another story of the communist academic functionary in postwar Eastern Europe.

We talk about Kundera's novel and about Kundera himself, who eagerly joined the Czechoslovakian CP as a teenager, cheered the communist take-over in 1948, became an unperson after Prague 1968, and emigrated in the mid-'70s. And about the airless, claustrophobic character of GDR life under communism. And about the mortality of memory. Should one preserve, forget, or laugh away the painful past?

August 21, 1968: when the Soviet T-64s came rumbling in.

Heike glances away, then raises her head slightly. The subject matter of Kundera's novel is indeed searingly personal for her in a way that it cannot be for her students, many of whom were not born until the 1970s. It is not just history, let alone History—and it is not just the political past. It is also her personal past.

"'The past is full of life, eager to irritate us, provoke or insult us, tempt us to destroy or repaint it.'" Heike is quoting Kundera again. She smiles.

Heike mentions how Kundera's characters suffer from *litost*, an untranslatable Czech word signifying an abject state caused by sudden insight into one's own soul-sickness. She reaches into her book bag for the Kundera novel and turns to a passage in which he writes of the Czech dissident Mirek: "He fought back his uncontrollable urge to reach far back into the past and smash it with his fist, an urge to slash the canvas of his youth to shreds." She pauses. Her own hands are clenched. Her voice drops; she recites from memory Mirek's thought before his arrest: "The struggle of man against power is the struggle of memory against forgetting."

Hesitantly, I mention the novel's protagonist, the unforgettable beauty, Tamina—exiled in Germany and working as a waitress—whose devouring passion is to retrieve the diaries that she abandoned in Czechoslovakia when she fled in 1968 after the Soviet tanks arrived. Heike nods gravely. Almost instantly, she finds the passage: "She has no desire to turn the past into poetry, she wants to give the past back its lost body . . . because if the shaky structure of her memories collapses like a badly pitched tent, all she will have left is the present, that invisible point, that mere nothing moving slowly toward death."

Heike closes the book, resting it atop my notepad.

# III

For Heike, disillusion came with Prague 1968. Until the late 1960s, she says, she thought that the weaknesses of socialism could be overcome.

"Prague, August 1968—when the Russian tanks rolled in. That was the watershed moment for me," Heike says. When the Czech Politburo under Aleksandr Dubcek openly defied Moscow during the heady spring of 1968, Heike was entranced. She admired Dubcek's Action Program, which renounced the Communist Party's legal monopoly on power, acknowledged other political parties, permitted freedom of the press, created market incentives, introduced small-scale private enterprise, and decentralized government control of industry—precisely those reforms that a collapsing Soviet economy would compel Mikhail Gorbachev to propose two decades later for the USSR itself as part of glasnost and perestroika. (A bittersweet joke made the rounds in Eastern Europe during the late 1980s: Q: What's the difference between Gorbachev and Dubcek? A: 20 years.)

Dubcek's reformist socialism resonated with the liberal proposals that some of Heike's colleagues discussed in local Party meetings, she says. In revulsion against a Soviet dictatorship that had dominated and exploited Czechoslovakia since the communist coup of 1948, progressive Czech leaders sought a "third way" between capitalism and communism: a nation both socialist and profoundly democratic. But the Soviet invasion in August meant that the Czech reforms never came to fruition.

Because Czechoslovakia was for many years the only country to which East Germans could travel without a visa—and because of its proximity on the southern border of the GDR, less than two hours from Leipzig—the events of August 1968 left an open wound on her generation, Heike says. The deepest anguish derived from the guilt of knowing that East German troops had helped put an end to the Prague Spring.

"Right then, I concluded that 'das bessere Deutschland' was a farce, an impossible dream," Heike continues. "Like my father, I couldn't look that nightmare [a failed socialism] in the face. 'Socialism can't be reformed from within'—again and again, that was the lesson, the lesson of all the uprisings in Eastern Europe before '68 and after." The system was Stalinism, not socialism. "But I couldn't bear to know that," Heike continues.

The rendezvous with disenchantment came, sooner or later, for nearly everyone, she says. And yet, there was no single shared moment, no common nationwide point of no return for renouncing the dream of *das bessere Deutschland.* And that was the hardest part, she says. Was the early postwar era of her father's generation really so different? I want to ask. But Heike effectively answers me: Each generation had its own unlessons, she says. Each generation had to unlearn and relearn for itself. Like those earlier communist pilgrims of the 1930s, who nurtured the flickering candle of Hope in exile or in concentration camps before the socialist sun rose over the eastern German ruins in 1945—through the pyres of the purges, the show trials, the mass executions, the Nazi-Soviet pact, and all the rest—successive generations of GDR citizens had to pass their own trials by fire in order to confirm their blind, unconditional faith. The tests were hardest if you actually lived in a communist country and saw your friends and family disappear or fall "out of favor" with the Party. Political romantics abroad could wax theoretical about "real existing socialism," but eastern Europeans had to live under it. And yet, even when everything else had been taken from you, Hope remained. For, as Dubcek later titled his autobiography, published posthumously: *Hope Dies Last.*

But die it eventually did. For nearly everyone in the GDR, the moment of recognition eventually came, Heike repeats. As though it were a long-resisted and deathly unpleasant initiation ceremony for the recalcitrant idealist. Or a belated coming-of-age, a second, belated socialist "Awakening." For Heike's paternal grandmother the date was 1953, when Russian troops ruthlessly suppressed the workers' uprising in East Berlin. For Heike's mother it was 1956, when the world turned upside down in the wake of Khrushchev's "Secret Speech," when the "Father of All Nations" suddenly stood revealed not just as a bad, "subjectivist" Party man but a murderer. For Heike's old Russian teacher it was 1957, when Party Chief Walter Ulbricht silenced Ernst Bloch and convicted the intellectual circle around the Aufbau publishing house, all of it eerily reminiscent of the postwar show trials elsewhere in Eastern Europe—indeed of the Soviet show trials of 1936–38. For Heike's older sisters it was 1961, when a desperate Ulbricht dammed up the westward flow of GDR migrants and erected "*den antifaschistischen Schutzwall.*" Even for Heike's resilient father, always the idealistic hard-liner, the date with the reality of "real existing socialism" finally came: in the mid-1970s, as the GDR began to "sell out to the fascists," when the half-hearted policy of détente pursued by Party leaders convinced him that the GDR would never offer a truly socialist alternative to West Germany.

And for each of them, the depth of the disillusion reflected the majesty of the myth and the duration of the dream. For the vision of paradise over the horizon had proven nothing more than a tantalizing mirage.

So Heike stayed. She did her work at the university. She taught her classes. She fulfilled her committee obligations, one of which included helping to plan the academic ceremony for the university's 575th anniversary in 1984. She published some articles on East European literature, invariably according to "the dialectical and materialist interpretation of History. . . . I would never have thought to have done otherwise," she says.

# IV

Yes, through it all she stayed, Heike says.

The words fall tonelessly. And then, her voice rising, Heike describes with awe the overwhelming autumn of 1989. Never in her own lifetime had Heike expected the Wall to come down. She had just, in the summer of 1989, taken her first trip to the West since adolescence, having been permitted to deliver a paper at a conference in Italy. A titanic battle seemed joined. Ronald Reagan's controversial 1987 speech ("Mr. Gorbachev, tear down this Wall!") was still ringing in European ears. And in mid-January 1989—just a few months before Heike's Italy trip—Honecker had made his much-quoted statement that the Berlin Wall would still be standing in the twenty-second century, "defending" the GDR against western imperialists.

"Do you think the Wall could fall?" several people at the conference in Rome asked her, Heike recalls.

"No, never, but maybe things are loosening up," she remembers answering. "The best proof of that is that I'm here, talking to you."

"No," she answers my question, with some irritation, it didn't occur to her not to come back.

But events were already beginning to overtake the Communist Party leadership. By late summer, voting with their feet, East Germans vacationing in Hungary began to force their way into the West German embassy in Budapest, willing to abandon everything, begging for asylum.

Heike herself was long past hoping for "socialism with a human face," she says. Confused and ashamed, yet at the same time transfixed with fascination, she gorged on West German TV beginning in August 1989. She watched an ever-increasing number of East German refugees flee their homes and seek asylum in the West German embassies in Prague and Warsaw. She watched Hungary open its border with Austria, resulting in 55,000 East Germans escaping to the West. And she watched the weeks of peaceful demonstrations on her doorstep in Leipzig, where the "October Revolution" began. Heike was too confused—and not hypocritical enough—to participate in the protests against the SED. She had been a *Nutzniesser* (beneficiary of the system).

But she watched. She watched throughout November, even after the Wall had fallen, as 300,000 Leipzig citizens marched peacefully through the streets, going from church to church carrying lighted candles. And almost as excitedly she watched the Velvet Revolution unfold in Czechoslovakia that same month, culminating in the return of the deposed Dubcek, who had spent most of the previous two decades repairing tools in a Slovak machine shop. She watched Dubcek's triumphant return to Prague, watched him stand on the balcony above Wenceslas Square, hand in hand with Vaclav Havel. The decent idealist was vindicated at last, as thousands jubilantly, indeed tearfully, roared their approval. Hope died last—but was reborn in joy.

Heike's own joy was mixed with shame. And even fear: In 1990, she thought she might lose her job.[2] Her husband, 57, did. His entire department of Marxist-Leninist philosophy was "wrapped up," summarily *abgewickelt*.

"'Early retirement,' he jokes, 'it's not so bad,'" Heike says, with a forced laugh. She pauses. "No, really he just sits at home and broods. The shame of it, and the guilt—never having taken a risk, never having stepped out of line, never having spoken up first. We'll take it to our graves."

Heike's eyes are bright with tears. She vouchsafes me the novel's closing line: "It takes so little, so infinitely little, for a person to cross the border beyond which everything loses meaning: love, convictions, faith, history."

Heike's voice is barely audible, but it floats onward, disembodied, dissociated. As if from a great distance, it speaks of the suffocating home that was the GDR.

Is this *litost*?

"The past—I can't laugh it away and I can't embrace it," Heike whispers.

The class bell slices the air, cauterizing the moment. Rising to leave, Heike glances at the *Aufbruch* sculpture, her face expressionless.

Mourning, remembrance, guilt, emptiness, homelessness, the vertiginous urge to throw off the past completely. *Nie wieder*: the unbearable lightness of being.

# V

Minutes later, I speak with Gerhard, 25, a graduate student whom a few of the younger students in the Orwell lecture recommended that I contact. Gerhard, a Ph.D. student in Slavic literature, did not attend my lecture on Orwell, whom he regards as "a socialist renegade."

We leave behind the *Aufbruch* sculpture, walking inside and up the stairs to his office cubicle. Gerhard speaks forcefully. He is a former student of Heike and says proudly that he is a PDS member—one of the few in a discredited, rump party that suffers the taint of the SED's failure, has shrunken overnight from 2.3 million members to 200,000, and boasts only seventeen representatives in reunified Germany's Bundestag. Having joined the SED in 1985, Gerhard had only been a member for four years before it fell apart. His view is a minority one, he says, but the task for him remains: to keep the flickering socialist torch aflame. When I respond that Heike and other Leipzig faculty seem to want to have nothing to do with the PDS, nor with politics or a reformed socialism, Gerhard waves his hand dismissively. "They're from another generation," he says.

I tell him I met earlier with Heike. I mention our conversation about Prague 1968 and Kundera.

Gerhard's smile vanishes. "She's from another generation," he says again, a note of weariness, or perhaps annoyance, slipping into his voice.

Suddenly Gerhard leans forward and grins. He says that when he thinks of Prague 1968 and middle-aged former Party members disillusioned with socialism since that date, another passage from Kundera, a scene from one of his stories, comes to mind and expresses his disgust with their quietism. Walking through downtown Prague, a man sees another man throwing up on the sidewalk. He comes up to him, shakes his head, and says: "I know just what you mean!"

Talk of the East German generation of '68 reminds Gerhard of *Der Tangospieler* (The Tango Player), by Christoph Hein, an eastern German author, which Gerhard read last year. A film version has just opened in Leipzig movie theaters.

Gerhard jumps up, goes into a cubicle across the hallway, and returns with a copy of the novel. I haven't read it; Gerhard explains that it is set chiefly during the spring and summer of 1968 and depicts the life of a thirty-six-year-old Leipziger named Hans Peter Dallow, a Slavic history professor whose specialty is the study of the working class in postwar Czechoslovakia. Two years earlier, Dallow had filled in as a piano player for a student revue. Without knowing what he was getting himself into, Dallow had found himself accompanying—in public—a ditty with improvised lyrics satirizing an aged head of state—obviously Ulbricht. In a Kafkaesque irony characteristic of totalitarian injustice, Dallow then lost his university job and was sentenced to twenty-one months in prison. Now free in mid-1968, he is utterly mired in the past—and in self-pity. Indifferent to the world-shaking events in Prague, the history behind which he had spent years professing, he is furious with everyone he meets. Nothing is important compared to the personal suffering he has endured. An inner émigré, Dallow can merely mouth, over and over: "I was only the tango player." His only concern is to have his name cleared and his former privileges restored.

The wheel does indeed eventually turn again. News arrives that Dallow can replace an old department colleague who, upon being informed by his students about the Warsaw Pact invasion of Prague, had injudiciously expressed public doubt that East German troops would ever march against a socialist brotherland. The opportunistic Dallow does not hesitate to resume his career. Our final glimpse finds him happily ensconced in his old apartment, playing Chopin on the piano in sweet triumph, as he watches East German TV clips of Czech women and children welcoming Warsaw Pact troops with flower bouquets.

Gerhard waves the paperback at me. *Der Tangospieler* offers insight into the mindset of the disillusioned SED generation of '68 today, he says. They play at remorse; they gaze at their navels. Whether guilty or not guilty, they are Guilty in the end. Gerhard flips to Hein's description of Dallow's image of the word "future" and reads aloud: "an enormous sheet of paper, white and terrifying."

Tossing the novel on the desk, Gerhard leans back in his chair. "Their failures aren't ours," he says of Heike and his other teachers. "We are not afraid of the future." He reminds me not to forget Marx's warning about the need to break the grip of "the dead hand of the past." Gerhard believes in moving on, in building a better future. He is indeed "from a different generation." But what separates him from his elders is not just a few decades; it is a chasm of experience. Their guilt—the legacy of years of disillusion and bad faith—is not his own, Gerhard says.

Gesturing expansively, his voice swelling, Gerhard declares: "Of course, they'll never make a mistake again; they'll never do anything again. It's perfect," Gerhard says, barely suppressing a derisive laugh. "If you do nothing, if you never get your hands dirty, you'll never make a mistake, you'll never be guilty! *Nie wieder!*' they say. Of course! How easy! Bury yourself in guilt, run from it!"

He looks hard into my face. "I'm still a socialist, still a utopian," he says. "Justice and decency for all! The ideals of socialism are still worth struggling for. We failed in the execution: the vision remains."

Another line from Kundera that Heike had quoted leaps out at me: "Totalitarianism is not only hell, but also the dream of paradise."

But I do not quote it. I listen and say nothing. For I am "only an American," I am from that Janus-faced thirty-something generation between Heike's and his own. I breathe the unbearably lighter air of America—indeed, of the American academy—where all is permitted but too little has mattered, precisely the opposite of the heavy atmosphere that has formed both of them. But clearly my intellectual world suffers from its own sorts of ideological conformity, doesn't it? Careerism? Status obsession? Gerhard races on:

"... And when I think of the relationship between the West and the Third World, of the resurgent xenophobia and anti-foreigner violence, of the neo-

*At the Fourth Party Congress in 1954, SED leaders continued, even after Stalin's death, to venerate him. Featured on the banner in the center of the stage are the four demigods of Marxism-Leninism in the early 1950s: Marx, Engels, Lenin, and Stalin. The banner on the left reads: "The strength of the Party is attributable to its unbreakable solidarity with the masses." On the right, the banner reads: "The strength of the masses is attributable to their linkage with the Party."*

Nazis on the march everywhere, I know we must do something, not merely run from the past.

"This country has been a microcosm of the whole world, a giant East-West laboratory to run one test over and over: capitalism or socialism? Which will it be? And that's still the question. Capitalism doesn't represent the absolute truth! Capitalism hasn't succeeded! And socialism hasn't failed—it still hasn't even been tried.

"We're still a microcosm. By the way we treat the foreign refugees, we reinforce or transform the relations between the industrialized and developing world. And those relations must be changed.

"Do I expect socialists to come to power in the next twenty or thirty years? No! Maybe never! But this much I do know: this capitalist system isn't capable of solving mankind's problems. When I think of this planet's future, of the children and of the Third World, I know this world mustn't—can't—go on as it always has."

I look across the table at that youthful face, in the springtime of hope. None of its features betray any twisted or fanatical idealism, no marks whatsoever disclose any receding line from moral righteousness to the *Realpolitik* of reflexive expediency and revolutionary justice.

The human face of socialism, its sincere and earnest voice echoing in my ears.

## POSTSCRIPT

Not until long after this conversation did Kundera publish his views of Orwell and *Nineteen Eighty-Four*. I was surprised to read his low estimate of Orwell—to whom he is obviously much indebted, both for his political criticisms as well as his literary vision. But I imagine that Kundera might respond in much the same way as he famously dismissed a political reading of *The Unbearable Lightness of Being* at an American conference in the mid-1980s. "Spare me your Stalinism!" Kundera scoffed. "It's a love story."

In *Testaments Betrayed* (1995), Kundera admires Diderot for introducing philosophical themes to the novel. But he calls George Orwell's *Nineteen Eighty-Four* "a bad novel": it is, he says, dogmatic, wooden, and burdened by literary characters who mouth prefabricated ideological shibboleths. Comparing Kafka's *Trial* to Orwell's *Nineteen Eighty-Four*, both of which are about an arrest and a trial, Kundera writes: "Orwell's novel itself joins in the totalitarian spirit, the spirit of propaganda. It reduces (and teaches others to reduce) the life of a hated society to the simple listing of its crimes."

This critique took me aback for two reasons. The first is that it is precisely the same critique that the Marxist Left has launched against *Nineteen Eighty-Four*. For instance, in the closing chapter of his monograph *George Orwell*, Raymond Williams castigates Orwell's "totalitarian" tactics of warning against totalitarianism in *Nineteen Eighty-Four*. Williams derides Orwell's vision on artistic grounds: " In the very absoluteness of the fiction," argues Williams, Orwell "committed himself to [the] submissive belief" in the historical inevitability of totalitarianism's triumph.[3] Kundera similarly condemns *Nineteen Eighty-Four* as a turgid, regressive ideological tract, concluding that if it can be called a novel at all, it is certainly a "bad" one:

> Orwell's novel is firmly closed to poetry; did I say novel? it is political thought disguised as a novel; the thinking is certainly lucid and correct, but it is distorted by its guise as a novel, which renders it imprecise and vague. So if the novel form obscures Orwell's thought, does it give something in return? Does it throw light on the mystery of human situations that sociology or political science cannot get at? No: the situations and the characters are as flat as a poster. Then is it justi-

fied at least as a popularization of good ideas? Not that either. For ideas made into a novel function no longer as ideas but as a novel instead, and in the case of *Nineteen Eighty-Four*, as a *bad* novel, with all the pernicious influence a bad novel can exert.

But to see Orwell's book as a "bad" novel may be a genre mistake. Strictly speaking, it is not a novel, for a novel *is* concerned chiefly with plot and character. *Nineteen Eighty-Four* is, therefore, not even a political novel. It is an anti-utopia, concerned with bringing to life an idea, a system—the totalitarian system of Oceania, which emerges as a virtuoso feat of characterization, a living reality: a Hitler and Stalin combined.

Kundera seems outraged as much by *Nineteen Eighty-Four*'s "influence" as by its substance, and he confuses the two. He calls it—fairly enough—"the book that for decades served as a constant reference for anti-totalitarianism professionals." But he denies (or "forgets") the historical reality from which *Nineteen Eighty-Four* emerged: the Gulag, the Holocaust, the bomb. What Williams had condemned as absolutist, Kundera dismisses as "reductive":

> The pernicious influence of Orwell's novel resides in its implacable reduction of a reality to its political dimension alone, and in its reduction of that dimension to what is exemplarily negative about it. I refuse to forgive this reduction on the grounds that it was useful as propaganda in the struggle against totalitarian evil. For that evil is, precisely, the reduction of life to politics and of politics to propaganda.[4]

But what about the possibility that *Nineteen Eighty-Four* is no "implacable reduction" but rather an accurate reflection of the reader's reality? What then?

That question forms the second reason why Kundera's deprecation of *Nineteen Eighty-Four* surprised me: My Leipzig University audience—especially the older adults, but even some students—found Orwell's novel provocative and powerful as a reading experience. And more: they considered it thoroughly relevant to life in the GDR, right down to the regime's bitter end.

Numerous elderly eastern Germans whom I interviewed during 1990–95 spoke in anguished tones about the "Orwellian" character of the early postwar era in the GDR. They were not "reducing" reality to politics. The father in the Stalinist concentration camp, the uncle sentenced to jail for carrying a sign in an anti-SED demonstration in June 1953, the older brother arrested by the *Stasi*: all that *was* their lived reality! It *was* their *erlebte Geschichte*! It is not an "exemplarily negative" slice of their past or "useful as propaganda." Rather, it constitutes a dominant feature of that past which overshadows their history and darkens it.

The eastern Germans with whom I spoke disagreed with Kundera's view: *Nineteen Eighty-Four* did indeed "live" for them. Some of them even suffered in order to procure and read it—such as young Baldur Haase. Perhaps *Nineteen Eighty-Four* is a lesser work of art, but it is, to borrow Orwell's phrase, "a good bad" novel. And even with its artistic deficiencies, it may have been a more powerful reading experience for eastern Europeans and Soviet citizens *because* of its deep connection with their reality. Orwell made it clear that he was writing a warning, that is, that he was acting as a moralist; Kundera writes as an artist more interested in exploring the possibilities of fiction than in attempting to turn the tide of history away from a calamitous outcome. Kundera seeks to create characters as living beings; Orwell is less interested in that than in changing human character or at least his readers' attitudes toward political and social life, in alerting people to the danger of certain tendencies in human character. My eastern German interviewees did not experience *Nineteen Eighty-Four* as a catalogue of crimes; it was true to their experience—if not their immediate personal experience, then the experience of their family or friends. Of course, Kundera lived inside the system and experienced it in its ordinary drabness. Orwell imagined it from the outside, from what he could gather from news accounts and the information of refugees. Kundera begins with art; Orwell starts from politics.

Yes, it was and still is their "reality." If the story of a Baldur Haase, a self-described "little servant of the state," is not convincing, might the word of Kundera's fellow writers and intellectuals prove more compelling? Would Kundera accept the testimony of his Parisian literary colleague Czeslaw Milosz, the Polish poet? Written in 1951–52, just two years after the publication of *Nineteen Eighty-Four* and based on his experience in the Stalinist cultural bureaucracy, Milosz's *Captive Mind* emphasized precisely the stunning *reality* of Oceania. Milosz wrote of his communist colleagues:

A few have become acquainted with Orwell's *1984*; . . . Orwell fascinates them through his insight into details they know well, and through his use of Swiftian satire. Such a form of writing is forbidden by the New Faith because allegory, by nature manifold in meaning, would trespass beyond the prescriptions of socialist realism and the demands of the censor. Even those who know Orwell only by hearsay are amazed that a writer who never lived in Russia should have so keen a perception into its life. The fact that there are writers in the West who understand the functioning of the unusually constructed machine of which they themselves are a part astounds them.

*Many GDR homes in the early postwar era included socialist shrines, known as the "Red Corner." These were home altars devoted to the socialist icons. Depicted here is a Stalin shrine of 1950. The caption reads: "Long live the best friend and benefactor of the German people—Joseph Stalin!"*

And what about the Soviet dissidents from whom we heard in chapter 3?[5] Liudmila Alexeevna of the Helsinki Watch Committee, who read *Nineteen Eighty-Four* in an "amateurish and even illiterate" Russian translation in the 1950s, nonetheless described its impact as "stunning." She added: "*Nineteen Eighty-Four* was about us. It was about our Big Brother, our Newspeak, our Ministries of Love and Truth."

Or Victoria Chalikova, who looked back in the late 1980s on how she and other dissidents had read Orwell in *samizdat*—and how he had "molded the spirit" of the Soviet intellectuals of her post-Stalin generation of the late 1950s and '60s:

> And how we used to read Orwell in Russia! In third and fourth typewritten copies and in pale Xerox copies *we* literally read "close to the text"—looking around while we put ourselves at risk, in a tightly closed room, alone or with one other person, just as in the novel Winston and Julia read the underground book. The book and life reflected one an-

other as if they were in a mirror! Yes, in spite of the prohibition against reading him, Orwell forced his way through at least to part of his Russian reading audience, about whom he had dreamed. *Animal Farm, Nineteen Eighty-Four*, and—to a lesser degree—*Homage to Catalonia* played their role in molding the spirit of the writers, historians, and publicists. . . .

Did Orwell address and capture the lived reality of millions under state socialism? Chalikova's words ring in my ears, as if in reply not just to Kundera but to ardent young Gerhard:

"The book and life reflected one another," Chalikova wrote, "as if they were in a mirror!"

# III.

## Man and Mentor,
## Myth and Monument

# 12

# Biographies and Biographers

## I

The previous scenes in this "afterlife" have shown how not just Orwell's work but also his life and literary personality have contributed to his reputation as the West's foremost literary Cold Warrior. The present scene centers on the various Orwell biographies and the issue of biography itself. In doing so, it illuminates a cultural process that recurs throughout Act III: how a cherished man and revered mentor is turned into a literary myth and even a cultural monument, i.e., how Orwell became "Orwell." Or how, in the previously quoted words of Malcolm Muggeridge, "the legend of a human being is created."

Orwell specifically requested in his last will and testament in 1950 that no biography of him be written. He didn't explain why, but he once told Susan Watson, his housekeeper in the mid-1940s, that he himself was the only person who could adequately write his biography—and that he would never do so. Indeed, he apparently had a low opinion of biography as a genre. Richard Rees, who served as Orwell's literary executor along with Orwell's widow

Sonia (Brownell) Orwell, once said that Orwell's request reflected a fear that he might be "written up extravagantly or luridly."

His anxiety was not unfounded. Orwell was a teenager at Eton (and already a rabid reader) during the vogue for biographies in the tradition of Lytton Strachey's anti-heroic *Eminent Victorians* (1918). No doubt young Eric Blair read Strachey's muckraking biography and its countless imitations. The popularity of Freud among intellectuals had also given rise in the 1920s and '30s to what Virginia Woolf initially heralded as the "New Biography" and what detractors soon termed "Stracheyism." Less-gifted followers of Strachey soon gave biography a bad name. In extreme reaction against the tendencies of nineteenth-century biographers toward hagiography, the "new" biographers were self-appointed idol-smashers and amateur psychoanalysts. Often proceeding on the flimsiest of evidence, they went far beyond Dr. Johnson's advice to explore "domestic privacies." Instead they trumpeted ill-founded or even false scandals, made wild use of literary devices such as symbolism and irony, conducted psychoanalytic autopsies, and proselytized for various ideological camps under the guise of objective biography.

Doubtless Orwell's hostility in his famous 1939 essay on Charles Dickens to the alleged attempts by G. K. Chesterton and T. A. Jackson to convert Dickens into a 1930s Christian and radical, respectively, stemmed from such biographical abuses as these. It was the age of "biografiction," conducted by those Joyce angrily called "the biografiends." The association of biography with debunking and sensationalism evidently stayed with Orwell throughout his lifetime. Just months before his death in January 1950, he advised his friend Julian Symons not to let his publisher pick a racy title for the biography of his brother, A. J. A. Symons. (Other British writers prominent during Orwell's lifetime—Auden, Eliot, Hardy, Kipling, Somerset Maugham—also took steps to prevent biographies, probably in part because they were similarly revolted by the degrading treatment afforded literary figures such as Wordsworth, Scott, Arnold, and Tennyson during the interwar period.)

Whatever Orwell's reasons for requesting no biography, his executors prevented access to his unpublished papers and quotation from his published writings, impeding a full-scale biography for three decades. Not until Bernard Crick's *George Orwell: A Life* was the story of Orwell's life told in full. Crick's biography, initially commissioned by Sonia Orwell, was published over her strenuous objections just weeks after her death in 1980. Responding to Sonia's discontent with Crick's emphasis on Orwell's radicalism and Crick's critical (if admiring) stance, the Orwell estate contacted Michael Shelden, an American academic, to write an "authorized" biography, *George Orwell* (1991). (His book's appearance induced Crick to revise and expand his 1980 biography the following year.) The year 2000 witnessed the publication of a third life of Orwell, this one by veteran literary biographer Jeffrey Meyers, who had already written excellent critical biographies of Fitzgerald, Hemingway, Frost, Edmund Wilson, and others.

# II

Richard Rees once stated that, had Orwell lived to witness the higher standard of postwar biography, he would have withdrawn his objections to the genre. Perhaps, but Orwell's own sense of integrity would have been sorely tested in the 1950s and '60s by the psychoanalytical interpretations of him offered by such critics as Isaac Rosenfeld, Delmore Schwartz, and Anthony West. Those men, accustomed to literary exegesis, wrote about Orwell as if there were no problematical relation between the man and the works. As a consequence they were much too ready to engage in psychobiography of Orwell's writings and to pin on him simplistic labels like "neurotic" and "sadomasochist"—and too complacent to do the biographical research necessary to comprehend the complex relationship between the man and his oeuvre.

Earlier biographers of Orwell disdained such a task, leaving it to Jeffrey Meyers to fill the gap. And he has done so with a display of industry and insight that warrants praise. Meyers's life is the first to engage in a sophisticated, well-researched biographical *and* psychological interpretation of Orwell's life. The result is a portrait much darker and more revealing about Orwell's sexual and private life than previous biographies.

Would the reticent Orwell have approved?

Probably not. But Meyers does not exaggerate or sensationalize. His biography devotes extended and nuanced attention to Orwell's psychology, the first time such a task has been undertaken. Meyers examines the contradictions in Orwell's personality and behavior, the relation between his literary vision and his temperamental makeup, and the role of his chronic, debilitating illnesses in shaping his outlook and motivations.

# III

Meyers's main argument is that Orwell essentially destroyed himself because he had a fixed, distorted image of himself as a hardy man of action who could invariably take risks and survive them. In Meyers's view, that delusion accounted for Orwell's self-punishing behavior: he practiced excruciating self-deprivation masquerading as toughness and tested his physical limits constantly.

Until the publication of the Meyers biography, I had always viewed Orwell's very modest living standard as a tribute to his willingness to practice his socialism, not just preach it. And I still believe that Orwell's severity toward himself had something soldierly and even heroic about it. (In different ways, it resembled that of Stafford Cripps, the brilliant early postwar Labour Party minister, and of T. E. Lawrence, a.k.a. "Lawrence of Arabia.") But Meyers is persuasive in arguing that Orwell's ascetical habits amounted to a masochistic streak. And this tendency induced him to deny himself even the minimal creature comforts necessary for his physical survival (and his wife's, too—Eileen was sickly and died at age thirty-nine in a botched hysterectomy). Orwell's austerities persisted long after he had ceased being a struggling writer; by the late 1940s he had achieved success, fame, and modest wealth with the publication of his last novels, *Animal Farm* and *Nineteen Eighty-Four*.

And yet in 1948, despite suffering periodic collapses from pulmonary tuberculosis, Orwell refused to leave the bleak island of Jura in the Scottish Hebrides to get a typist in London for *Nineteen Eighty-Four*. (Against doctor's orders to do no work and rest fully, he insisted on typing the manuscript himself.) He thus subjected himself to Jura's horrible winters in 1948 and 1949—Orwell's "Jurassic period," in Meyers's sardonic phrase—after having just spent several months in a Scottish sanatorium for tubercular treatments.

Meyers shows the link between Orwell's saintly reputation and his self-sacrificing, indeed self-punishing personality. As we have seen, Orwell relished his monkish poverty. Meyers quotes one friend from the 1930s, Jack

Common, who describes Orwell in Nietzschean terms: "[H]is theme is hardness, which is curious, because his physique denies that this is his need. His theme is hardness and action. That is reiterated while all the while it saddens me to see how obviously he needs love and repose."

Orwell's asceticism did not begin on Jura. As Meyers notes, "Orwell's compulsion to live an arduous and exhausting existence in Jura was typically perverse and even suicidal." For instance, in the 1930s, when Jack Common knew him, Orwell insisted on living in (and subjecting his new bride Eileen to) revolting sewage problems in a run-down house in Wallington, outside London. During this decade he pushed himself constantly, never really taking a rest (let alone a vacation), and collapsing numerous times from sheer exhaustion and illness—and yet he continued to go on, even enlisting in a loyalist militia during the Spanish Civil War. (He received a bullet in his windpipe in 1937, which left him voiceless for weeks and permanently weakened his speaking voice.) Indisputably, he was a soldier of the spirit, but he erroneously fancied himself physically tough and able to withstand all kinds of bodily traumas. That delusion contributed to his early death from tuberculosis, at the age of forty-six, in January 1950.

Meyers partly attributes the darkness of *Nineteen Eighty-Four* to Orwell's declining health and the bleakness of life on Jura. He goes into excruciating detail in discussing the treatment for tuberculosis in the 1940s and Orwell's physical agonies. This discussion does shed some light on Orwell's great novel, particularly the suffering of his fictional hero Winston Smith during the torture scenes in room 101. Meyers's point is well established: Orwell himself had been living in such a room.

But despite his agony, Orwell was driven to finish *Nineteen Eighty-Four*. Meyers believes that this was the decision that brought about his death. "The creation of *Nineteen Eighty-Four* virtually killed Orwell and the novel's vision of the future is correspondingly grim." Meyers concludes his chapter on Orwell's last year: "Orwell's life in essence was a series of irrational, sometimes life-threatening decisions. All these risky moves were prompted by the inner need to sabotage his chance for a happy life, but the life he chose supplied the somber material of his art."

That formulation strikes me as excessive: Did Orwell's socialist convictions play no role in his life decisions? And if so, were they entirely delusive? Moreover, is rationality the final criterion of good judgment? The man who ventured down the Wigan Pier mines and fought against fascism on the Aragon front in Catalonia might have acted for non-rational—though not necessarily irrational—reasons. I believe that we can credit Orwell with a higher degree of self-understanding than Meyers allows.

Meyers's provocative suggestion that Orwell was motivated by a suicidal urge—what Freudians would call a "death wish"—is the most controversial claim of his biography and is one that Meyers had advanced in some of his previous critical studies of Orwell. Meyers's psychological interpretation of Orwell follows the approach first advanced in 1956 by the writer Anthony West, the illegitimate son of Rebecca West and H. G. Wells (Orwell's boyhood literary hero, with whom Orwell was acquainted and about whom he later published some sharp criticisms). Nevertheless, Meyers does not turn Orwell into a "case history." Nor can this book be reduced to the category of "psychobiography." As the aforementioned facts of Orwell's life attest, Meyers has strong evidence for the psychological basis of his conclusions. Moreover, his interpretation is really only an elaboration of the views of Orwell's second wife, Sonia, and some of his friends, such as T. R. Fyvel.

Nonetheless, despite agreeing with Sonia about Orwell's masochistic tendencies, Meyers is quite severe on her. Following the lead of Shelden, who first devoted (critical) attention to her, Meyers suggests that Sonia was a repressed lesbian and notes her ambivalence toward men and disgust with heterosexual relations. Although Orwell affectionately sketched her portrait in the figure of Molly, the mare in *Animal Farm*, and made her the model for Julia in *Nineteen Eighty-Four*, he did not see a great deal of her before their deathbed marriage in October 1949. (She never visited him in Jura or in his Scottish hospital during 1946–48). He had met her in mid-1945, in the offices of *Horizon*, and impulsively proposed marriage to her shortly after his wife Eileen's death that spring. (Sonia was one of three women to whom Orwell proposed in rapid succession, all of whom refused him.) Back in London in 1949, he again begged her to marry him and this time she agreed.

Orwell wished Sonia to take care of his adopted five-year-old son, Richard, or at least share her bequest with him. But she adopted the name Orwell, not the son. (Her official married name was "Blair.") While some friends of Sonia's believed that she married Orwell for mercenary motives, Meyers views her not as a gold digger, but as a literary huntress seeking big game and fast fame. By 1949, Orwell was becoming a rich and famous author. He was also one who would make no sexual demands, who indeed would soon be dead.

What is the truth about Sonia and George? Opinion is divided, with biographers as well as friends of the couple taking opposing sides. For instance, Orwell's biographers take a dim view of Sonia's motives for marrying Orwell. Although he may be accused of prurience, Meyers does not hedge in quoting his interviews with friends of Sonia Orwell, who believe that she had a tormented attitude toward sex. Basically, they think of her as a sexpot, a tease who flirted with men but then turned cold. Sonia's closest friends were elderly dowagers and male homosexuals. Meyers considers her domineering, short-tempered, and an appalling literary snob. Shelden is in basic agreement with Meyers. (Sonia was still alive when Crick was writing his biography; he does not discuss her in detail.)

Although my focus here is on the biographies of George Orwell, it is important to note that Meyers's (and Shelden's) view of Sonia Orwell is disputed by Hilary Spurling in her memoir of Sonia, *The Girl from the Fiction Department: A Portrait of Sonia Orwell* (2002). A close friend of Sonia during the last decade of her life, Spurling depicts Sonia as generous, impulsive, confused, and naïve—partly in love with Orwell and yet also entranced by the London literary scene. All observers agree, however, that the true love of her life was the French philosopher and friend of Sartre, Maurice Merleau-Ponty, with whom she broke off an affair just months before her marriage to Orwell, only to resume it within days of his death (and break off again soon thereafter—permanently).

Spurling's is a lone, if moving and heartfelt, voice; unlike the full-scale biographies of Shelden and Meyers, of course, she has authored a short biographical "portrait" based largely on her own memories and on recollections and correspondence from Sonia's friends. Spurling charges that Orwell's biographers have "systematically blackened" Sonia's reputation—but she does not quote a single line or specifically contest even one claim from any of the biographies. She merely cites a negative remark of Crick about Sonia, written in a letter eleven years after the publication of his biography. Spurling's informants are entirely limited to those sympathetic to Sonia; the portrait almost exclusively presents testimony favorable to Sonia.

Indeed Spurling mentions hardly a word critical of Sonia, except to reiterate that she was sometimes rash or foolish or wildly romantic. Where are the "greedy," "superficial" sides of Sonia that other observers (even friends such as David Plante, in *Difficult Women*) have noted? (For instance, Spurling does not mention incidents such as the fact that Sonia insisted that the CIA introduce her to Clark Gable before she gave the agency permission to film *Animal Farm*.) Instead Spurling emphasizes Sonia's innocence and idealism; she says that Sonia married Orwell (and also her second husband, Michael Pitt-Rivers) "for nobly disinterested motives." Unlike Shelden and Meyers, however, her evidence to support such a view of Sonia's relationship to Orwell before the marriage is slight. While I am inclined to agree with Spurling that Orwell's friends (and biographers) have been hard on Sonia—certainly they have scanted her "extraordinary warmth, her radiance, her passionate altruism"—Spurling's portrait is one-sided. It does not simply "disentangle the truth." Rather, her close-up of Sonia seems ultimately skewed by friendship and not entirely convincing.[1]

# IV

The special contribution of Meyers's life of Orwell is that it fills an important gap in the biographical literature. Bernard Crick's analytical approach focused on Orwell's outer life, especially on Orwell as a political writer, while Michael Shelden concentrated on Orwell's literary and private life, though without detailed literary criticism of Orwell's writings. Whereas Crick practiced a form of scholarly austerity, a kind of Brechtian distancing whereby he presented acquaintances' discrepant images of Orwell and renounced any grand synthesis of them into a portrait of Orwell, Shelden took a traditional empathic approach, including speculation about Orwell's motives and his inner life. Crick limited himself to a biography of "externality," as he termed it, arguing that "memory unsupported by documentation is not to be trusted." Indeed Crick explicitly titled his book a "life" of Orwell, because the word "biography" he said, had come to acquire since Boswell's *Life of Johnson* a "romantic" meaning: "the portrait of a 'character.'"[2] By contrast, Shelden insisted, "a character must come to life on the page . . . by the biographer's willingness to look at the world through the subject's eyes." What Crick dismissed as the "empathetic fallacy," Shelden defended as a necessary "extension of sympathy and imagination." What Shelden castigated as biographical positivism, Crick championed as fidelity to the empirical facts.[3]

In a sense, Meyers integrates the approaches of the first two biographies. He does the necessary essential biographical legwork of visiting old friends and old haunts as well as presenting conflicting testimony where pertinent, yet he also devotes himself both to the psychology of Orwell's inner life and to the literary tradition that Orwell inherited and influenced.

Crick's biography was commissioned by Sonia Orwell, though she soon disavowed it and tried to block publication because she found it "too political, too dry, and too unsympathetic." Shelden began his biography after Sonia's death and after receiving authorization from Orwell's literary executor, Mark Hamilton. Between them—and the pioneering two-volume Orwell biography published in the 1970s by Peter Stansky and William Abrahams—it would have seemed as if there were little else to say about George Orwell.[4]

But Meyers felt that a third biography was warranted after the final volumes of the long-awaited *Complete Works of George Orwell*, edited and expertly annotated by Peter Davison, appeared in 1998. A monumental achievement of 8,500 pages that comprises virtually everything that Orwell ever wrote, *The Complete Works* is a twenty-volume labor of a lifetime. Meyers makes extensive use of Davison's edition and is, of course, the first biographer to do so. His biography is thus neither the commissioned nor the authorized biography, but rather the first truly literary biography—both in the sense of its emphasis on Orwell's literary influences and legacy and in its reliance on the entire corpus of Orwell's writings. Meyers also gives attention to Orwell's politics, but not at the expense of inattention to Orwell's personal life and private demons.

Perhaps the most powerful—and least publicized—of those demons was sexuality. Meyers does not spare Orwell the psychological scrutiny and severe judgment that he accords Sonia. Meyers reports fully, yet without undue or excessive detail, both on Orwell's affairs and on his unrequited loves. One of those was Lydia Jackson, a close friend of Eileen. In her memoir, *A Russian's England*, Jackson (under her pen name, Elisaveta Fen) records that she once allowed (out of pity for a sick man) Orwell to kiss her during a 1939 visit to him in a sanatorium. Orwell hoped thereafter to become her lover, which mortified her. Meyers mentions this incident—which he is the first biographer to relate—as an example of Orwell's sexual neediness. Jackson recalled that she tried to be "kind" to Orwell because she regarded his advances as a hapless urge to assert his masculinity in the face of his body's decay. Summarizing his psychosexual conclusions in an essay after the biography's appearance, Meyers writes:

> He yearned to be rich, handsome, and a devil with the ladies. Women were always important to him, and his weird proposals to Celia Paget and Anne Popham [practically on first acquaintance] revealed the hopelessly romantic side of his character. His desperate longing for love—a theme in all his novels—lies at the core of his life and work, and was responsible for his deathbed marriage to Sonia, the model for Julia in *Nineteen Eighty-Four* (and for Molly, by the way, in *Animal Farm*). He had a noble character, but was also violent, capable of cruelty, tormented by guilt, masochistically self-punishing, and sometimes suicidal.[5]

In a compelling essay, Tzvedan Todorov suggests a related line of thinking about Orwell compatible with Meyers's viewpoint; his essay, in fact, preceded Meyers's biography by more than a decade. In writing *Nineteen Eighty-Four*, argues Todorov, Orwell was confronted with a "tragic dilemma." Doctors told him he might be able to recover on the condition that he rested, "in other words that he stopped writing." But, notes Todorov, Orwell's life had already been "reduced precisely to this one activity. Nothing else interested him. He had, in sum, a choice between death and non-life: if he wrote he died; but if he didn't write he no longer lived."

According to Todorov, Orwell resolved this dilemma, however painfully, by choosing to complete *Nineteen Eighty-Four* "even at the cost of killing himself." Todorov cites this fatal choice as an instance of Orwell's "egoism," which Orwell had mentioned in his essay "Why I Write" as the typical author's first motive for writing. This manifestation of egoism, believes Todorov, was merely the extreme outcome of the self-absorption that had made it possible for Orwell to put his wife Eileen to the most strenuous demands even while he was pursuing other women. Todorov acknowledges that the standard defense for an author who left us masterpieces is: "model husbands don't make great writers." But Todorov disputes this: "Just as aesthetic success in Orwell's writing always derived from great political concern, I think that a greater concern for individuals, also for those surrounding him, would have rendered his books more powerful, not less. What is sometimes missing in them is an attention to concrete facts and individual characters: the principles, even when right, do not leave room enough for these and a novel does need individuals."[6]

How extreme was Orwell's "egoism"? How "noble"—to use Meyers's word— was Orwell's character? Lionel Trilling once praised Orwell as "not extraordinary" (in his 1952 introduction to the American edition of *Homage to Catalonia*)—a characterization that reportedly infuriated Sonia Orwell, who considered it a backhanded compliment.[7]

Shelden implicitly followed Trilling's line of thinking and explored Orwell's private life with imagination and empathy, making Orwell a more accessible, sympathetic figure than does Crick or Meyers—and perhaps a more unexceptional one. But some readers objected that Shelden rounded off Orwell's edges. In a mixed review, Steven Marcus remarked that Shelden's biography "contains one large and consistently apparent flaw. It tries continually to 'normalize' Orwell, to make him seem like some ordinary, sensible person, distinguished from others only by his gift for writing, when this is clearly not the case."[8]

Marcus was the first to characterize Orwell as a "virtuous man," the phrase that Lionel Trilling made famous in that introduction to *Homage to Catalonia*. (Marcus, a graduate student of Trilling, made the remark to him in conversation.)[9] Implicitly disagreeing in 1993 with Trilling, Marcus finds Orwell's life "extraordinary," at least in its unity and centripetal force. Orwell's life "has an extraordinary integral impetus to it."

And Marcus goes on to present an analysis that could serve as a gloss for understanding the power that Orwell's literary voice derives from the perception of the authenticity of his life. Writes Marcus: "Part of Orwell's singular moral authority as a writer is connected to the reader's sense of the connection between what is on the page and the lived experience it articulates and impels. But that life and those writings are themselves, in addition, vivid refractions of the historical era through which Orwell's experiences were compounded." Marcus is struck by "the peculiar coherence of Orwell's life and work." Their rich and complex coherence, Marcus believes, renders Orwell such an integral part of his epoch and lends his character such integrated self-possession that, however attractive he indeed remains to intellectual grave-robbers because of his cultural prestige, their pursuits will always and inevitably fail. Concludes Marcus: "None of them can succeed in these undertakings of theft. He belongs to himself and to the historical world of which he was an active and creditable part."

And yet, perhaps not entirely. Since the 1980s, "Orwell" increasingly belongs also to novelists and the fictional world. For in addition to the standard biographies, Orwell has experienced an unusual form of literary afterlife: biographical novels speculating about his struggles as a man and writer. David Caute's *Dr. Orwell and Mr. Blair* (1994) and Thurston Clarke's *Thirteen O' Clock* (1984) are two of the more recent examples. The former imagines how Blair-Orwell became the author of *Animal Farm*; the latter fictionalizes the emergence of *Nineteen Eighty-Four* in the context of Orwell's illness and last days. This was not the first time that novelists had drawn on Orwell's life and work, but now novelists had thematized them fictionally. The novels of Caute and Clarke go far beyond the few previous fictionalized treatments of Orwell's life written by his friends, such as Stevie Smith's novel, *The Holiday* (1949), which featured Orwell in a cameo role as Basil, an old Etonian who drones on incessantly about population decline, moral bankruptcy, and "scanty panties." Or Anthony Powell's twelve-volume *Dance to the Music of Time*, where Orwell appears briefly as Alf, Viscount Erridge, Earl of Warminster, an eccentric, idealistic revolutionary.

# V

Despite the passing of 1984, Orwell continues to be a writer who provokes arguments and commands news headlines. Perhaps the biggest in recent years have involved the much-publicized charges that Orwell was a McCarthyite fink who compiled lists of crypto-communists near the end of his life. Meyers's biography is the first Orwell study to respond to these allegations.

In July 1996, the U.K. Public Records Office released documents which showed that Orwell fed names of communist fellow-travelers to the British Foreign Office shortly before his death. This was actually old news, but the

Orwell estate had not released all the details and had restrained scholars and biographers from publishing the full story. Interviewed by Celia Paget, Arthur Koestler's sister-in-law (to whom Orwell had proposed marriage in 1945), Orwell told the Foreign Office his impressions of the political orientations of certain people and whether they should or should not be trusted as propagandists and approached to write for the Information Research Department (IRD). Paget had just begun working for the IRD, which had been created in January 1948 by Attlee's Labour Government to furnish "support to genuinely progressive and reformist elements withstanding the inroads of Communism" by publicizing anticommunist information. The IRD subsidized publications (such as *Tribune*) that championed "social democracy as a successful alternative to Communism."[10]

Following the arguments advanced by Davison, Crick, Robert Conquest, and others, Meyers rightly notes that, seen in the political context of 1949, Orwell's behavior seems not only defensible but commendable. He was only noting that the citizens he named were not suited to write pro-British propaganda. (Moreover, Orwell was no McCarthyite: he strongly supported the civil rights of British communists. For instance, he opposed any purge of them from the British Civil Service.)

But even as these revelations about Orwell's involvement with British and American intelligence agencies were being headlined in the mainstream press and trumpeted by the Marxist Left, Orwell's life was again becoming the object of fascination as the year 2003 approached—the year of the centennial of Orwell's birth. In addition to the biography of Sonia by Hilary Spurling, several critical studies of Orwell appeared, along with a pair of children's books and the reissue of previously published books about Orwell.[11] The publication of three new biographies of Orwell was also announced for 2003.[12] But unlike the case with 1984, the so-called "Year of Orwell," when *Nineteen Eighty-Four* managed the unprecedented feat of topping the fiction bestseller lists for weeks, 2003 witnessed no popular "Orwellmania" frenzy of the kind we discussed in chapter 1. Instead the Orwell centennial turned out to be primarily an academic affair.

Still, the periodic recurrent headlines about Orwell's work attest at least to this much: *pace* Fitzgerald, there are indeed second acts in some literary lives, at least in the case of the Englishman under discussion here. For the fact is that Orwell remains a significant literary presence and a political writer whose voice and arguments still figure in public debate. Just as he was a half-century ago, he continues to arouse controversy among intellectuals across the political spectrum, from Left to Right—as the next three scenes make clear.

# 13

# Orwell, Marx, and the Marxists

## I

George Orwell has been esteemed as a man and exalted as a mentor by literary and political intellectuals located at virtually every point along the ideological spectrum except—and it is a large exception—the far Left. Indeed, the roles in which the Marxist Left has typed Orwell—heretic, renegade, traitor, turncoat—have cast him as a heavy, an impersonator, a stooge, a villain clad in bogeyman black. Orwell has in fact stood as one of the Left's leading *dramatis personae non grata* for more than a half-century.

Ever since the August 1945 publication of *Animal Farm*—and arguably since the appearance of *The Road to Wigan Pier* in March 1937, in which Orwell first castigated the British Left for its Stalinist prostrations—he has been scripted as the scapegoat in the Marxist repertory of radicalism. Because Orwell's powerfully expressed criticisms of social*ists*—which were aimed at protecting and strengthening social*ism*—gave "ammunition" to the enemy, many radicals have dismissed them as a betrayal of the Left. Orwell's broadsides against his fellow socialists were delivered with such rhetorical cleverness and virtuosity that it was easy to remember his catchwords and forget his argument. This fact has allowed British Marxists since Orwell's day to dismiss his criticisms as the obtuse rants of a hatemonger, the screeds of a cynic ignorant of the history and tenets of Marxism.

This scene highlights these charges as it examines Orwell's Marx and the Marxists' Orwell. Among our concerns are the following: Who was Karl Marx for George Orwell? What did Orwell think of Marxism as a philosophy of man, society, and history?

The short answer is this: Orwell respected what he did know of Marx, but he objected to Marxism's scientific pretensions, to its doctrines of violent revolution and class struggle, to its economic interpretation of history, and to its view of art.

We will also be exploring a converse pair of questions: Who was George Orwell for the Marxists who came after him? What influence has Orwell exerted upon the radical Left in Britain during the last several decades?

Here again, the answer can be summarized quickly. Indeed, the headline from a posthumous critique of Orwell's work—"Prisoner of Hatred"—perfectly captures the history of Orwell's reception by the far Left. Given the biting satires on Stalinism in his last two books, this hostile reception is not surprising.

Thus, our aim in examining Orwell's Marx and the Marxists' Orwell is twofold: first and chiefly, to clarify Orwell's anti-Marxist tradition; second, to call attention to the British Left's long-running battle with Orwell and its strenuous efforts to *dis*claim him for the socialist fold.

## II

An American conservative once remarked that Orwell "arouses fiercer pro- and anti-reactions than any writer since Marx."[1] The judgment is arguable, but the comparison is apt, especially in regard to both men's receptions on the Anglo-American far Left. Just as the strongest negative response to Marxism during the 1930s and 1940s in Britain came not from the Right, but from Orwell and other non-Marxist radicals, the most hostile reactions to Orwell have come not from conservatives but from Marxists.

Among the many disputes about Orwell on the Anglo-American Left is the issue of how well Orwell knew Marx's writings. Various passages in Orwell's books directly echo or mock famous statements from *The Communist Manifesto,* such as *The Road to Wigan Pier's* closing line: "You have nothing to lose but your aitches." Orwell once explained that he wrote *Animal Farm* by working out Marx's theory of class struggle from an animal's point of view: "Our labor tills the soil, our dung fertilizes it," Old Major declares, "and yet there is not one of us that owns more than his bare skin." Yet although such inversions and parodies are cleverly handled, they indicate no thorough understanding of Marx on Orwell's part; Orwell as polemicist evidently invoked such passages and ideas because they were so well-known to his public. He never devoted any sustained attention in his writings to Marx or to Marxist theory. His attitude toward and grasp of Marx must be constructed from acquaintances' testimonies and scattered references, many of them in his journalism.

Friends, scholars, and biographers disagree about his knowledge of Marxism. Richard Rees, Orwell's closest friend, recalled one meeting in the 1930s in which Orwell "astonished everybody, including Marxist theoreticians," with his "breathtaking Marxist paradoxes and epigrams, in a way as to make the sacred mysteries seem almost too obvious and simple."[2] Orwell read Marx "with care and understanding" yet "in an open and critical spirit," contends Alex Zwerdling in *Orwell and the Left,* further maintaining (in a claim short on supporting evidence) that Orwell's essays reveal a "detailed familiarity" with Marx and "a fundamental admiration for his contribution to the socialist movement."[3]

On the other hand, both Orwell's biographer Bernard Crick and renegade Marxist intellectual Isaac Deutscher are skeptical about Orwell's familiarity with Marx. Crick judges that Orwell never read Marx closely.[4] Deutscher, who roomed with Orwell in Germany as an *Observer* war correspondent in 1945, insists that Orwell simply couldn't understand Marxism: "the dialectical-materialist philosophy had always been too abstruse for him."[5]

It is an important clue to the extent of Orwell's knowledge of Marx that his was clearly the "old" Marx of the *Manifesto* and *Capital*. Because he did not read German, he could not have known, at least not directly, the "young" Marx of the 1844 *Economic and Philosophical Manuscripts,* first published in

1932 in German, suppressed during Hitler's years in power, and not translated into English until 1960. Thus, Orwell's Marx was some variant of the mature "revolutionary" Marx, who emphasized class struggle, historical materialism, and violent revolution, not the young "humanistic" Marx interested in consciousness, alienated labor, species being, and evolutionary change. Likely Orwell would have been more sympathetic toward this "early" Marx. For both Orwell's own brand of democratic socialism and his objections to Stalinist ideology suggest that he opposed, without realizing the whole of Marx, precisely the excesses of the "old" Marx embodied in the crude Marxism of the 1930s. (In fact, an argument advanced outside the English-speaking world during that decade, usually by disenchanted former communists, was that Stalin, unfamiliar with Marx's full corpus, had misunderstood, overemphasized, and vulgarized the "old" Marx's concepts of revolution and historical materialism). Orwell stood in the parliamentary tradition of English socialism, in the line from Robert Owen to William Morris, though he shared neither Owen's sentimental utopianism and faith in technology nor Morris's primitivism. Orwell also did not see himself as a Fabian "gradualist," and he reacted strongly against the administrative socialism of the Webbs and Shaw, which he despised as a cult of efficiency and machine worship.

It is likely that Orwell knew more about Marxism than he let on in *The Road to Wigan Pier* and *Homage to Catalonia*. In both books he assumed the stance of the intellectual naïf and earthy skeptic, probably for rhetorical effect. By portraying himself as a man of common sense and by exaggerating the suddenness and force of his conversion to socialism when confronted by the suffering English miners and unemployed, Orwell depicted his former self as that of a skeptic and truth-seeker. He thereby disposed the average reader to identify more readily with his dramatic conversion.

Certainly Orwell knew people in the early 1930s who were familiar with Marxist ideas. One of his Hampstead bookshop acquaintances in the early 1930s was among England's first Trotskyists (Reg Groves), a roommate was a fellow-traveling poet (Michael Sayers), another roommate was a Jewish socialist intellectual and later Orwell's managing editor at *Tribune* (Jon Kimche), and Orwell's landlady and landlord (Mary and Francis Westrope) were long-standing Independent Labor Party activists. Both Mrs. Westrope and Eugene Adam (an Esperantist proselyte and the French lover of Orwell's favorite aunt, living in Paris) visited, separately, the Soviet Union after Stalin's accession to power—and both returned angry and disillusioned.

Although Orwell described himself in this period as a "Tory anarchist," his anti-imperialism and close ties with Esperantists who espoused an international fraternity through a single world language gave him a temperamental affinity with libertarian and democratic socialism: the trips to Wigan Pier and Spain provided emotional passion for his deepening socialist convictions. Crick concludes that Orwell had been "brooding" about socialism for a long time, and that his trips to Wigan Pier and Spain made his final commitment more explainable, dramatic, and convincing.[6]

Neither before nor after his commitment to socialism in 1936, however, did Orwell ever treat the writings of Marx and Engels with any special reverence. His response to Marxist theory and praxis was always that of a workaday journalist's, addressed to the moment and to the layman. Both his infrequent references to Marx and his contempt for theorizing about dialectical materialism arise from this stance. Orwell believed that his dispute in the 1930s and 1940s was not with Marx but with Marxists, and he was little concerned with adjudicating rival claims to Marx's mantle.[7] Orwell viewed himself as a socialist conscience and pamphleteer. These are the twin keys to all of his pronouncements on Marx and Marxist theory generally.

Nevertheless Orwell could and did distinguish sharply between "Marx" and the "Marxism" of his day. In "Marx and Russia" (1948), written at the same time as *Nineteen Eighty-Four*, Orwell remarked that "Communism" meant "two different things, only rather tenuously connected: a political theory and a political practice." Orwell noted that Marx's vision of "world revolution" had been "modified" by the Soviet Union to mean "conquest." "Dictatorship of the proletariat" likewise meant in practice "the dictatorship of a handful of intellectuals, ruling through terrorism."[8] As for English socialists, Orwell declared in *Wigan Pier* that "the worst advertisement for Socialism is its adherents." He deplored the fact that "Bolshevik commissars (half-gangster, half-gramophone)" and "shock-headed Marxists chewing polysyllables" had come to represent "Socialism" in the average man's mind. Orwell used the term "orthodox Marxist" invidiously, usually with reference to intellectuals who supported Stalin uncritically and thus closed their eyes to Soviet history, toeing the party line like puppets on a string. "Only the educated are completely orthodox," Orwell wrote. "I have yet to meet a working miner, steel-worker, cotton-weaver, docker, navvy, or what not who was 'ideologically' sound."

"Das Kapital socialists," "book-trained socialists," and "orthodoxy sniffers" were Orwell's other favorite deprecatory terms for Stalinist intellectuals.[9] The labels were polemical yet not unfair. Orwell had rightly seen that many Left intellectuals had betrayed Marx's vision of socialism, turning a worker's struggle for equality into a meaningless "pea-and-thimble trick with those three mysterious entities, thesis, antithesis, and synthesis."[10] Orwell criticized such Marxist intellectuals, he once explained, "not because they were intellectuals but precisely because they were not what I mean by true intellectuals."[11] "True" intellectuals thought independently and spoke out fearlessly, Orwell said, whereas the intelligentsia of the Left imported its language and ideas prefabricated from Moscow.

Orwell told working-class friend and writer Jack Common in 1938: "What sickens me about left-wing people, especially intellectuals, is their utter ignorance of the way things happen."[12] "The sin of nearly all left-wingers from 1933 onwards," Orwell declared in his 1945 essay on Arthur Koestler, "is that they have wanted to be anti-Fascist without being anti-totalitarian."[13] Many intellectuals, judged Orwell, were power worshipers who had sold out their socialist principles by subordinating freedom of thought to tyranny by clique. Lacking physical and intellectual courage themselves, leftists and pacifists often covertly admired brute strength. Orwell saw this cowardice as representative of the otherworldly, puerile schoolboy outlook of the entire English Left: "A twelve-year-old boy worships Jack Dempsey. An adolescent in a Glasgow slum worships Al Capone. An aspiring pupil at a business college worships Lord Nuffield. A *New Statesman* reader worships Stalin."[14]

Or as Orwell once said of *New Statesman* editor Kingsley Martin: "The bloody fool seems to think war is a cricket match."[15]

# III

Orwell never devoted any sustained attention to Marxist theory. He approached it piecemeal, as his experience supported or clashed with its doctrines. Orwell's distance from the "orthodox Marxist" (a term he used invidiously) of his day is apparent when his own views on fundamental Marxist doctrines are considered:

SCIENTIFIC SOCIALISM. Orwell considered Marx's "scientific socialism" invalidated by history itself. Marx had not discovered "laws of history" in the relations among society's productive forces. "In our age," Orwell wrote in 1944, "the followers of Marx have not been much more successful than the followers of Nostradamus."[16] But Orwell did not fault Marx as a prophet so much as he castigated those English leftists of the 1930s whose interpretations of European events since World War I were "so mechanistic" that they "had failed to foresee dangers that were obvious to people who had never even heard the name of Marx."[17]

Marx himself seems to have struck Orwell as a gifted yet historically limited thinker whose utopian visions of a worker's paradise had been perverted in Russia by "professional revolutionaries" not "answerable [to] the common people" and rendered obsolete in the West by the lessons of Hitler and Stalin.[18] Orwell saw that Marx was very far from anticipating James Burnham's vision presented in *The Managerial Revolution* (1941), of oligarchies run by middle-class bureaucrats—the scenario for *Nineteen Eighty-Four*. Orwell in effect grouped Marx with Twain, Kipling, Wells, and Gandhi—all nineteenth-century thinkers who "did not understand the nature of totalitarianism."[19] Orwell believed that Marx the rationalist and revolutionary had taken for granted that the ends of socialism were democratic and that, after the socialist revolution, "History" would by itself create a better humanity. Marx had underestimated the dark side of human nature and neglected to consider the existence of such human qualities as those represented by Comrade Napoleon of *Animal Farm* and O'Brien of *Nineteen Eighty-Four*. In Orwell's view, "scientific" socialism had thus shown itself to be just as "utopian" as the socialisms of Owen or Fourier. Orwell is explicit about this last point in *Nineteen Eighty-Four*. So abused was the word "science" by the Left and Right in the 1930s that Oceania has no Newspeak word for it: evidently every Party concept is "scientific."

REVOLUTION. It is worth noting that Orwell's two Marxes were a black poodle (his pet dog "Marx") and an old, hoarse pig who sings his revolutionary hymn "Beasts of England" with lyrics that echo the *Internationale* and to a tune that is a crazy cross between *My Darling Clementine* and *La Cucuracha*. Orwell's use of "Marx" is certainly not without irony. Orwell bought the poodle on his return from Spain, where he had been outraged by the Stalinist-inspired suppression of his P.O.U.M. (United Marxist Workers Party) militia, a dissident Left group of anarchists and Trotskyists affiliated with Britain's Independent Labor Party (which Orwell joined in 1938). Old Major in *Animal Farm* is a portrait of Orwell's ambivalent attitude toward Marx. Very different from his two younger followers, the plotting Napoleon (Stalin) and the self-absorbed, oratorical Snowball (Trotsky), Old Major is a "majestic-looking pig" with a "wise and benevolent appearance." He closes his speech to the animals: "This is my message to you, comrades: Rebellion!" In "Beasts of England," Old Major envisions the day when the harness will vanish from animals' backs and "riches more than mind can picture" will be theirs.[20]

Orwell scoffed at the utopianism that is explicit in these lyrics, preferring to live in the possible world and work for a better one. In 1943 he bluntly told *Tribune* readers:

> The real answer is to dissociate Socialism from Utopianism. Socialists are accused of believing that society can be—and indeed, after the establishment of socialism, will be—completely perfect.
>
> The answer, which ought to be uttered more loudly than it usually is, is that Socialism is not perfectionistic, perhaps not even hedonistic. Socialists don't claim to be able to make the world perfect: they claim to be able to make it better.[21]

When one Marxist told him that under socialism people would no longer feel like they were at the mercy of irresponsible and unpredictable powers, Orwell tersely replied: "I notice that people always say 'under Socialism.'"[22] Orwell suspected bourgeois and intellectual Marxists of lusting for power. Moreover, although he was a self-declared "democratic socialist" and Labour Party supporter all his life, "riches more than mind can picture" was not his idea of socialism: "All that the working man demands is . . . the indispensable minimum without which human life cannot be lived at all. Enough to eat, freedom from the haunting terror of unemployment, the knowledge that your children will get a fair chance, a bath once a day, clean linen reasonably often, a roof that doesn't leak, and short enough hours to leave you with a little energy when the day is done."[23] Commenting on this modest program, Richard Rees remarked: "He doesn't say whether he means a hot or cold bath. I hope he means a hot bath."[24]

Orwell's socialism was present-oriented, not directed like Marx's toward some apocalyptic moment of violent revolution in the unspecified future. As a democratic socialist and pragmatist, Orwell would have sanctioned, with proper qualification, the notorious declaration of Marxist revisionist Eduard Bernstein, the so-called "father" of "democratic socialism" in pre–World War I Germany: "What is generally called the ultimate goal of socialism is nothing to me: the movement is everything."[25] Bernstein meant that socialism was a way of life to be sought in the here-and-now, not a paradise to be realized at the end of History.

Probably Orwell would have been surprised to find one of his "European intellectuals" voicing similar sentiments four decades earlier. Bernstein (whom Orwell probably never read) saw that several specific predictions of Marx were not being realized: capitalism was not collapsing, the middle class was not disappearing, and the workers' lot was not worsening. Bernstein insisted that it was a futile dream to live in the future and to insist on the sudden and total triumph of socialism: the aim of socialism should be to enrich workers' daily lives.

Bernstein (1850–1932), who began editing the newspaper of the outlawed German Socialist Party shortly before Marx's death and who died one week before Orwell's first book appeared, may fairly be seen as a missing link between them. Bernstein bears unusual affinities with both Marx and Orwell. As a personal friend of Marx and a German Jew similarly exiled in London, as Engels's heir apparent and literary executor and as the editor for many years of his party's official organ, Bernstein represents important continuities within Marxism and illuminates the relations among Marxism, Germany, and England. By virtue of his empirical outlook, his partial acceptance of Fabian ideas, and the ferocious attacks from virtually every major continental socialist of his day, which he suffered after his return to Germany, Bernstein offers insight into Orwell's brand of "English" socialism and into the role of ideology on the Left. Returning to Germany in 1901 after twenty years in England, Bernstein reacted strongly against German Social Democracy's quickly ossifying orthodoxy in the late 1890s, much as Orwell opposed the abstract socialism of the English leftists of the 1930s.

Bernstein and Orwell insisted on the democratic element in socialism. But what Orwell supplied through his personal experience of the Wigan miners and Spanish workers, Bernstein supplied through Kant. Influenced by the "Back to Kant" movement in Germany at the turn of the century. Bernstein closed *Evolutionary Socialism* with the motto, "Kant Against Cant." Bernstein called for a return to Kant not in the sense of immersion in Kantian episte-mology; rather, he urged Social Democrats to embrace Kant's critical spirit in order to "keenly and critically examine our inherited dogma."[26] As a way of stressing personal liberty, Bernstein invoked Kant against Marx's Hegelian view of man as a strictly communal being. Freedom was Bernstein's Kantian check beyond which socialism's drive for justice could not go.[27]

But Orwell repeatedly insisted on what Bernstein had sometimes failed to voice emphatically: socialism's "ultimate goal" must be kept firmly in mind. The "essentials," wrote Orwell in *The Road to Wigan Pier*, were the active wish "to see tyranny overthrown" and to unearth socialism's oft-forgotten cor-nerstones of freedom and equality. "Justice and liberty! Those are the words that have got to ring like a bugle across the land."[28] The aim of socialism, said Orwell, was not to *improve* capitalism but to *transform* it. Social reforms were the means to a bloodless, democratic, "English" social revolution, not ends in themselves: by "social revolution" Orwell simply meant the radical transfor-mation of the property-owning system: "a fundamental shift of power."[29] This, he insisted with Bernstein, could occur through the democratic process; it need not entail acts of violence or civil war. But Orwell allowed in *The Lion and the Unicorn* (1941) that "a bitter political struggle" necessitating violence might be necessary.[30] He neither envisioned nor advocated a gradual political transformation through a series of peaceful transitions from capitalism to socialism. During the darkest days of the war in 1940, he argued for "war-Communism"; the war could and must precipitate a British socialist revolu-tion—or Hitler would triumph. By late 1941 Orwell recognized that the war could be won without a socialist revolution. He supported, with reservations, the Labour government that came to power in 1945.

HISTORICAL MATERIALISM. Orwell faulted Marxism for failing to take sufficiently into account how local conditions could give rise to different forms of socialism. Subtitled "Socialism and the English Genius," *The Lion and the Unicorn* was concerned with the conditions for a specifically *English* revolution and an *English* form of socialism, not with the continental and orthodox Marxist kinds. In *The Lion and the Unicorn* Orwell defined "socialism" as the Marxist Left would have ("common ownership of the means of production"), but he was in many ways more radical in his general conception of the term than in his specific political proposals. His six-point program in that book consisted of radical domestic reforms (nationalizing industries, increasing educational opportunities, fixing a minimum wage, limiting incomes) and decolonization proposals of the sort adopted by the postwar Labour government and even by some non-socialist countries.

Orwell's central theoretical dispute with Marx was with the economic motive as the basis for human behavior and history. "The main weakness of Marxism," he told *New Statesman* readers in 1940, is "its failure to interpret human motives":

> Religion, morality, patriotism, and so forth are invariably written off as "superstructure," a sort of hypocritical cover-up for the pursuit of economic interests. If that were so, one might well ask why the "superstructure" has to exist at all? . . . Apparently because human beings can only put faith in their full powers when they believe they are not acting for economic ends. But this in itself is enough to "suggest" that superstructural motives should be taken seriously.[31]

As a pluralistic theory and heuristic principle giving emphasis, rather than sanctity, to economic explanations, the Marxist theory of history was valuable, Orwell thought. "Marxism may possibly be a mistaken theory," he wrote in 1944, "but it is a useful instrument for testing other systems of thought, rather like one of those long-handled hammers with which they tap the wheels of locomotives. Tap! Is this writer a bourgeois? A crude question, ignoring much . . . and yet illuminating."[32]

Orwell was little interested in psychoanalysis or academic psychology as theories of human behavior (though his wife Eileen had a Master's degree in psychology). Richard Rees, writing of Orwell's "psychological incuriosity" with regard to psychoanalysis, said that he never once heard Orwell mention Freud or Jung.[33]

Orwell's criticism of historical materialism nonetheless amounted to its neglect of psychology, its failure to account for human drives in non-material terms. Although skeptical of the adequacy of the explanations of psycho-analysis and academic psychology for human behavior, Orwell nonetheless based his criticisms of historical materialism on its psychological shallow-ness, its failure to account for human beings' drives in non-material terms. "The basic trouble with all orthodox Marxists," Orwell said in 1936, "is that, possessing a system which seems to explain everything, they never bother to discover what is going on in other people's heads."[34] Orwell believed that Marxism did not account sufficiently for power hunger and leader worship. Though he makes no reference in his corpus to Alfred Adler, who lectured extensively in Britain in the 1930s, Orwell's "psychology of power" in *Nine-teen Eighty-Four* corresponds in several crucial respects to Adler's ideas.[35]

Probably Orwell's animus toward "Freud" and "psychology" as a discipline was another instance of his distaste for theory and system-building. For if we remember that he was concerned that leftists devise effective rhetorical strat-egies and that literary critics know the backgrounds of writers, it is clear that Orwell considered a grasp of "psychology"—understood simply as an aware-ness of people's attitudes and motives—vitally important to both politics and literature.

CLASS CONFLICT. Orwell believed that national identity and religion, far from being masks for class conflict, were often the real issues at stake in po-litical controversies. "Patriotism is finally stronger than class-hatred," Orwell claimed. And as much as anything else, his contempt for "Europeanized" Left intellectuals was that they were not patriotic Englishmen. "They take their cookery from Paris and their opinions from Moscow. In the general patriotism of the country they form a sort of island of dissident thought."[36]

Social divisions, he thought, were not necessarily economic in nature, nor did all ideas directly and mechanically reflect class interests—or become in-validated by such a genesis. "If no man is ever motivated by anything else except class interests, why does every man pretend that he is motivated by something else?" Orwell asked. "Superstructural" factors like religion and patriotism, he thought, "may be causes as well as effects. As it is, a 'Marxist' analysis of any historical event turns out to be a hurried snap judgment based on the principle of *cui bono?*—something like the 'realism' of the saloon-bar cynic who always assumes that the bishop is keeping a mistress and the trade-union leader is in the pay of the boss."[37] Reviewing an English Communist's account of the British class system in 1936, Orwell moaned that it was "like watching somebody carve a roast duck with a chopper."[38] Orwell acknowledged that the economic approach could explain a good deal about ideology and class oppression, but it did not explain either the "heroic snobbishness" of the English middle classes or the stratification within the middle class itself. Far from disappearing amid a progressive division of the capitalist world into two great classes, as Marx had predicted, the middle class was stretching out to encompass the upper and lower classes, Orwell observed. Middle-class ideas were spreading among the lower class, and the gradual tendency in Britain, furthered by World War II, was toward "wip[ing] out most of the existing class privileges."[39]

AESTHETICS. No doubt Orwell enjoyed his friend Cyril Connolly's famous parody of England's Left poets (Auden, Spender, C. Day Lewis) in "Where Engels Fear To Tread":

> M is for Marx
> and Movement of Masses
> and Massing of Arses
> and Clashing of Classes.[40]

Orwell himself adopted the radical slogan of the 1930s, "All art is propaganda." But he gave it a different twist, adding, "but not all propaganda is art."[41] To Orwell the slogan meant not that aesthetic integrity should be subordinated to ideological purity, but that every creation is rooted in a set of values and therefore possesses a political "tendency"—even if it is only the passivity and noninvolvement of a Henry Miller. Like his Marxist contemporaries, Orwell was more interested in a writer's "message" than in his technique, though he maintained in his essay on Yeats that political tendency was reflected in even the smallest details of a writer's work. For this position, Orwell was sometimes misidentified by reviewers as a Marxist and, after

*Animal Farm*, as a Trotskyist ("that Trotskyist with big feet," in H.G. Wells's memorable phrase) or even as a disillusioned former fellow-traveler or Party member (like his friend Arthur Koestler). Orwell rejected the dominant radical orthodoxy of the 1930s that a bourgeois or "reactionary" writer must be a "bad" writer. To the contrary, said Orwell, "by and large, the best writers of our time have been reactionary in tendency."[42]

Orwell always insisted that a writer's work—including the work of "reactionaries" such as Kipling, Yeats, Eliot, and Pound—should be judged on grounds independent of their politics. Orwell was in effect reaching back past the rigid literary policies of Lenin and Stalin to the broad aesthetic attitudes of Marx and Engels, more fully developed by Plekhanov, all three of whom recognized the literary excellence of writers ranging from Sophocles to Balzac even when they disagreed with their politics. And he was anticipating, if not the theoretical reformulations, at least the direction of some of the developments in neo-Marxist thinking on the complicated relations between base and superstructure, exemplified by the fruitful work on artistic production, form, and genre by Marxist literary theorists such as Walter Benjamin, Theodor Adorno, Lucien Goldmann, Fredric Jameson, Raymond Williams, Terry Eagleton, and others. Probably Orwell would have found the theoretical apparatus of most of these thinkers heavy and pretentious. But Orwell and these Marxist revisionists would have been in firm agreement that it was monstrous for Left critics to claim, in Orwell's words, "that any book whose tendency one disagrees with must be a bad book from a literary point of view."[43]

# IV

Yet beginning with the 1937 publication of *The Road to Wigan Pier*, members of the communist press, including the General Secretary of the British Communist Party,[44] began making precisely such claims about Orwell's own work. By 1946 the anarchist George Woodcock could fairly conclude: "Ask any Stalinist today what English writer is the greatest danger to the Communist cause and he is likely to answer 'Orwell.'"[45] As we noted at the outset of this chapter, the headlines alone from communist publications reviewing *Nine-*

*teen Eighty-Four* and *Shooting an Elephant* in 1949–50 indicate Orwell's official standing on the far Left during the next several years: "The Nightmare of Mr. Orwell," "Prisoner of Hatred," "Maggot of the Month."[46]

Raymond Williams later summarized the picture that the young radical of the period held of Orwell, a portrait that suggests Williams's own enduring anxiety of influence:

> In the Britain of the Fifties, along every road that you moved, the figure of Orwell seemed to be waiting. If you tried to develop a new kind of popular culture analysis, there was Orwell; if you wanted to report on work or ordinary life there was Orwell; if you engaged in any kind of socialist argument, there was an enormously inflated statue of Orwell warning to go back. Down into the Sixties political editorials would regularly admonish younger socialists to read their Orwell and see where all that led to.[47]

Williams's attempts to disengage himself from Orwell continued through the 1970s and finally erupted into open hostility at the decade's close. Orwell's "impression of consistent decency and honesty" was an "invention," declared Williams, prodded by the editors of the *New Left Review,* in an interview in *Politics and Letters* (1979). "I am bound to say, I cannot read him now."[48] Williams pronounced Orwell "an ex-socialist"—a conclusion that echoes that of another of the father figures of the British New Left, the Trotskyist Isaac Deutscher, who included Orwell on his index of misguided Left apostates in *Heretics and Renegades* (1955).

These verdicts recall again the Stalinist Left's judgment on Orwell in the 1930s. Williams's later views on Orwell echo those of A. L. Rowse, a contemporary of Orwell's for whom the running battle continued unabated, in articles and reviews, for almost five decades after their skirmishes began in the 1930s. In 1984, Rowse excoriated Orwell as "anti-*la condition humaine*" and condemned Orwell as a pessimist and polemicist whose work promoted a "deformation of the spirit of man": "Orwell denied art; and that I detest in him."[49]

Or as Williams put it in his essay for *Marxism Today,* "*Nineteen Eighty-Four* in 1984," which dismissed Orwell not because of Marxist aesthetics but on psychobiographical grounds, *Nineteen Eighty-Four* was an "irrational projection" of Orwell's understandable fears about a future far worse than even Hitler's Germany or Stalin's Russia. The novel, maintained Williams, was an overreaction that constituted "a cancellation of inquiry and argument, and therefore of the possibility of truth."[50]

The stance of the Marxist intellectuals in Britain toward Orwell has changed little in the last six decades. Having fixated on Orwell and blown him up into "an enormously inflated statue," they brand him an anti-socialist and imagine that he wields a club "warning you to go back." And so Orwell still stands today as a nightmarish shadow figure somehow blocking the far Left's advance beyond the Stalinist orthodoxies of the interwar and early postwar eras.

Already in the 1970s, Williams wrote that Orwell's influence on the Left was "diminishing" and would continue to do so.[51] Insofar as Orwell remains unpopular among Marxists, radical feminists, and neo-Marxist leftists, Williams was right, as the title alone of Scott Lucas's *George Orwell and the Betrayal of Dissent* (2003) indicates.[52]

But Orwell endures as a significant landmark in the intellectual landscape of the twenty-first century. The vogue for Williams among British radicals and Marxist academics notwithstanding, he is a minor presence in contemporary cultural life compared to Orwell. Nor is Williams's "sub-literate prose" (in the phrase of Christopher Hitchens) likely to win him new generations of readers. Indeed, the derisively humorous prediction advanced by British conservative Geoffrey Wheatcroft (adapting a line from Byron) may indeed be borne out: "Raymond Williams will be read when George Orwell is forgotten—but not until then."[53]

# V

"If only he had foreseen how great his intellectual influence would be," Orwell once mused, Karl Marx might have repeated himself "more often and more loudly" to prevent ideologues from manipulating his rhetoric and perverting his historical vision.[54] One could with justice voice a similar thought about Orwell's contested legacy.

But as Old Major would have woefully discovered, had he lived to witness Boxer's fate and the Rebellion's outcome, no ordinances, no matter how explicit, will guarantee that an author's self-interpretations will also be History's: the paintbrush of orthodoxy could deface even the Seven Commandments of Animalism.

# 14

# Orwell, the Catholics,
# and the Jews

## I

What of the attitude of Orwell, a professed atheist, toward religion and the Judeo-Christian tradition—and of the attitudes of Christians and Jews toward him? A passing remark of Orwell in a *Tribune* column illustrates the relationship. Speaking of the high literary reputation in England of communist fellow-traveler Sean O'Casey, Orwell remarked in 1945: "[A] dog does not praise its fleas, but this is somewhat contradicted by the special status enjoyed in this country by Irish Nationalist writers."[1]

Likewise, despite a career marked by biting attacks against believers, especially Catholics, Orwell was warmly received in religious circles. His acclaim in the American Catholic press began even before the U.S. publication of *Animal Farm* (1946) with the appearance a few months earlier of *Dickens, Dali, and Others*. "Mr. Orwell is a man we Catholics ought to get on reading terms with," a reviewer for the Jesuit magazine *America* declared, "for he is very definitely on our side."[2]

Nothing could have been further from Orwell's professed intent. In 1931 he explained to Christopher Hollis, a fellow Etonian and Catholic acquaintance, why he regularly read the Catholic press: "I like to see what the enemy is up to."[3] Typically Orwell found that "the enemy" was up to no good. As a Catholic myself, I sometimes feel chagrined when I hear him talk in such terms, and I like to imagine that he might have seen the present-day Church differently. But the fact remains: Orwell pulled no punches in his war of words with "the enemy." After spotting a Bible Society sign noting that the local Protestant shop did not carry the Catholics' Douay bible, Orwell wrote in August 1931 to a friend: "Long may they fight, I say; so long as that spirit is in the land we are safe from the RCs."[4]

Much of Orwell's work shared that anti-Catholic spirit. He mocked the Catholic (and Anglican) priesthood and notions of heaven in *Down and Out in Paris and London* and *A Clergyman's Daughter*.[5] For instance, although Orwell most obviously satirizes the Anglican priesthood in *A Clergyman's Daughter* through the figure of Reverend Hare, he ridicules Catholicism even more unreservedly. Mr. Cameron is a Roman Catholic convert and Knype Hill Conservative Club member whose children teach a parrot to say, "*Extra ecclesiam nulla salus*" ("No salvation outside the Church"). Schoolmaster Victor Stone favors more ritual in the parish, more of "the real Catholic worship of the real Catholic Church." Like her father, the devout Dorothy Hare at the novel's opening fears that the "Roman fever" of the Anglo-Catholic movement will ruin her parish. In *Down and Out*, Orwell mocks the Catholic practice of venerating saints (as when starving Valenti mistakes a painting of prostitute Suzannah May for Saint Eloise and prays to her).

Moreover, Orwell's attacks against "the Church" continued throughout his career. He frequently denounced "Romanism" as the ecclesiastical equivalent of Stalinism in his journalism and in *The Road to Wigan Pier*, and he castigated the Spanish Church in *Homage to Catalonia*. This onslaught against organized religion and religious belief continued with the satiric figures of Moses the Raven and Sugarcandy Mountain in *Animal Farm*, and with O'Brien's power-crazed rhetoric associating political with religious orthodoxy in *Nineteen Eighty-Four*.

Yet Orwell's passing comment that Graham Greene "might become our first Catholic fellow-traveler"[6] was nevertheless in effect applied, with a sharp shift in emphasis on the phrase's last two words, to Orwell himself by post-war critics. "There is no reason why, at least in Chestertonian geography," one Catholic critic put it shortly after Orwell's death, "one should not travel the path to Rome by way of the road to Wigan Pier. . . . In this vale of tears we are all fellow-travelers."[7]

As we shall soon see, tributes like these from believers—and posthumous conversions of Orwell—became frequent during the 1950s. Christopher Hollis argued (in a full-length critical study of his work) that Orwell "half-understood" the need for God and that a great number of his opinions "only made sense on the assumption of an implicit acceptance of a future life."[8] Indeed, despite Orwell's frequent and scathing assaults on "the stinking RC," his enthusiastic reception in Catholic periodicals has rivaled that of many leading Catholic writers.[9] Catholic intellectuals have compared Orwell and his work favorably with Chesterton, Hilaire Belloc, Evelyn Waugh, Charles Peguy, Leon Bloy, Jacques Maritain, and Greene.[10] Orwell invited many of these comparisons, for he had written with qualified admiration on Chesterton, Maritain, and Frank Sheed; and he knew Waugh and Greene personally and respected much of their work.[11]

Furthermore, despite indications of mild anti-Semitism in *Down and Out* and Orwell's firm opposition to Zionism, prominent New York Jewish intellectuals associated with *Partisan Review* and *Commentary* (Philip Rahv, Lionel Trilling, Isaac Rosenfeld, Irving Howe) admired Orwell's writings and helped introduce him to an American reading public.[12] Although Malcolm Muggeridge judged Orwell to be "at heart strongly anti-Semitic,"[13] most Jewish critics of the 1940s saw him as a supporter of Jewish causes, and Orwell clearly considered himself (in essays like "Anti-Semitism in Britain") a defender and friend of the Jews. Many of his personal friends were Jewish, including T. R. Fyvel, Arthur Koestler, his publisher Fred Warburg, and *Tribune* editors Evelyn Anderson and Jon Kimche.

Sometimes Orwell confused questions of Judaism and anti-Semitism, lumping religious belief, culture, ethnicity, and politics together. Close attention to the pattern of Orwell's remarks linking Judaism, anti-Semitism, Catholicism, Anglicanism, and communism shows how curiously antinomian his thinking was and how schematized and blinkered by politics his religious thought could be. He frequently compared and contrasted these "-isms" according to criteria like political power, popularity among intellectuals, and the role of doctrinal orthodoxy. Thus, examination of Catholic and Jewish intellectuals' responses to Orwell's work sheds light on the larger pattern of Orwell's political reception on the Right and Left; it also shows how observers can mistake selected aspects of a writer's work for his entire corpus.

# II

It is startling to discover, when one pieces together scattered journalistic references, how often the lines of Orwell's thought on Catholicism, communism, and anti-Semitism ran on parallel tracks. So preoccupied was Orwell with questions pertaining to Catholics and Jews in light of English political conditions that he saw these two religious groups in diametrically opposed terms, never giving attention to anything like a shared Judeo-Christian tradition. Orwell invariably judged both Catholicism and Judaism from the outside and by quantitative measures, never asking (as he did so effectively in exploring the outlooks of tramps and miners) how members themselves see their faiths, what alleged needs specific faiths satisfy for their members, or how different faiths contribute to British society. Often he identified the outlooks of "Catholics" and "Jews" not by their popular membership but by a tiny number of vocal intellectual adherents—a practice that he sharply criticized in *The Road to Wigan Pier* when writing of how "book-trained socialists" treated Marxist intellectuals as if they actually spoke for left-wing workers.

Orwell saw Catholicism as intellectually fashionable, hierarchically structured, and conservative or even fascist in political influence. In contrast, he saw Jews as non-doctrinaire in belief, free from a ruling hierarchy, radical-liberal in political tendency, and victimized by anti-Semitic prejudice. These three criteria—fashion, power and organization, and political tendency—governed virtually all of Orwell's reflections on the two groups. His views can be summarized briefly under these headings:

FASHION. "Anti-Semitism," Orwell declared in condemning Ezra Pound's wartime radio broadcasts for Mussolini, "is simply not the doctrine of a grown-up person." In a deathbed journal entry, Orwell remarked of Evelyn Waugh,

"One cannot really be a Catholic and grown up."[14]

Orwell's resonant language here—linking faddish anti-Semitism and Catholicism with what he viewed as the schoolboy mentalities of most Oxbridge-educated London intellectuals of the 1930s—is representative of his tendency to organize religious topics in compartmentalized extra-religious categories. He particularly despised Catholicism because he saw it as an intellectual fad. He concluded a 1948 column comparing communist intellectuals of the 1940s with Catholic intellectuals of the 1930s: "if you do not like Communism, you are a Red-baiter. . . . Similarly, when Catholicism was almost as fashionable among the English intelligentsia as Communism is now, anyone who said that the Catholic Church was a sinister organization was promptly accused of swallowing the worst follies of No-Popery organizations, of looking under his bed lest Jesuits should be concealed there, of believing stories about babies' skeletons dug up from the floors of nunneries, and all the rest of it." Orwell concluded on a note of self-congratulation: "But a few people stuck to their opinion, and I think it is safe to say that the Catholic Church is less fashionable now than it was then."

In remarks like these, one suspects that Orwell the iconoclast is chiefly intent on decrying fashion. "There are two journalistic activities that will always bring you a comeback," Orwell told *Tribune* readers in 1944: "One is to attack the Catholics and the other is to defend the Jews." Orwell relished comebacks. He seems to have delighted in printing samples of *Tribune*'s correspondence labeling him "THE JEW-PAID EDITOR . . . IN THE PAY OF THE YIDS. . . . YOU ARE A FRIEND OF THE ENEMIES OF BRITAIN."[15]

Yet Orwell's criticism of Catholicism and anti-Semitism may also be attributed to his self-proclaimed hatred of authority and his overwhelming empathy for victims and underdogs.[16] Here and elsewhere, it seems clear that Orwell's deep fellow-feeling disposed him to defend the weak and the ostracized against the strong, almost irrespective of politics.

POWER AND ORGANIZATION. Orwell rightly saw that power worship had itself become an intellectual fad, typified by intellectuals' admiration for Stalin and Hitler. But Orwell maintained that London intellectuals' attraction to Catholicism was a similar form of power worship. The popularity of anti-Semitism and Catholicism among intellectuals was linked, Orwell thought, to gross disparities in the political influence of Catholicism and Judaism. In "Anti-Semitism in Britain" (1945), he argued that Jews in Britain were "not numerous or powerful enough" to pose a "problem." He dismissed talk of surreptitious Jewish political and financial influence, remarking that Jews owned no more than a few department-store chains and a couple of newspapers. Instead Orwell spoke of the Jews as if they approximated some lost William Morris–like English ideal of medieval socialism, for they "have failed to keep up with the modern tendency toward big amalgamations and have remained fixed in those trades which are necessarily carried out on a small scale and by old-fashioned methods."[17] Although *Nineteen Eighty-Four*'s Emmanuel Goldstein is the image of the Jew-as-intellectual, when Orwell thought of the Jews in Britain he often thought not so much of intellectuals as of a common people, many of them refugees clinging to standards of craftsmanship and to a dissenting tradition—two signal characteristics of nineteenth-century English Nonconformity.

But when Orwell spoke of Catholicism, he invariably referred to intellectuals—and intellectual converts at that. In part this was a polemical strategy designed to exaggerate and undercut Catholic influence. Orwell knew very well that most of Britain's two million Catholics were poor Irish laborers.[18] And he certainly knew also that far less than 1 percent of Catholics in Britain were "intellectuals," let alone intellectual converts.

Yet Orwell interpreted the conversion of prominent intellectuals to Catholicism (including Chesterton, Christopher Hollis, Evelyn Waugh, Monsignor Ronald Knox, and Arnold Lunn) as comparable to the power worshipping of dedicated Stalinists and Nazis. For unlike T. S. Eliot, most intellectual converts had not embraced Anglicanism, Orwell noted, but rather "the Church with the world-wide organization, the one with a rigid discipline, the one with power and prestige behind it."[19] According to Orwell, Catholic writers like D. B. Wyndham Lewis and J. B. Morton combined foreign-leader worship with a hatred of England. They "denigrat[ed] England and [the] Protestant countries generally," along with "every English institution—tea, cricket, Wordsworth, Charlie Chaplin, kindness to animals, Nelson, Cromwell, and what not."[20] Orwell maintained that the rigid doctrines that "orthodox" Catholics upheld handicapped them severely as writers. He considered the paucity of good novels by Catholics proof that "orthodox believers" were "intellectually crippled" and "mentally unfree": "The fact is that some themes cannot be celebrated in words, and tyranny is one of them."[21]

On the other hand, Orwell argued, cradle Catholics were more patriotic and less crankish. Spiritual roots, patriotic spirit, and appreciation for ordinary life went together, Orwell thought. The deep feeling of Chesterton for the common man and English popular culture explains Orwell's otherwise peculiar fondness for him.

POLITICAL TENDENCY. The collaboration of the Spanish Church with Franco in the Spanish Civil War hardened Orwell's anti-Catholicism, though his hostile attitude is already evident in pieces written years before the civil war. He considered Catholicism's overall political tendency to be plainly fascist, distinguishing it from Anglicanism, which did not "impose any political 'line'" on its followers. Orwell did not doubt, in late 1941, that "the bulk of the hierarchy and the intelligentsia would side with Germany" against "godless Russia" if given the chance.[22]

But hatred of Russia was not, Orwell believed, the prime reason for Catholic pro-fascist sympathies. "The Roman Catholic ideal," Orwell claimed, is always "in favour of private ownership and against Socialist ownership and 'progress' generally." He noted with contempt that several Catholic intellectuals had successively supported Mussolini, Franco, and appeasement. Only an obsessive anti-Catholicism, however, could have led Orwell to overestimate so grossly the Church's power in his observation that, if James Burnham's vision of an "American Empire" prevailed as a countervailing force against potential USSR global hegemony, "the strongest influence in it would probably be that of the Roman Catholic Church." Although Christian Socialism and Catholic socialist parties were widely supported on the Continent, Orwell also insisted in "Toward European Unity" that the Church's existence made "true Socialism impossible, because its influence is and always must be against freedom of thought and speech, against human equality, and against any form of society tending to promote earthly happiness."[23]

Jewish anti-fascist convictions in the 1930s and 1940s were clear to everyone, but Orwell believed that Judaism's emphasis on individualism and the political effects of Britain's mild anti-Semitism had combined constructively to render Judaism itself compatible with progressive political goals. The absence of a bureaucratic hierarchy in Judaism, coupled with a deplorable anti-Semitism that had severely limited government and military career opportunities for Jews, had resulted in the Jews' general exclusion from the official circles that bred rightist mentalities. Nevertheless, Orwell considered Zionism no better than Jewish Stalinism. He criticized what he deemed *Tribune*'s postwar "overemphasis" in support of Zionism. Indeed, he once declared to *Tribune* editor and Labour Party leader Aneurin Bevan that British Zionists were only "a bunch of Wardour Street Jews who have a controlling influence over the British press."[24]

# III

Still, despite Orwell's criticism of religion in general and Catholicism and Zionism in particular, by the mid-1950s critics had, paradoxically, turned him into a Crusader-by-impressment, a foot-dragging religious fellow-traveler. One could well understand it if Orwell had merely been reclaimed posthumously as a radical Dissenter in the Protestant tradition. He saw himself as an agnostic and a freethinker; he was confirmed in the Anglican Church and requested an Anglican burial service.[25] Unsurprisingly, Protestants uninterested in "Chestertonian geography" and "the path to Rome" have hailed Orwell as a pilgrim Christian without faith. The most notable example is Alan Sandison's book-long effort to locate Orwell within the Protestant tradition of Luther, Milton, and Bunyan. "[He] out-Protestants the Protestants in disregarding the institution and getting back to first principles, reviving and reasserting them with fundamentalist passion. . . . Orwell's instinct is that of *homo religiosus*."[26]

But what did Catholics and Jews see in Orwell that appealed so strongly to their religious sensibilities? Why were Catholics willing to overlook, even welcome, his harsh criticism of the Church?

Catholic and Jewish critics in the 1950s eagerly adopted the posthumous Orwell as an ally and champion because they discerned a special integrity in his writings and style of life. They also found in his work parallels with their own views, perceived his quickly rising reputation, and thus sought to use him as a weapon in their own internal politicking against or inside the Left.

Catholic writers noted explicit affinities between Orwell's views and their Christian outlook. Placing V. S. Pritchett's famous obituary characterization of Orwell as "a kind of saint" and "the conscience of his generation" within a Christian framework,[27] they came to see Orwell as Chesterton's "good agnostic," or as Orwell's Christian friend Richard Rees phrased it, "a religious or 'pious atheist.'"[28] The influence of Pritchett's characterization is noticeable in the remark of the Jesuit priest John Kelly in 1957: ". . . people are beginning to speak of him as a saint. . . . They use the word in no orthodox sense, but it is easy to understand and to sympathize."[29]

By contrast, liberal Jewish writers—especially New York intellectuals affiliated with *Partisan Review*, such as Rahv, Trilling, and Howe—identified similarities between Orwell's anti-totalitarian politics and their own. The latter group appreciated Orwell's attack on anti-Semitism as a secondary matter. To them, it was simply another telling example of Orwell's courageous outspokenness against injustice. Thus, while seizing upon different elements in Orwell's work, leading members of both groups believed that they had discovered in Orwell a colleague in spirit (if not ideology) and a brilliant anti-Stalinist spokesman.

Catholics admired Orwell's uncompromising independence of mind, accepting his criticism as the fire of a man passionately committed to the truth. Headlined "The Testimony of an Honest Man," a 1953 *America* review of *Such, Such Were the Joys* drew attention to Orwell's attacks on the Spanish Church, on Chesterton's anti-Semitism, and on Catholic propaganda and fascist tendencies. The reviewer concluded: "This is a ruthlessly honest book. . . . It should be required reading for conscious Catholics."[30] Catholic critics took Orwell's criticism willingly because he chastised the left-wing intelligentsia no less harshly. He "never sacrificed integrity for [Left] 'orthodoxy,'" one Catholic reviewer put it approvingly—precisely what Orwell refused to do with Christians, too.[31]

Orwell also seemed to Catholic intellectuals a man who, after all, was really in their camp, a man whose "instinct," as Sandison expressed it, was indeed "that of *homo religiosus*." For in his realization that modern man's decaying belief in immortality was "the major problem of our time," Orwell recognized, said one reviewer, that "the fundamental problem of the world is spiritual."[32] In this view Orwell clearly differed from Marxists, technocrats, and other leftists whom Church supporters typically opposed. Their agreement with Orwell on the need to restore what Orwell called "the religious attitude," by whatever means, struck many Catholic intellectuals as more important than their differences. Catholic readers also found that they shared with Orwell some longstanding antagonists, such as "the birth-control people." Orwell and Catholicism's common meeting-ground in criticism of left-wing Russophiles indicates as well that Catholic critics identified with, and found appealing, the conservative aspect of Orwell's stance.

Although Orwell himself pointed out that Catholicism and conservatism should not be automatically equated,[33] his surprisingly cordial reception among Catholics in the 1950s does mirror in microcosm the wider pattern of his enthusiastic postwar reception among political conservatives generally.

Whether writing for neoliberal or conservative organs, some postwar Catholic critics converted Orwell, implicitly or explicitly, from a Church-hater into a man of grace, just as some conservatives, like Russell Kirk and Christopher Hollis, transformed Orwell the left-wing Labour Party supporter into a disillusioned anti-socialist and would-be Conservative, respectively.[34] "One thing he never forgot: 'When men stop worshiping God, they promptly start worshiping man, with disastrous results,'" a 1955 *America* reviewer reminded his readers, quoting Orwell. The reviewer added: "Anyone who can understand this is surely not far from the seat of understanding and grace." The following year Conservative M. P. Christopher Hollis wrote: "[H]is main complaint against the Conservative Party was that it failed to conserve. Man, he thought, needed ownership of property in a simple straightforward way, to know, to see and to handle what was his own." Orwell's objection to conservatism, said Hollis, lay with those Conservative politicians who had betrayed conservatism's ideals: "Orwell despaired of the Conservatives because the Conservatives despaired of Conservatism."[35]

Such interpretations demanded that critics overlook or suppress evidence about Orwell's life and writings. Both reclamation efforts were facilitated by misunderstandings about *Animal Farm* and *Nineteen Eighty-Four*. Despite their criticisms of religion, the frontal assaults of these books on Stalinism (and the British Labour Party) popularized Orwell as an anticommunist Jeremiah. The widespread circulation of this image made it easy for 1950s and 1960s Catholic intellectuals, and conservatives generally, to minimize or gloss over differences with Orwell—especially since most of his anti-Catholic *Tribune* criticism was not widely known until the 1968 publication of *The Collected Essays, Journalism and Letters of George Orwell*.

# IV

It would be an exaggeration to say that Jewish intellectuals in Britain and America in the 1950s exalted Orwell primarily, or even largely, because he opposed anti-Semitism. Of course, the Jewish anti-Stalinist writers associated with *Partisan Review* admired Orwell's sympathetic portrait in *Nineteen Eighty-Four* of Leon Trotsky (né Lev Bronstein), represented by scapegoat figure Emmanuel Goldstein. And Jewish intellectuals on both sides of the Atlantic supported and appreciated Orwell's unequivocal condemnation of anti-Semitism in widely reprinted essays like "Anti-Semitism in Britain" (first published in the 1945 *Contemporary Jewish Record*, *Commentary*'s forerunner). One Jewish literary critic went so far in 1975 as to argue that Oceania symbolizes Nazi Germany and Winston Smith specifically represents a Jewish victim tortured into submission. In 1982 even Zionist sympathizer T. R. Fyvel, editor of London's *Jewish Chronicle*, remarked on Orwell's foresight in anticipating that Zionism might lead to Israeli militarism. Orwell also appeared in *Commentary*'s first issue (November 1945), later telling Fyvel that he read the magazine regularly and was "amazed" by how many of his favorite writers were Jewish.[36]

But most Jewish intellectuals have identified with Orwell for broadly political and humanistic, rather than sectarian, reasons. Like American leftists generally, most American Jewish liberals in the 1950s looked upon Orwell as the model liberal, the exceptional man of both conscience and action—Lionel Trilling's celebrated "virtuous man." Like Catholics, Jewish writers respected what seemed to them Orwell's unimpeachable integrity. *Partisan Review* editor Philip Rahv honored Orwell "for his singular directness and honesty" by giving him the first Partisan Review Award in 1949. Thus, whereas the Catholics' Orwell was para-Christian, the Jewish liberals' Orwell was post-Christian—Philip Rieff's exemplary figure of the contemporary "postliberal-Christian imagination."[37]

Yet as *Partisan Review*'s London correspondent (1941–46) and its first solid, regular link with the London literary world, Orwell also served the magazine in ways he probably never fully realized. He brought *Partisan Review* into contact with Cyril Connolly's *Horizon* and the London intelligentsia, which furthered its aim to become America's "leading cultural quarterly," a magazine in close touch with European avant-garde and intellectual currents. Engaged in New York intellectual battles with Stalinists (who wrote for journals like *Mainstream*, the *New Masses*, and *Masses and Mainstream*), *Partisan Review* published in its pages the work of Orwell, Koestler, Ignazio Silone, and André Gide, thereby linking Orwell's name with ex-Communists and giving some readers the impression that he too was a disillusioned former fellow-traveler or Party member.[38]

# V

Many observers have fairly noted that Orwell had "a blind spot" when it came to religion, dismissing it as an otherworldly evasion of the problems of the here-and-now. "Religion," which Orwell often discussed in the singular as a monolithic and anachronistic institution, was not a subject to which he directed sustained attention. Both as a force in people's lives and simply as a system of belief, "religion" seemed to him on the historical wane, a topic hardly worthy of one's attention except as it impinged on the pressing problems of poverty, imperialism, and totalitarianism. This attitude sometimes led him to absurd assertions, like the one in *The Lion and the Unicorn* (repeated in *The English People* despite an editorial reader's protests) that "the common people are without definite religious belief, and have been so for centuries." That statement overlooked the importance in Britain of nineteenth-century Methodism (to cite just one piece of contradictory evidence) and the multitude of people like Mr. and Mrs. Pithers in *A Clergyman's Daughter*, whom Orwell ridiculed for their superstitious faith.[39]

"Religion" to Orwell amounted to "pie-in-the-sky." When he thought of believers, he dealt in stereotypes like Mr. Pithers, who says to his wife at the end of each suffering day, "Never you mind, my dear, we ain't far off from Heaven now."[40] Often Orwell voiced the reductive and simple-minded opinion that socialist and "progressive-minded people" believe in and engage themselves in "this world," while people of religious faith believe in the escapist "other world."

Orwell once pointed out that the meaning of Marx's famous aphorism, "religion is the opiate of the masses," was that people created religion because it supplied a real need—the need for human brotherhood. Orwell agreed with Marx on this score, maintaining in his interpretation of Marx that religion was not "a dope handed out from above."[41] But Orwell often talked in his journalism and through figures like Moses the Raven as if religion were precisely a drug from the sky. In Orwell's post-Enlightenment view, the intellectual disburdenment of religion was a stage in the species' progress toward maturity. To be a skeptic was to be "grown up." And yet, when Orwell directly confronted the work of a believer like Chesterton, Greene, or Waugh, he could overcome his knee-jerk response and recognize the quality of the thinker's mind and his work's value. (Waugh visited Orwell in the hospital during his last months and allegedly returned with the report that Orwell was "very near to God." When Waugh's remark got back to him, Orwell groused with a smile, "Waugh is about as good a novelist as one can be while holding untenable opinions.")[42]

Orwell's "hard-headed" this-worldly orientation and his emphasis on individual human dignity probably align him more closely to rationalism, humanism, or personalism than to any established religion, and some followers of these philosophies have also inducted Orwell as an honorary member.[43] But nowhere in his work does Orwell make any specific references to these schools of thought. Despite unmistakable affinities between his apparent religious thinking and these philosophies, and also the fact that he had good friends (like humanist Brenda Salkeld) who identified themselves by such names, Orwell never bothered to align himself formally with these groups or to call himself by these or any other sectarian labels. This disregard doubtless has made it more possible even for groups to which Orwell was openly antagonistic, like Catholics, to interpret his occasional religious pronouncements as reconcilable with their own central preoccupations.

During the countdown to 1984 in the early 1980s, neoconservatives such as Norman Podhoretz and socialists like Irving Howe asked "where Orwell would stand today" on political questions ranging from the nuclear freeze to the comparative merits of Soviet and American foreign policies.[44] Observers like Raymond Williams, Mary McCarthy, and Richard Rees had voiced similar questions during the '50s and '60s about Orwell's possible positions on the Suez crisis and the Vietnam War, for example. The question, "If Orwell were alive today," is still being raised in the twenty-first century, and we will devote extended attention to these and other speculations in later chapters. But it is interesting to note here that a Catholic reviewer of *The Collected Essays, Journalism, and Letters of George Orwell*, writing in 1969, while conceding that predictions about what Orwell's views would be in the 1960s were "interesting if futile," could not resist asking what Orwell's attitude would be toward the Church "in the post–Vatican II and post–*Humanae Vitae* period."[45]

And indeed, what about the first decade of the twenty-first century? What would Orwell say about the Church in light of John Paul II's inter-faith initiatives with Judaism—and with Islam? About the Church's "pro-life" movement against abortion and euthanasia? About the scandals and episcopal cover-ups of priests molesting children? About ongoing Church controversies over celibacy, married priests, and the proposals for ordaining female clergy? What would he say about Israeli militarism? About Zionism and the Palestine Liberation Organization? What would he say about international terrorism and the U.S.-led war against it?

As a liberal Catholic with a long-standing interest in Jewish culture, politics, and faith questions, let me conclude here with my own tuppence of speculation. At least this much, I believe, can be said: surely Orwell would find it more difficult than he did in the 1930s and '40s to maintain his simple dichotomies regarding Catholicism, communism, and anti-Semitism, or to locate the Roman Catholic Church as unequivocally aligned with the contemporary Right. (And doubtless he would still be interested in knowing "what the enemy is up to.")

Of course, these questions—and their many answers—are in a sense absurd. Orwell has been dead more than a half-century, and it is impossible to extrapolate from a man's writings what he would say about events after his death. And yet most Orwell critics admit straight off that, while the questions *are* absurd, they still feel drawn to ask them. All this further attests to a syndrome that is prevalent among intellectuals of all stripes and sects—and to which an upcoming scene will devote extended attention: W.W.G.O.D.

# 15

# Canon Fodder for the King's English

## I

Orwell's status as nearly "every intellectual's big brother" has its curricular counterpart: his exalted standing as a canonized author in student reading lists. In this scene we glimpse the haloed "St. George" of the classroom, the Model Stylist and Defender of the King's English.

A useful source for insight into Orwell's reputation in the schools is available: the questions in instructors' composition manuals. These manuals place Orwell's personality center stage, spotlighting his "virtue" and "integrity." The study guides do likewise, uncritically identifying the writer's "pure" style with the man's "saintliness." "Orwell's style shows the simple, self-conscious quality of his own personality," declares the Cliff's Notes for *Animal Farm*. The Monarch Notes for *Animal Farm* calls Orwell "a sort of modern-day saint" and asserts that Orwell and Eileen Blair had "an ideal relationship," since both of them were "saintly ascetics."

And yet, like everything else about Orwell's legacy, his canonization in schools and universities raises much larger questions. To begin with the most basic one: How do books become canonized in British and American curricula?

Amid all the calls during the last two decades to "open up" the canon, this practical question has gone largely unexplored. Much excellent research has been conducted on the theoretical issues involved in canon formation and on the politics of literary criticism. Public discussion of the "assault on the canon" began in the 1980s and '90s in the wake of widely selling books such as Allan Bloom's *Closing of the American Mind*, E. D. Hirsch's *Cultural Literacy*, Charles J. Sykes's *ProfScam*, Roger Kimball's *Tenured Radicals*, and James Atlas's *Book Wars*. The issue of how certain books and authors become "canonical" is, then, an important one in cultural and curricular politics. But the concrete historical-institutional conditions whereby works gain such status remains a neglected topic by literary scholars. In particular, the canonization of Orwell in school curricula discloses many of the institutional and historical factors conditioning the inclusion and exclusion of a writer's work in Anglo-American classrooms.

# II

The present scene is set inside a schoolhouse. But we encounter here no gruesome Room 101. Rather, this scene focuses on the place of Orwell's late fiction in secondary school English curricula, a focus that clarifies Orwell's canonical status and pedagogical treatment.

Orwell's last two books have long been curricular mainstays: *Animal Farm* is a high-school staple and *Nineteen Eighty-Four* is also widely taught in Anglo-American schools. By contrast, Orwell's essays are only occasionally assigned, usually in advanced composition classes. Moreover, with the exception of the use of selected essays such as "Politics and the English Language" or "Shooting an Elephant" in introductory college rhetoric and expository writing courses, Orwell's essays are rarely encountered in most universities. Nor, apart from the special attention occasionally accorded *Nineteen Eighty-Four* in courses devoted to the utopia or the modern novel, are any of his other works usually taught in the academy—as if in ironic imitation of their author, who never attended university. But neither is Orwell so easy to teach to high school students. His work—so simple on the surface—is characterized by a challenging complexity when one looks more closely at the allegorical correspondences of *Animal Farm*, the satirical referents of *Nineteen Eighty-Four*, or the plain-man persona of the essays.[1]

Like most countries, neither the United States nor Britain has a national syllabus of required school texts. In the United States, individual schools or school districts usually establish curricula. Only elementary school textbooks are chosen at the state level (and only in twenty-two states). The traditional British "set book" policy, however, in which readings are "set" for external examinations by regional Examination Boards in cooperation with their Local Education Authorities, introduces a greater measure of uniformity and consensus about appropriate school texts—though by no means a national canon. Orwell's work—specifically *Animal Farm* (1945)—first entered English Ordinary-level classes (sixteen-year-olds) in the 1950s. Composed of examiners and teachers, Examination Boards for O-level (and sometimes for the AO [Alternative Ordinary] level) began prescribing *Animal Farm* every three or four years after 1958.[2] The fable is also often read in British classes before the O-level year, as early as the age of thirteen, whether or not it is later studied for the external examinations.[3] *Animal Farm* appears to have entered American eighth- to tenth-grade classrooms at roughly the same time.

Why did *Animal Farm* join *Great Expectations* as a standard fiction assignment in many Anglo-American classrooms in the late 1950s? "It is such a useful teaching text for pupils of a wide range of ability," wrote one British educational official. "It is short, entertaining, makes a suitable impact, and is acceptable at a variety of levels."[4] Surely brevity, readability, perceived literary merit, and sufficiency to the assigned task and grade level have been significant considerations, as in the case of such mainstays as *Great Expectations*. But politically wary teachers might justly cast a cold eye on claims that such explanations fully account for the sudden rise of *Animal Farm* to canonical status in the schools.

Consider, for instance, the Introduction to the 1956 Signet edition of *Animal Farm*, written by C. M. Woodhouse, who praises Orwell lavishly. Woodhouse goes on to cite a passage in Orwell's essay, "Why I Write," in which Orwell declares how the Spanish Civil War defined his political faith:

"Every line I have written since 1936 has been against totalitarianism. . . ." Woodhouse halts there: the ellipses are his own. And thus he vaporizes Orwell's closing ("and for democratic socialism, as I understand it") and, along with it, Orwell's radicalism.

We have already mentioned in chapter 4 that the 1955 film adaptation of *Animal Farm* was covertly funded by the CIA. Here it is germane to mention that Woodhouse was a chief cultural official in Britain's version of the the CIA—he worked for both the Secret Intelligence Service (SIS) and the Information Research Department (IRD) in the early Cold War era, during which time he coordinated joint projects with the CIA. Among his IRD activities were to oversee clandestine participation by British intelligence in the sponsorship of the Congress for Cultural Freedom and *Encounter*, both of which were discovered in the mid-1960s to have been largely financed by CIA front organizations. Woodhouse also arranged with Orwell's publisher, Fred Warburg, to lend Secker & Warburg's name as the distributor of *Encounter*—and Warburg no doubt helped smooth the way for Woodhouse to contribute the introduction to *Animal Farm*'s Signet edition, which went on to sell several million copies in the next three decades.[5]

The point here is not that Anglo-American intelligence agencies conspired to institutionalize *Animal Farm* as required reading in the schools. Rather, it is to suggest that formalist or pedagogical explanations for the fable's postwar success are quite insufficient. Overall, while it is difficult ever to establish precisely how a book is taught by individual teachers, evidence such as Woodhouse's introduction and the widely used CIA-backed Cold War film adaptation of *Animal Farm* (in which Woodhouse and Warburg played cameo roles),[6] is significant. At a minimum, these facts point to the structural fit in the early postwar era between the demand, whether overt or implicit, for anticommunist propaganda and for a "simple lesson" like *Animal Farm*. Orwell's little fable filled, as probably no other contemporary work could, a public need during the Cold War era to confront the communist menace, especially in the schools, and thereby safeguard impressionable youth.

And here we should pause to consider further how the Cold War and the cultural politics of literary criticism in the early postwar era (1945–52) generated a climate that helped canonize another literary figure in the 1950s—William Faulkner. At first glance Orwell and Faulkner would seem unlikely analogues: the Englishman an accessible novelist and democratic socialist, the American Southerner a densely intricate stylist and (not overtly political) traditionalist.

Yet Faulkner's work and reception, especially after his 1950 Nobel Prize, shared with that of Orwell certain significant features that made him extremely attractive to Cold War critics as a Western humanist and thus an anticommunist bulwark. Both Faulkner and Orwell were perceived as quintessential representatives of native traditions (Faulkner's "Americanness" and "Southernness"; Orwell's "Englishness"). Both were anti- or noncommunist liberals. Both could therefore be championed in the late 1940s and early 1950s by the same cultural elites—the anti-Stalinist New York intellectuals (especially Lionel Trilling and Irving Howe) and the "nonpolitical" New Critics. Despite Faulkner's regionalism and Orwell's sometimes parochial Englishness, these two groups of critic-intellectuals presented the two novelists as "tragic" writers of pure, individualistic "universal visions."[7] Both writers won important literary awards at the same historical moment (Orwell's 1949 reception of the first Partisan Review Award, Faulkner's Nobel Prize). Both also rejected the realism of the 1930s. Faulkner did so in a series of radically inventive, sometimes surrealistic, experimental novels between 1927 and the early 1940s (*Sanctuary*; *The Sound and the Fury*; *Absalom, Absalom!*; *Go Down, Moses*). Orwell abandoned realism and documentary writing after the 1930s to write a politically committed fable and a dystopia, "didactic fantasies" that made him "the missing link between Swift and Kafka."[8]

Thus, at the very time when anticommunist fears were resulting in strict legislation against "seditious" teaching in American schools and universities, a broad coalition of intellectual leaders was embracing a new formalistic aesthetic.[9] In his excellent *Creating Faulkner's Reputation*, Lawrence H. Schwartz explains the connection between anticommunist ideology and literary formalism during the early Cold War, and how this combination served to elevate Faulkner:

> In the context of . . . the emergent cold war, there was a need to find an important nationalist writer. . . . Had the aesthetic values of the 1930s persisted or had anti-Communism not become prevalent, Faulkner could not have achieved renown.

The ideological component of this struggle [for postwar freedom and democracy] was . . . anti-Communism. The literary form of anti-Communism was a repudiation of the heritage of naturalism and realism. The critics and writers involved with this shift in cultural emphasis put forward a formalist aesthetic that became the dominant mode of criticism in the postwar era, and advocated a solipsistic literary modernism. . . . The liberal aesthetics traditionally associated with naturalism and socially conscious literature came to be identified with the "totalitarianism" of the Soviet Union and Stalinist politics. Ahistorical art-for-art's sake formalism was adopted as the aesthetics of postwar America and became redefined as cultural liberalism. . . . [10]

Schwartz concludes:

[A] great new American novelist [was needed] to represent the dominance of Western humanist values. Ultimately, Faulkner's work was championed and canonized because his often supremely individualistic themes and technically difficult prose served an ideological cause. [11]

On this view Faulkner did subtly what Orwell did overtly: he promoted the values of the "free world" against Stalinism. This claim implies no conspiracies or even collusion among postwar literary elites, let alone by Faulkner and Orwell themselves: rather it is a matter of two writers being integrated into a new culture of postwar conservative liberalism. Faulkner and Orwell proved superior candidates to fit the needs and aspirations of the cultural *Zeitgeist*. Each writer could function within a distinctive educational tier: Orwell's "accessible," overtly anti-Stalinist novels could work directly against the communist threat, and thus be institutionalized at the school level; Faulkner's "difficult" fiction could operate indirectly and could serve in college literature courses, where (because technical virtuosity was valorized by modernism) content was now secondary to form. So Faulkner would take the "high" canonical road, Orwell the "low."

Such observations are not meant to dismiss casually the interpretation of Orwell as a Cold Warrior or to embrace a leftist reading of postwar cultural history. Indeed, I believe that Orwell was indeed a "Cold Warrior" as well as a democratic socialist, and that—rightly or wrongly—he saw these positions as mutually reinforcing and jointly necessary rather than contradictory.

Rather, my aim here is to challenge all those reductionist approaches and glib orthodoxies that are so readily applied to Orwell. To criticize simplistic, indeed tendentious, anticommunist readings of *Animal Farm* is not to endorse or take a pro-Soviet or pro-communist stand. The Cold War critics who claimed Orwell for their side often exaggerated the communist menace at home—as in the "Red Scare" era during the McCarthy era of the early 1950s. But their worries about Soviet imperialism and communist tyranny were by no means unwarranted—least of all in the Soviet Union itself.

# III

Although a 1955 secondary school survey showed that *Nineteen Eighty-Four* (1949) was one of thirty novels most commonly read by college-bound seniors, it was not widely taught in schools until the early 1960s.[12] Its entry into senior high school classrooms at this time marks a second stage in Orwell's canonization in the schools. (The timing should remind us that, although Cold War politics no doubt conditioned how Orwell's work was taught, it was a necessary but not sufficient condition for the canonization of both Faulkner and Orwell. It was not the primary factor in the selection of their books for classroom use.)

*Nineteen Eighty-Four* occupies a different, and less secure, place than *Animal Farm* in school canons. Invariably, *Nineteen Eighty-Four* is read at more advanced grades: it belongs to what could be called the "senior high school canon," whereas *Animal Farm* would normally be classed in the "junior high school canon." In the United States, *Nineteen Eighty-Four* has been most frequently read in the twelfth grade, sometimes as a science fiction novel.[13] In England *Nineteen Eighty-Four* has sometimes been set for A[dvanced]-level (eighteen-year-old) students, though (except during 1983–84) it has never been so popular an examination text as *Animal Farm*.

Numerous reasons account for *Nineteen Eighty-Four* being less commonly taught than *Animal Farm*. In America, its greater length has probably deterred teachers from assigning it. Whereas teachers not bound to anthologies are frequently encouraged to innovate in their selection of poems, plays, and short fiction for syllabi, curricular guides have often advised caution in the choice of full-length novels, since a month or more of class time may be required for a novel.[14] Parents and educators have also found the love scene between Winston and Julia objectionable; a few school boards have even banned *Nineteen Eighty-Four*. Controversy about its sexual content was probably a key factor in its delayed entry into American schoolrooms. Even during the McCarthy era, parental opposition to *Nineteen Eighty-Four* on moral grounds was evidently more powerful than anticommunist support for it on political grounds. (In fact, one comprehensive retrospective survey in the 1970s found that *Nineteen Eighty-Four* "never failed to appear" on postwar lists of censored books.)[15]

In England, where censorship in the schools is rarely a community issue, the examination structure largely explains why *Nineteen Eighty-Four* is less often set as an exam book than *Animal Farm*. *Nineteen Eighty-Four* does not easily fit examiners' expectations for texts at either the O- or A-level. Understandably, it is often regarded as too difficult to be an O-level set book. The A-level exam for which *Nineteen Eighty-Four* could be set is the "Practical Criticism" exam, where traditional critical standards (organic unity, character development, etc.) have often made it appear inappropriate, a "failed" novel possessing insufficient literary merit.

# IV

During the much-publicized "countdown to 1984" in the early 1980s, a third stage in Orwell's curricular reputation emerged, during which his work temporarily became near-ubiquitous, with even some of his earlier or minor writings entering classrooms. An enormous upsurge of interest in *Nineteen Eighty-Four*, along with much of Orwell's other work, occurred at all educational levels in Britain at this time. *Nineteen Eighty-Four* was widely taught, with some school principals even requesting that special O-level exams be devised at school expense.[16] Longman issued special school editions of *Animal Farm* and *Nineteen Eighty-Four* in 1984. Orwell's essays were also set for A-level exams by many examination boards in 1983–84.

Meanwhile, in the United States, entire college courses were devoted to

*Nineteen Eighty-Four* during the title year. Political theory, sociology, and history courses made increasing use of *Burmese Days*, *Keep the Aspidistra Flying*, and *Coming Up For Air*. The prominence of Orwell and *Nineteen Eighty-Four* during the 1980s was reflected even in E. D. Hirsch's *Cultural Literacy* (1987). "Orwell" is one of the few items that "every American needs to know," as the subtitle of Hirsch's book proclaims. Orwell is one of only three postwar British authors—along with Aldous Huxley and Agatha Christie—cited in Hirsch's famous appendix. And Big Brother is the only postwar fictional name on Hirsch's list.[17]

An equally revealing, if less spectacular, instance of the change in Orwell's reputation in the schools since the 1950s is identifiable in the study questions of the British set book editions and American study guides. Notice: (1) the absence of ideologically motivated questions, and (2) how the authors of the study questions, obviously influenced by Orwell's reputation as a prophet, approach analysis of *Nineteen Eighty-Four* via game-playing. The following examples are representative:

- Discuss the presentation of the proles in *Nineteen Eighty-Four*. Is Winston right to think: *If there is hope, it lies in the proles?*

- Discuss the part played by dreams and memories in *Nineteen Eighty-Four*.[18]

- Prove the current president is Big Brother, then prove by use of doublethink that he or she isn't.

- If you were George Orwell, would you be pleased or displeased by the world political scene today?[19]

Given the wide name recognition and tremendous prestige of "Orwell" as a cultural icon, it is unsurprising that the political use of his work also re-emerged as an issue during the 1980s and 1990s. This time, however, it arose within a series of larger U.S. educational disputes between the Left and Right, including America's image in the schools, the censorship of allegedly "obscene" books, and the canon-formation controversy.

Whereas in the 1970s British radicals were charging that *Animal Farm* was

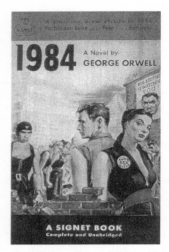

*The Signet edition of* 1984 *sold several million copies;* Animal Farm *and* 1984 *have together sold more than forty million copies in sixty-two languages since their publication in the 1940s.*

used in high schools as anti-Soviet propaganda, in the 1980s American neoconservatives were protesting that *Nineteen Eighty-Four* was being taught as if it applied not just to totalitarian states but also (or chiefly) to the Western democracies. Meanwhile, the New Right was organizing lobbying efforts to proscribe *Nineteen Eighty-Four* on religious or sexual grounds. At the same time, inevitably, civil libertarians such as the editors of *Penthouse* used the occasion to warn against the coming specter of a right-wing *Nineteen Eighty-Four*.[20]

These Left/Right skirmishes culminated in late 1984, helping to fuel a fierce, and still continuing, public debate about American higher education focused on literary canonization, cultural literacy, multiculturalism, and the fate of the Western humanist tradition. The Orwell scuffle of 1984–85 was an early round in a long bout.

The triggering event was a conference on Orwell held at the University of Minnesota in April 1984. Outraged by left-wing and poststructuralist papers on *Nineteen Eighty-Four*, which interpreted it as an attack on bourgeois democracy rather than Stalinism, a conservative history professor, Arthur Eckstein, published a severe critique of the conference in the *Chronicle of Higher Education* in mid-October 1984. His essay was quickly publicized in the *Washington Post* by Pulitzer Prize–winning columnist Jonathan Yardley, a cultural conservative who presented Eckstein's article the following week as sorry evidence of the politicization of the humanities by radicals. All this occurred just days before the publication in November 1984 of *To Reclaim a Legacy*, the controversial report from the National Endowment for the Humanities by its chairman, Secretary of Education William J. Bennett, on the deplorable state of humanities education in America. (The NEH, along with the Minnesota State Humanities Council, had funded the Minnesota conference.) Bennett bemoaned the overt politicization of the humanities and urged educators to re-establish "a common culture rooted in civilization's lasting vision, its highest shared ideals and aspirations, and its heritage."

Bennett's report—along with scholarly essays and magazine articles during 1982–85 by Hirsch, Chester Finn, and others—triggered a heated debate in the literary academy, and it was in this context that the radical reply to Eckstein and Yardley was delivered in late 1985 by Ronald Sousa, one of the Minnesota conference's organizers.[21] After mocking Eckstein's article as "a parody of the discourse of William Bennett" and suggesting that Eckstein "was probably up for a program directorship at the Endowment," Sousa addressed the "common culture" issue. He observed that the Left/Right split over *To Reclaim a Legacy* "breaks down—very much as with the battle over Orwell's *NEF* [*Nineteen Eighty-Four*] in 1984—according to whether one sees culture and tradition (read . . . '*Western* Culture and Tradition,' presumed to be paradigmatically universal) as more or less uniform and their interpretation as unproblematic for all 'right-thinking' individuals." Sousa said that the reception of Bennett's report and of *Nineteen Eighty-Four* reflected an "all-out struggle for interpretive predominance" between the Left and Right. The stakes, he said, were control of the agenda of the literary academy. The "NEFism" of liberal humanists, Sousa argued, amounted to white male "cultural imperialism." It authorized a mode of reading guaranteed "to reject cultural diversity and deny any specificity of cultures other than our own. . . ."[22] Sousa concluded:

> Bennett and Eckstein's "value-free" "correct" readings of cultural artifacts [are] in fact a very value-loaded first ploy—consciously understood as such or not in what is a totally political posturing. . . . [T]he traditionalist camp's predesignated mode of reading (grounded in the liberal humanist notion that the reading of somehow-predesignated "great works" is somehow abstractly good for the "individual's" soul) thereto attached, represents . . . a cultural politics. It is a politics of dehistoricization and its dissemination is through criticism and teaching. Moreover, its primary historical target is the very development, since the mid–1960s, of a range of critical stances, most of them decidedly anti-traditional. . . .[23]

Similar arguments about Orwell's plain style had occurred between the Left and liberal-Left in the 1960s and 1970s. Here they resurfaced in the '80s in the context of the Left/Right culture wars and the new round of the Cold War stimulated by the escalation in tensions between the Reagan administration and the Andropov-Chernenko regimes. Already in the 1970s Mina Shaughnessy had warned that Orwell's plain style was "'common' only to readers who have been long apprenticed to the literary culture."[24] But Shaughnessy noted that Orwell's deceptive complexity meant that such patient apprenticeship was a necessary and more difficult task than some teachers might think. In order to understand even an accessible author like Orwell, her argument implied, readers needed a greater understanding of Western "common culture" than it at first appeared. By contrast, Sousa, however knowingly or unawares, was subtly criticizing Orwell along with traditionalist arguments for cultural literacy. For the plain style of Orwell *is* analogous to the "value free," "correct" style of the traditionalists. It reflects, as another radical critic phrased it, a "drastic simplification at the heart of liberalism," which posits a "theoretical individual" apart from any community or social structure.[25]

Orwell was indeed a liberal humanist. The author of *Burmese Days* was also a fierce anti-imperialist and a staunch supporter of Indian independence. Yet at the same time he was Anglocentric in his outlook and writings. Furthermore, he believed in the Great Tradition of English literature, though he held that the canon of the 1940s was too narrow.[26] Those paradoxes, of course, say nothing about where Orwell might have stood, if he had lived, in the canon conflicts that still break out today. But both radicals and conservatives flatten out his paradoxes, pretending that Orwell can be read as simply pro- or anti-canon. They do so in order to bolster their own positions by constructing a family pedigree, with Orwell as a distinguished ancestor—the patron "St. George" of an ideological camp. They "reclaim a legacy" that never was.

# V

A fourth phase of Orwell's Anglo-American reputation in the schools has opened in the last fifteen years. Only in the late 1980s did canon-formation emerge as an issue in Great Britain, and its ultimate consequences for Orwell's institutionalization in British curricula remain unclear. Indications are that

Orwell (along with Auden and the Movement writers) is still a favored writer, given that the exclusion heretofore of almost all modern authors at A-level has resulted in a new canonization wave featuring mostly those postwar authors who are already esteemed outside academe by critics. A canon designed for greater diversity along ethnic and gender lines, however, will probably ultimately downgrade Orwell. As the high canon "makes room" for under-represented women and minority authors, it is less likely that a white male like Orwell will remain.[27] As one British examiner explained the trend emerging in the 1990s: "There is a move toward setting more contemporary authors from different societies and cultural backgrounds."[28] He mentioned the novels of V. S. Naipaul—who has since received the Nobel Prize (2002)—as examples.

Recently, English examining boards have begun to face the fact that only four percent of students taking A-level English exams go on to study English at universities. Courses and exams are being devised for "the other 96 percent," which will "draw on a far wider range of sources" than the traditional canon[29]—and Orwell has therefore made only an occasional appearance since the early 1990s.

At O-level, the so-called sixteen-plus reforms occurred throughout the 1990s, which merged syllabi and examinations at O-level with the (technical and vocational) Certificate of Secondary Education into a new General Certificate of Secondary Education (GCSE) program. This egalitarian reform is the most important event in British education since the 1944 Education Act. Of great significance is the fact that all GCSE candidates will study a common syllabus, so that Britain now has something approaching a regional "core curriculum." As a result, Britain seems to be moving toward greater centralization at O-level and greater diversity at A-level. Interestingly, Orwell is still among the most frequently taught authors at O-level.

In light of recurrent GCSE reforms and the recent canon-formation discussions in Britain, it may be of interest to list the GCSE set texts for prose, as specified by England's four examining boards. Although GCSE set texts vary from one year to the next, the following list is representative of the preferences of British examining boards in recent years. Because I have rarely seen such lists published in the United States, let me present it in full here: I believe it will be of keen interest to literary scholars. Significantly, almost all recommended authors are twentieth-century writers. Orwell is among the most frequently cited (see box at right).[30]

In the United States, despite the prominence of the canon debates, and with the exception of some fundamentalists' efforts to exclude *Nineteen Eighty-Four,* clashes about the use of Orwell's works in the schools and universities ended with the passing of 1984. But the contrary views of the academic Left notwithstanding, Orwell continued to be exalted by secondary school educators. In the mid-1970s a double image of Orwell as prose laureate and guardian was institutionalized in the United States by the National Council of Teachers of English (NCTE), which began making annual awards in Orwell's name. This development constitutes the chief landmark of the fourth stage in Orwell's curricular reputation: official canonization. Following what it called Orwell's "intention to expose inhumane propagandistic uses of language," the NCTE's Committee on Public Doublespeak now presents the ironic tribute of the Doublespeak Award to an (un)deserving public figure. The NCTE also bestows the George Orwell Award for Distinguished Contribution to Honesty and Clarity in Public Language. No other English or American writer has prompted the establishment of tributes to his or her legacy by an official national body like the NCTE; certainly no other author bears both positive and ironic awards in his or her name.[31]

Yet in the universities, Orwell is notable for his sudden absence; he "dropped out" of college, as it were, shortly after 1984. By the 1990s Orwell's fiction and nonfiction had largely disappeared from upper-division college literature courses, the result of an odd confluence of received truths: *Animal Farm* and *Nineteen Eighty-Four* are "high-school reading," the essay is not really "literature," an "untheoretical" writer and critic is of little contemporary value, and the "realistic" tradition of the modern British novel is inferior. How these four judgments have solidified and interacted, and how they have structured Orwell's academic reputation by level and genre, says much about the contemporary literary academy. And on this discordant note, indicating how the canon-formation process has operated to *exclude* as well as include Orwell as a canonized author, this scene closes.

Orwell's relative absence from the high canon owes much to three factors in the literary academy, which remains the chief arbiter of canons at all levels: the enduring allegiance of English professors to formalism, the rise of literary

## NORTHERN EXAMINING ASSOCIATION

Michael Anthony, *Green Days by the River*
Stan Barstow, *Job*
E. R. Brajthwaite, *To Sir with Love*
Charles Dickens, *Great Expectations*
Graham Greene, *Brighton Rock*
Merle Hodge, *Crick Crack Monkey*
D. H. Lawrence, *Selected Tales*
Harper Lee, *To Kill a Mockingbird*
Joan Lingard, *Across the Barricades*
D. McDonald, *The Hummingbird Tree*
George Orwell, *Animal Farm*
Nevil Shute, *A Town Like Alice*
John Steinbeck, *Of Mice and Men*
Mildred Taylor, *Roll of Thunder,*
   *Hear My Cry*
Mark Twain, *Huckleberry Finn*
H. G. Wells, *The Time Machine*

## SOUTHERN EXAMINING GROUP

Chinua Achebe, *Things Fall Apart*
Stan Barstow, *Job*
Emily Brontë, *Wuthering Heights*
John Christopher, *The Guardians*
Charles Dickens, *Great Expectations*
F. Scott Fitzgerald, *The Great Gatsby*
Graham Greene, *Brighton Rock*
Ernest Hemingway, *The Old Man and*
   *the Sea*
Geoffrey Household, *Rogue Male*
D. H. Lawrence, *Selected Tales*
Harper Lee, *To Kill a Mockingbird*
Robert O'Brien, *Z for Zachariah*
George Orwell, *Animal Farm*
George Orwell, *Nineteen Eighty-Four*
A. de Saint Exupery, *Night Flight*
Jack Schaeffer, *Shane*
Nevil Shute, *No Highway*
John Steinbeck, *Of Mice and Men*
Mark Twain, *Tom Sawyer*
Evelyn Waugh, *Decline and Fall*
H. G. Wells, *The Time Machine*

## LONDON AND EAST ANGLIAN GROUP

Chinua Achebe, *Things Fall Apart*
Michael Anthony, *Green Days by the River*
Stan Barstow, *Job*
Emily Brontë, *Wuthering Heights*
Anita Desai, *The Village by the Sea*
Charles Dickens, *Great Expectations*
Malcolm Fain. ed., *Four Modern*
   *Storytellers*
Graham Greene, *The Power and the Glory*
Ernest Hemingway, *The Old Man and*
   *the Sea*
Geoffrey Household, *Rogue Male*
D. H. Lawrence, *Selected Tales*
Harper Lee, *To Kill a Mockingbird*
Doris Lessing, *The Grass is Singing*
Joan Lingard, *Across the Barricades*
Joan Lingard, *Into Exile*
James V. Marshall, *Walkabout*
V. S. Naipaul, *Miguel Street*
Robert O'Brien, *Z for Zachariah*
George Orwell, *Animal Farm*
George Orwell, *Nineteen Eighty-Four*
John Steinbeck, *Of Mice and Men*
John Steinbeck, *The Pearl*
Mildred Taylor, *Roll of Thunder,*
   *Hear My Cry*
Mark Twain, *Huckleberry Finn*

## MIDLAND EXAMINING GROUP

Charles Dickens, *Great Expectations*
Graham Greene, *Brighton Rock*
Harper Lee, *To Kill a Mockingbird*
John Steinbeck, *Of Mice and Men*

theory, and the influence of the Marxist Left. Not only is Orwell's fiction not abstruse—and therefore unlikely to attract exegetically minded formalists or poststructuralists—but Orwell was also an unsystematic, "unsophisticated" sociological critic. He was no theorist: indeed he castigated grand theory. Moreover, although Orwell has many admirers among humanist intellectuals and English composition teachers, his legacy has gone largely unrecognized by the academic Left—which, in the broad sense, exerts a key shaping force on the high canon. Marxist-oriented criticism has remained popular in graduate studies programs in English literature—for example, in cultural studies—and this has worked decidedly to Orwell's disadvantage. Radical academics are still wary of embracing the twentieth century's fiercest critic of the Left.

Consider, for instance, Orwell's cultural criticism. Orwell is arguably the grandfather of British cultural studies, given his deep influence on Raymond Williams, E. P. Thompson, and Richard Hoggart. Indeed, as Christopher Hitchens has recently argued in *Why Orwell Matters* (2002), Orwell may be even credited with having decisively contributed to Marxist-oriented postcolonial studies. Yet the hostility of Williams and Thompson toward Orwell has induced most radicals to overlook this debt and to condemn or ignore Orwell. Indeed, a new ideological critique of how Orwell's influence has "stifled alternative thinking and debate for decades," written in the tradition of British cultural studies by Birmingham professor Scott Lucas, is titled *George Orwell and the Betrayal of Dissent* (2003).[33]

Lucas's views reflect a wider consensus and have exerted influence in British left-wing educational circles; his new book follows closely upon a short biography of Orwell, and Lucas's web site reports that he is at work on a textbook devoted to Orwell. As his work demonstrates, most Left academics doing cultural studies today—and ultimately shaping the academic literary canons—look at continental, Marxist-oriented thinkers such as Louis Althusser, Pierre Bourdieu, Slavoj Zizek, Antonio Gramsci—and to Williams himself—as their exemplars, not to Orwell.

# VI

The diverse responses to Orwell's life and work—from literary academics, British Marxists, Anglo-American Catholics, prominent Jewish intellectuals, Soviet journalists, East European dissidents, and virtually every species of promoter and proselyte—all attest to a remarkable fact about his legacy that goes well beyond these groups and beyond the urge to claim (or dis-claim) him for one's side. To an extent probably unequaled by any other modern writer, George Orwell has induced both admirers and detractors to prophesy about his likely opinions on events since his death at mid-century.

As we now exit our schoolroom scene of "Orwell" as St. George, we shift our gaze to behold another spectacle. Now the spotlight moves to Orwell the *raisonneur*. For just as Orwell was a witness to his time, "Orwell" has been a far-seeing witness to events since his death: his extraordinary posthumous reception history has registered responses to almost every pressing issue facing Anglo-American intellectuals since 1950, from McCarthyism to Vietnam to Nicaragua to the Gulf War to the so-called New World Order and the American-led invasion of Iraq. Scarcely a major political issue has arisen in the last half-century that has not moved his readers to ponder What George Orwell Would Say—and Do.

# 16

# W.W.G.O.D.?

## I

You see the placards waved at every rally of Christian evangelicals, as well as at many gatherings of Catholics and mainline Protestants: "W.W.J.D.?" The question is intended as a guide, a prod, a summons to action among the faithful. Nothing else is written on the posters; no further explanation is needed for those in attendance. For they can read "the signs of the times." The proper stand on any political or social issue is supposedly as clear as the conscience-pricking question itself: What Would Jesus Do?

And yet secular intellectuals are not without their own oracle, and (with the exception of the Marxist Left) the coveted (and presumed) patronage of their patron saint knows no bounds. In fact, as we saw in chapter 14, even some religious believers revere "St. George" Orwell.

"The most heterogeneous following a writer can ever have accumulated," said his close friend, George Woodcock, of Orwell's "faithful."[1] "W.W.G.O.D.?" they ask recurrently. (Why not simply an Orwell web site, a cyberspace hotline named www.GOD?) As a headline in the *New York Times*

*Book Review* on the one-year anniversary of the al-Qaeda attacks did indeed phrase it: "What Would Orwell Do?"[2]

# II

Yes, the question seemingly arises whenever a public issue provokes a major intellectual debate and splits the ranks of the Left and/or Right. Then "St. George" is called to arms, with his battle-certified catchwords from *Animal Farm* and *Nineteen Eighty-Four* packed in the polemical arsenals of his self-appointed mouthpieces, ready to be fired at the drop of his name. (Just days after 9/11, Geoffrey Wheatcroft suggested that British soldiers shipped out to Afghanistan should pack Orwell's essays in their knapsacks.)

More than a half-century after his death, Orwell remains "a writer well worth stealing," as he once said of Dickens. Since his death, his soul has been up for grabs. Today, polemically minded intellectuals are still playing what pundits refer to as "that wonderful parlor game" called "What Would Orwell Have Stood For Today?"[3] The "game," as we shall soon see, has its illicit darker sides: mantle-stealing, body-snatching, and political grave-robbing. It's an ideological shell game (usually with clever sleight-of-hand), whereby the participants move Orwell's coffin to the left or right.

"What Would Orwell Do?" intellectuals ask. When Judith Schulevitz popped the question in the September 2002 *NYTBR*, she bemoaned "Orwell-mongering," especially in the form of prophecies claiming Orwell's authority, which range from predictions about what he would celebrate (or condemn) nowadays, to amusing exercises such as "identifying an Orwell for our time."

As so often happens, however, Shulevitz herself could not resist throwing in her own tuppence to the W.W.G.O.D. game (as neither, sometimes, can I: see chapter 14). Commenting on *Why Orwell Matters* (2002) by Christopher Hitchens—whom she acknowledged as a prominent nominee for "Orwell of our time" status—Schulevitz advances a claim that even Hitchens himself has never explicitly made. Shulevitz argues that Hitchens' position on military policy and geopolitical strategy since 9/11 is the one that Orwell would have likely taken, if his "change of heart in 1940 is any guide. That's when it became obvious that Nazi Germany was about to invade England, and Orwell

stopped being a pacifist and began to excoriate British leftists for their de-
featism and the moral equivalence he felt they drew between the British
Empire and Nazi Germany."[4]

A few months earlier, in March 2002, on the occasion of the forthcoming
American publication of *Why Orwell Matters*, I had the opportunity to join
Hitchens in an amusing round of the "W.W.G.O.D." game myself[5] under
the auspices of a PBS broadcast devoted to "The Orwell Century."[6] That title
was chosen, a PBS assistant producer told me, because "Orwell's history is
the history of the twentieth century." Indeed—and it even promises, as we
shall see, to become the early history of the twenty-first.

# III

The W.W.G.O.D. game is chiefly played by literary-political critics and
intellectual journalists, though many others also try to walk in Orwell's foot-
steps and fill his large shoes. In 2002, a columnist for the *New York Observer*
nominated Christopher Hitchens and Andrew Sullivan as successors for
Orwell's mantle. And they are only the top candidates among his liberal British admirers. There are also American contenders, conservative nominees,
and others across the political spectrum—even in non-English speaking countries.

W.W.G.O.D. is usually a frivolous exercise that reflects more of an interest
in Orwell's personality than his serious work. And yet such speculations also
contribute to his legacy—even if they only serve to extend and confuse it,
rather than to clarify it. They are partly responsible for his ongoing visibility,
because they link him to currently prominent intellectuals and literary celeb-
rities, such as Hitchens, Sullivan, Susan Sontag, Martin Amis, Norman
Podhoretz, and many others. Just as these writers benefit by association with
Orwell, Orwell receives a new lease on life. Just as they identify with him and
seek to drape themselves in his mantle, he casts a lengthening shadow of
influence. Indeed, throughout his afterlife, Orwell has been a writer with
very long coattails.

In an earlier study of the "making and claiming" of Orwell's reputation, I
spoke about the "If Orwell Were Alive Today" predictions. Even more so

than in the case of W.W.G.O.D., such prognostications are usually no more than an innocent guessing game. As the Orwell centenary passes, the "If Orwell Were Alive Today" game remains highly popular among his would-be claimants.

Yet it has occurred to me in recent years that there are at least four varieties of claiming. What distinguishes these varieties is the depth of emotion and topical range they evince, from curious and wide-ranging to impassioned and narrow.

The first type of claiming begins with a polite insistence on Orwell's "relevance." One emphasizes how "contemporary" Orwell remains. The focus of attention may be broad or narrow, but the tone is often that of a respectful sigh. W. H. Auden's lament of 1971 is representative: "Today, reading his reactions to events," wrote Auden, once a victim of Orwell's attacks on "the pansy Left," "my first thought is: Oh, how I wish that Orwell were still alive, so that I could read his comments on contemporary events." Auden, after pronouncing Orwell, a self-professed atheist, a "true Christian," ran through his list: drugs, trade unions, birth control, nationalization, student demonstrations. "What he would have said I have no idea. I am only certain he would be worth listening to."[7]

But a claimant may concentrate on a single topic that is of special concern. The following excerpt from Geoffrey Wheatcroft may serve as an example of this gentlemanly art of merely referring (and deferring) to Orwell's example. Wheatcroft is looking back in 2002 on the British response to the Queen's golden jubilee, the fiftieth anniversary of her accession to the throne:

> Not least [Orwell] would have understood very well what we have been witnessing in England this year—both the renewed simple un-political patriotism of ordinary people and the resentments of the left-wing intelligentsia about whom Orwell once wrote so sharply. What took place in the summer was a celebration not merely of the Queen, but of us, the nation she reigns over. And a most benign and nourishing celebration it was. . . . Orwell would have known why. Orwell saw the purpose of monarchy.[8]

Let us also hear an example from the Left, headlined "Orwell's *1984*—Our Reality" in the *Catholic Worker* in 2003. Here we see Orwell's relevance asserted with greater urgency and in alien terms (e.g., with jargon such as "binary opposites"):

> In *1984*, there are three superstates which collaborate with one another to keep the war going. The ascension in our world of one state to superpower status has not altered the basic scenario. There has been neither peace nor its much vaunted dividend since the rise of the United States to global dominion at the end of the Cold War. In our world, too, war is perpetual. The current drive by the Unites States government to launch an offensive against Iraq is not, as it is nearly always characterized, a new war initiative. Rather, it is a continuation of the massive 1991 attack on Iraq: 110,000 combat missions, 885,000 tons of bombs, the deaths of 200,000 Iraqis. . . .
>
> The ritual of Two Minutes Hate is played out on a daily basis in homes throughout North America, as media images flash across the screen identifying the enemy of the moment—Manuel Noriega, Fidel Castro, Osama bin Laden, Saddam Hussein—as the epitome of evil. The demonization of such figures is part of a larger tendency in western thought to construct the world in terms of binary opposites which establish western superiority.[9]

Another variant of this first mode of Orwell-claiming is the tentative, nuanced academic stance, as exemplified in the opening and concluding paragraphs of John Newsinger's excellent study, *Orwell's Politics* (1999). Newsinger's "intended contribution to Orwell's legacy" disputes Bernard Crick's claim to Orwell on behalf of the left wing of the Labour Party, yet still defends Orwell both from his conservative claimants as well as his Marxist attackers. Newsinger places renewed "emphasis on Orwell's left-wing credentials, on the influence that the ideas of the revolutionary left had on his thinking," justifying his predictions about Orwell's posthumous politics by constructing an immutable figure: "The Orwell of the late 1940s." Newsinger's strategy is to imagine "how the Orwell of the late 1940s" would have stood—presuming that both Orwell and political conditions would have remained essentially static:

What would Orwell have thought of . . . developments [after his death]? This is, of course, a dangerous question to ask because we can have no idea how his thinking would have developed if he had lived into the 1950s and 1960s, let alone to the present day. Nevertheless, it is possible and worthwhile to suggest how the Orwell of the late 1940s, whose opinions we do know, would have responded. Without any question, he would have welcomed the downfall of Communism. . . . At the same time we can also be certain that he would have regarded the former Communist countries' embrace of the free market with some alarm. The great increase in social inequality and poverty, the rise of a new class of robber barons, many of them former Communist apparatchiks, the growth of racism and nationalism, and the outbreak of bloody wars, would all have filled him with horror. The Orwell of the late 1940s would have hoped that developments would have progressed in a socialist direction. One suspects that confronted with the phenomenon of New Labour [under Tony Blair] he would have regarded his change of name from Blair to Orwell as astonishing prescience.

Newsinger returns to these issues in his conclusion:

As a last point, let us consider Orwell's relevance today. We obviously have no way of knowing how he would have responded to the great expansion of Western capitalism in the 1950s, a boom that completely falsified his belief that private enterprise was doomed. This is the key unanswerable question. Would he have concluded that the inequality, poverty and injustice that had made him a socialist could now be remedied without the overthrow of capitalism? Would he, as his neoconservative admirers argue, have been so impressed by the success of the capitalist system as to stop being concerned about such peripheral issues, such peripheral people? This would have been the key determinant of his later political development.

We are perhaps on stronger ground considering how he would have responded to the Anglo-French invasion of Egypt and the Russian invasion of Hungary in 1956. Unless some profound rupture had occurred in his politics amounting to apostasy between 1950 and 1956, he would have opposed both invasions.[10]

Here we can see unfolding a not-infrequent tactic in this first type of claiming, especially common among academic claimants: to start diffidently with a provisional claim to Orwell's relevance, then to grow bolder even in the course of a single page. Such moves may be thought of as instances of "creeping claiming," whereby a would-be claimant slowly advances his stake to Orwell's legacy. Newsinger continues:

> What of his attitude towards nuclear weapons or the Vietnam War? How would Thatcherism, the return of mass unemployment, increasing social inequality and the rise of New Labour have affected him? Speculation reveals more about the attitudes of the person doing the speculating that it can about someone who died in 1950. Nevertheless, what we can say with complete confidence is that Orwell, with all his faults and weaknesses, was an enemy of injustice and inequality, that he believed democracy in Britain was perverted by the power and influence of the rich, that he championed civil liberties, that he opposed the exploitation of the so-called Third World, that he opposed tyranny and was an enemy of the class system. Moreover he thought it a duty to fight against these evils, to try and help create a better, never a perfect, but a better world. While we cannot know how Orwell would react to the world we live in today, what we can be absolutely confident of is that his writings still affect the way his readers respond to contemporary developments, still inspire resistance.[11]

Within a few sentences, Newsinger has crept far in staking his claim to a "revolutionary" Orwell. Newsinger begins by conceding "we have no way of knowing" Orwell's posthumous stands but concludes his book "absolutely confident" that Orwell's writings "still inspire resistance"—a confidence apparently unshaken by the numerous conservative claimants for whom Orwell renews respect for stability, tradition, patriotism, and even law and order.

A second species of claiming is imbued with greater passion and often covers a narrower range of topicality. This is the phenomenon that I called "claiming by acclaiming" in my *Politics of Literary Reputation*. Usually, the acclamation celebrates those positions of Orwell similar to the claimant's own—or how the positions of the claimant's opponents resemble Orwell's own adversaries. An instance of this second sort, which often buries opponents as it grave-robs St. George, is the following passage from *National Review* on the "bad thinking and bad language" of the postmodern theorists Judith Butler and Homi Bhaba: "If George Orwell were alive today, he would beat these people into submission with a London phone book. . . . 'Why drag Orwell into this? Well, because he is the secular saint of clean writing and clear thinking.'" The *National Review* columnist adds that, when Rudolph Giuliani proposed curtailing a remedial reading program at City College, the *New York Times* compared the move to "ethnic cleansing."[12] To *National Review*, such a cleansing—or rectifying—was "worthy of Stalin": "Ethnic cleansing—a true Orwellian word, worthy of Stalin when describing what happened in the former Yugoslavian or Rwanda. But here at home it turns Orwell on his head. Here it is a euphemism to allege or elevate a 'crime' that has not occurred at all."[13]

Meanwhile, on the Left, Nat Hentoff uses Orwell in conjunction with drawing an analogy between China and the prospect of a Chinese Olympics and Hitler and the Nazi Olympics:

> The Embassy of China has sent a letter to members of Congress attacking the Lantos-Cox resolution that opposed granting Beijing the 2008 Olympics. The letter charges that "any attempt to deny China's right to host the Games is a challenge to the universal principle of human rights."
>
> Would that Orwell were alive to savor this peerless piece of shameless hypocrisy!
>
> We shamed ourselves in 1936. Do we want to leave "a glow of pride" among the commanders of the prison labor camps in China in 2008?[14]

In both of these examples, we see that the claimant is not content with a polite assertion of Orwell's "relevance"; instead the admirer intensifies the claim and asserts Orwell's pertinence with decided impertinence.

Sometimes this sort of acclamation takes the form of a heartfelt wish or wistful plaint. Wrote a *Tribune* reviewer, after the publication of *The Collected Essays, Journalism, and Letters of George Orwell* in 1968, "Orwell, thou shouldst be living at this hour. England hath need of thee." From the Right, a reviewer for the *Financial Times* voiced similar sentiments: "It would be impossible to count the occasions in the eighteen years since his death that I and many others have asked the question, 'What would Orwell think about that?' He was, in life, and has remained, part of our conscience as twentieth century citizens, and very especially, part of our consciousness as Englishmen."[15]

The third and fourth sorts of claiming are quite similar, but one centers more on predictions and the other on calls to action. The third and most familiar type is the "If Orwell Were Alive Today" prognostication. This kind of claiming is often less impassioned than "claiming by acclaiming," but it is usually much more explicit. "What would Orwell think about political events today?" goes the query. What immediately follows is an attempt to forecast Orwell's overall political trajectory and present-day political allegiances, and sometimes even his specific policy stands. Passionate or not, the first two types may be thought of as "weak claiming" or "soft claiming," since they make no overt claim to Orwell and merely imply or insist on Orwell's "relevance." But the "If Orwell Were Alive Today" guessing game consists of outright pronouncements—and, as such, invariably amounts to a strong claim for his mantle.

A mixed variant of this third category of claiming combines "soft" claiming of Orwell with a gentle yet firm nudging of his coffin in one's direction. Some old friends of Orwell have indulged in this mixed form. The pronouncement of Orwell's literary executor and possibly his closest friend, the normally reticent Richard Rees, is one example. Rees, a conservative, suggested that Orwell would have generally supported America's conduct of the Vietnam War. Writing in late 1969, just a few weeks before his death, Rees allowed that Orwell would have criticized America. But Orwell would first have put the Left's own house in order, Rees said. Orwell would have stressed the yawning difference between America and the communists, much as his later writings did the difference between Churchillian "imperialism" and Stalinist "totalitarianism."

> I knew Orwell intimately for the last twenty years of his life, but I always hesitate, after a friend's death, to make public guesses, based on the privilege of friendship, about his probable views on current events. But ... something that should be obvious to every reader of Orwell. ... In my opinion it is practically certain that Orwell would have consid-

ered much of the propaganda against American involvement in Vietnam to be, at best, politically and morally imbecile. No doubt he would have disagreed with some of America's handling of the problem, but it is certain that he would have had much more to say about the Soviet Union's handling of Czechoslovakia; and as for all those who talk about American "imperialism" and equate it, and even compare it unfavourably, with Chinese and Russian tyranny, they should congratulate themselves that he is no longer here to give them a piece of his mind. He was a pessimist, no doubt, but he would not have compared the Western world of 1969 with the communist world. He would have known that 1969 is not yet *Nineteen Eighty-Four*.[16]

A more recent example of this variant is a statement by Ben Pimlott, who was acquainted during his boyhood with Orwell (Pimlott's godmother was Gwen O' Shaughnessy, sister-in-law of Orwell's first wife Eileen). Pimlott muses on whether Orwell "would recognize Tony Blair's England"—and answers, somberly, in the negative. For Pimlott, Orwell is a "beloved," indeed quixotic figure of "stern whimsicality," a man from an era long gone. In 2001, Pimlott looked back more than a half-century to recount his childhood memories from the 1940s of the already-famous writer, and his romantic image of "Orwell the failure" is one that seems to have enduring appeal for unworldly intellectuals:

> I remember George as a difficult, often exasperating, yet beloved specter, whose name conjured up muddy boots and dirty fingernails, adventures in foreign parts and a stubbornly masculine failure to be practical. For me, Orwell's stern whimsicality has ever since been bound up with a preaffluent world that no longer exists—of long-faced, heavy smoking, *New Statesmen and Nation*-reading men (and a few women) who regarded a commitment to history, literature, and the public service as taken-for-granted attributes of any civilized human being. . . . To see him today as altogether fallible, struggling for most of his adult life to find a voice and earn his crust, does not diminish his work. . . . In place of the god or prophet, we discover a "degenerate moderate modern semi-intellectual" (his self-description) trembling on the edge of failure.[17]

But some admirers do more than nudge. An aggressive pusher is George Scialabba, a regular contributor to *Dissent* and the *American Prospect*, who plays the "If Orwell . . ." game with carefree gusto, unabashedly identifying Orwell's politics with his own. Like Newsinger, he appears quite confident that Orwell would have maintained his radical outlook (and "associate with the unsexy democratic left"). But Scialaba does not practice "creeping claiming"; he begins with a feisty, strong assertion:

> "If Orwell Were Alive Today" seems to me a perfectly legitimate, even useful, game. What would he stand for and against now?
>
> I think Orwell would associate himself with the unsexy democratic left, notably *Dissent* and the *American Prospect*. He would abhor the market fundamentalism of the *Wall Street Journal*, scoff at the identity politics of the *Nation*, heckle the self-congratulatory tough-mindedness of the *New Republic*, and mock the apocalyptic pessimism of the *New Criterion*. He would disagree forcefully with Robert Conquest. . . . Conquest was an enthusiastic supporter of Thatcherism and Reaganism. . . . Orwell probably would not have been.
>
> And given his aversion to cant and his reluctance to march in a parade, Orwell might have made an unexpected remark or two on the subject of Sept. 11, 2001. He might, in particular, have wondered aloud why the heinous terrorist murder of 3,000 Americans was a turning point in history, while the death of several times that number of non-Americans every day from the effects of malnutrition, inadequate sanitation, lack of medical care and other poverty-related conditions—a state of affairs that the amount earmarked for the wealthiest 1 percent of Americans by the Bush administration's tax cuts would go a long way toward remedying—is simply . . . history.
>
> Now it's the reader's turn. What if Orwell were alive today . . . ?[18]

The best-known instance of "strong claiming" in this third type occurred in the heated exchange between Norman Podhoretz and Christopher Hitchens in 1984. Podhoretz, the neoconservative editor of *Commentary* magazine, had written a controversial essay during the "countdown to 1984" for *Harper's*. "If Orwell Were Alive Today," ran the cover headline of the January 1983 issue, atop a full-cover drawing of Orwell. Podhoretz's essay was a concerted, sustained attempt to "claim" Orwell for the neoconservative camp, for which he, Podhoretz, had become one of the leading spokesmen. Orwell was a "forerunner" of neoconservatism, Podhoretz said.[19] Orwell would have castigated the peace movement as pacifist-neoisolationist, and he would have stood fast against détente as an accommodation to "Soviet imperialism." He would probably have also allowed that democratic socialism had failed and should be abandoned, for he might well have realized, like the neoconservatives, that "the aims of what *he* meant by socialism [had been] realized to a very great extent under capitalism, and without either the concentration camps or the economic miseries that have been the invariable companions of socialism in practice." Podhoretz concluded:

> . . . I find it hard to believe that Orwell would have allowed an orthodoxy to blind him [to socialism's failure] more than he allowed any other "smelly little orthodoxies" to blind him to the truth about the particular issues involved in the struggle between totalitarianism and democracy: Spain, World War II, and Communism. In Orwell's time, it was the left-wing intelligentsia that made it so difficult for these truths to prevail. And so it is too with the particular issues generated by the struggle between totalitarianism and democracy in our time, which is why I am convinced that if Orwell were alive today, he would be taking his stand with the neoconservatives and against the Left.[20]

Podhoretz was aiming here at nothing less than providing neoconservatism with an unimpeachable intellectual pedigree. He was well aware of what he was doing, noting that to have "the greatest political writer of the age on one's side" gave "confidence, authority, and weight to one's own political views." By emphasizing Orwell's hatred for "the left-wing intelligentsia" of his time, Podhoretz was also skillfully providing the present-day Left with an undesirable family tree, traceable to the British pacifists and communists of Orwell's day.

In reply, British leftist Christopher Hitchens argued that Orwell, since he had helped found the anarchist-sponsored Freedom Defence Committee, would have opposed "the McCarthy persecutions" "unequivocally." Regarding Vietnam, Orwell "hated colonialism," said Hitchens, and he "would have seen the essential continuity of American intervention with the French colonial presence. . . . [H]e would have seen through the obfuscations (lies, actually) of the Kennedy and Johnson administrations." Hitchens closed: "I wish Orwell were alive today. The democratic socialist camp needs him more than ever. I would also dearly like to have his comments on the sort of well-heeled power worshipper who passes for an intellectual these days."[21]

Finally, then, we move to the fourth variant of claiming, a sort of would-be grand slam: W.W.G.O.D. The concern here is less with what Orwell would think than with the action he would take. The appeal is to Orwell the outspoken critic, the militiaman, the fumigator of those "smelly little orthodoxies" that the claimant finds abhorrent.

The W.W.G.O.D. game is invested with intense energy and sweeping scope: it escalates the claim to identification and is often played with deadly seriousness. W.W.G.O.D has frequently arisen in the new century in relation to such hot-button issues as the war on terrorism, Israeli militarism, and other (chiefly) international issues that may lend themselves to a militant stance, pro or con. "What Would Orwell Do?" the player asks. And he bolsters the credibility of his position, as well as his own authority, by establishing that Orwell would do the same thing he would do—whatever "the same" might be.

I have not yet mentioned the move in the W.W.G.O.D. game to "disclaim" Orwell, which is especially popular on the Left. But there the players' scope of interest is usually much narrower. Frequently only the first two types of claiming apply to *dis*claiming: either the disclaimant issues a pointed disavowal of Orwell's relevance, amounting to a curt dismissal of him and his work, or the critic delivers an impassioned critique of Orwell's alleged pseudo-radicalism, often accompanied with sharp contempt for his intellectual integrity or political acumen—Orwell wasn't a "true" socialist or a "true" intellectual. The *locus classicus* of this type of disclaiming is Mary McCarthy's famous dismissal of Orwell in her essay-review of *CEJL* in the *New York Review of Books* in January 1969. (The *NYRB* had taken a radical stand against the war and had even given instructions on one issue's cover on how to construct a Molotov cocktail.) To McCarthy, Orwell was a "political failure" because he left "no fertile ideas behind him to germinate." McCarthy's Orwell was mired in nostalgia. He was "typical of a whole generation of middle-class radicals (myself included), whose loudest spokesman was Orwell." But though

Mary McCarthy felt the urge to pose the "if," she was no more certain than Auden about the "then":

> It is impossible, at least for me, to guess how he would have stood on many leading questions of the day. Surely he would have opposed the trial and execution of Eichmann, but where would he be on the war in Vietnam? I wish I could be certain that he would not be with Kingsley Amis and Bernard Levin (who with John Osborne seem to be his main progeny), partly because of his belligerent anti-Communism, which there is no trying to discount, and partly because it is modest to oppose the war in Vietnam: we are the current, squealing "pinks." I can hear him angrily arguing that to oppose the Americans in Vietnam, whatever their shortcomings, is to be "objectively" totalitarian. On the other hand, there was that decency.
>
> And what about CND [the Campaign for Nuclear Disarmament]? He took exception to the atom bomb, but as a "realist" he accepted the likelihood of an atomic confrontation in a few years' time and computed the chances for survival. . . . I cannot see him in an Aldermaston march, along with long-haired cranks and vegetarians, or listening to a Bob Dylan or Joan Baez record or engaging in any of the current forms of protest, the word "protest" would make him sick. And yet he could have hardly supported Harold Wilson's government. As for the student revolt, he might well have been out of sympathy for a dozen reasons, but would he have sympathized with the administrators?
>
> If he had lived, he might have been happiest on a desert island, and it was a blessing for him probably that he died. [22]

# IV

And yet, as the diverse responses of intellectuals across the ideological spectrum attest, Orwell has not "died." Or rather, he is continually resuscitated by readers eager for his *pronunciamentos*. This remarkable aspect of his legacy goes well beyond the urge to claim (or disclaim) him: his extraordinary posthumous reception history has registered responses to almost every pressing issue facing Anglo-American intellectuals since 1950, from McCarthyism to Vietnam to the European Union to the West's anti-terrorism campaign. Nor have the stakes to Orwell's legacy since the 1990s been advanced only by intellectuals. A prominent claimant on the Right has been Rupert Murdoch, chairman of News International and owner of the *Sun* newspaper (among others). In a lecture in October 1994, Murdoch argued that the free market had prevented the triumph of totalitarianism as envisaged by Orwell and that News International had helped keep free "the crystal spirit" that Orwell had celebrated in a poem on the Spanish Civil War. (That poem had also served as the title of anarchist George Woodcock's much-praised critical study of Orwell).[23]

Murdoch engaged chiefly in "claiming by acclaiming" here; Orwell's luster served to burnish his larger claims for capitalism. Nor was Murdoch the only public figure to do so. In 1993—on St. George's Day (April 23) no less—the Tory Prime Minister John Major moved Orwell's coffin rightward. Seeking to reassure his Conservative audience by invoking the association between Orwell and English (or, as political necessity dictated he call it, "British") values, Major reiterated support for Britain's presence in the European Union and for the idea of "Europe" generally. But he insisted that "British" values and traditions, "the best of Britain," would endure under all circumstances:

> Distinctive and unique . . . Britain will remain in Europe. Fifty years from now Britain will still be the country of long shadows on country grounds, warm beer, invincible green suburbs, dog lovers and pools fillers and—as George Orwell said—"old maids bicycling to holy Communion through the morning mist" and—if we get our way—Shakespeare still read even in school. Britain will survive unamendable in all essentials.

British liberals ridiculed Major's claim. Wrote a *Guardian* contributor: "If Orwell were alive today, I suspect he would write a very much more troubled piece, one which was far less reassuring than the affectionate register of the eternal English verities. . . ."[24] Even conservatives were embarrassed by Major's casual borrowings from *The Lion and the Unicorn* and *England Your England.* As Geoffrey Wheatcroft later acknowledged: "That vision of England was never true, and is less so today."

Orwell was invoked on a variety of issues throughout the 1990s. Outraged in 1995 with the Clinton administration's pro-diversity policies, a conservative columnist equated liberals' support for affirmation action with progressives' sympathies for Stalinism in Orwell's day. "Shocking the Gollanczes [Victor Gollancz was Orwell's pro-Soviet publisher] was not a side effect of writing *Animal Farm*, but rather part of its purpose. . . . But what are all our latter-day Gollanczes defending now? If Orwell were alive today, he would surely be writing *Affirmative Action Farm* instead."[25]

Yet most claimants of Orwell's mantle coveted his authority to buttress their geopolitical stands. "Orwell" was drafted to address various conflicts and controversies in international policy: the Gulf War, the Bosnian war, trials of Serbian war criminals at the Hague, and similar issues. "Orwell Was Right About War" was the headline of one conservative column in 1999 on the "failures" of peacekeeping missions during the 1990s in Somalia, Rwanda, Angola, and the former Yugoslavia. The article promoted the *Realpolitik* of war hawks such as Edward Luttwak. "Used incorrectly," argued the columnist—i.e., whenever "peacekeepers are sent to separate belligerents before wars have run their natural course"—peacekeepers *extend* conflicts, not resolve them. The article then drew the Orwellian lesson: "Luttwak and Orwell were right: War is Peace."[26]

Meanwhile, examining a different set of international issues, another columnist apparently took a trip to the Golden Country and "dreamed I saw George Orwell last night." Enraged about the hypocritical doublethink of politicians on the world stage, the resurrected Orwell told the slumbering columnist:

> All this doublespeak about war crimes is appalling. Why should we try Milosevic and not prosecute Ariel Sharon as a war criminal? After all, evidence clearly implicates him in the massacre of hundreds of Palestinian people inside the Sabra and Shatila refugee camps in Lebanon. Likewise the Turkish government has killed Kurds for many years and brutally suppressed their language and culture. But Turkey, like Israel, is a U.S. ally. And what about Kissinger—the wholesale murder in Viet Nam, Cambodia, and east Timor? And what about the assassination of Salvador Allende in Chile?

On waking, the journalist drew this moral:

> Orwell would have applauded the treasuring of civil liberties and other freedoms in the U.S., but he would deplore deep patterns of indoctrination and the intellectual infirmity and political propaganda that undermine so-called democratic processes. He would remind us that both *Animal Farm* and *1984* constituted critiques of Anglo-American capitalist democracy as well as Soviet and Nazi totalitarianism.[27]

Another journalist agreed, noting both that attention to the abridgement of civil liberties should begin at home and that Orwell would need to update his anti-utopia. The sophisticated technologies of government snooping have now advanced well beyond the Orwellian telescreen to invisible surveillance such as the implanted microchip:

> If Orwell were alive today, his new novel might predict even more dire government acts, such as implanting chips in people's bodies to monitor them around the clock.
>
> Well, that's already fact, not fiction.
>
> Applied Digital Solutions, Inc., says the chips can also be used in cases where patients are unable to speak and, when combined with satellite-tracking devices, could help locate lost Alzheimer's patients.
>
> Civil-rights activists say the chip eventually could be used to track people anywhere and everywhere, crushing the final vestiges of personal privacy.
>
> As Orwell would say: Big Brother is watching you.[28]

# V

Yes, what "if Orwell were alive" today, in the twenty-first century? As the predictions cited in the winter 2003 *Catholic Worker* suggest, the clamor to claim Orwell took off in earnest after 9/11. Indeed Orwell has been loudly and repeatedly claimed and declaimed and counter-claimed—and disclaimed—by the Left and Right on international policy since September 11, 2001. The Afghan bombing campaigns, Islamic fundamentalism (or "Islamic fascism," as Christopher Hitchens terms it), the U.S. "war on terrorism," the "assault" on American civil liberties: these and other issues have received his posthumous pronouncements, with Orwell trotted out on some issues as both a hawk and a pacifist.

Stage Left is the full-page advertisement headlined "George Bush Channels George Orwell" that ran in the Sunday *New York Times* (November 3, 2002). The ad, sponsored by TomPaine.com, featured a grinch-like president sporting large floppy ears and two eyeballs projecting the numerals "19" and "84." The ad began in bold face: "As President Bush wages his war against terrorism and moves to create a huge homeland security apparatus, he appears to be borrowing heavily, if not ripping off ideas outright, from George Orwell's *Nineteen Eighty-Four. . . .*"

The ad compared current events and the policies of the Bush administration to the world of Oceania. For instance, Oceania is perpetually at war against a vague and ever-changing enemy. The war against terrorism conducted by Bush "is almost as amorphous . . . but Bush is clear on one point: The war will continue indefinitely." The ad equates Bush with Big Brother: "He has quietly achieved the greatest expansion of executive powers since Nixon. His minions cultivate an image of infallibility and impugn the patriotism of anyone who questions his leadership." According to the ad, Big Brother's ever-watchful eye via the telescreen is imitated by the Bush administration too. For instance, the new TIPS program would employ citizens as spies for alleged law enforcement. And the Justice Department, thanks to the hastily passed U.S.A. Patriot Act, wields sweeping new powers to monitor phone conversations, Internet usage, business transactions, and library records. The ad concludes: *"Nineteen Eighty-Four* was intended as a warning about the evils of totalitarianism—not a how-to manual."[29]

From the Right, the *Austin Review* in July 2002 ran a story headlined "Newspeak Totalitarianism." It criticized those who spoke of the attacks on the World Trade Center in New York City and the Pentagon in Washington D.C. as the "events" or the "tragedy," insisting that they must be called "terrorists attacks." The conservative columnist Lee Congdon, professor of history at James Madison University, argued: "PC regulars have mounted a massive media campaign to persuade people that those who express doubt concerning the peace-loving impulses of Islam are vile slanderers, guilty of crimethink." Leftist reporters, said Congdon, avoid the word "terrorist" and instead use "militant," since it "evokes an image of a courageous and uncompromising freedom fighter." The essay concludes: "One wonders . . . if Orwell ever envisioned the kind of linguistically constructed surreality that now forces Western minds into desired channels. One thing that remains certain: Were he alive today, he would be among the leading defenders of Oldspeak."[30]

Meanwhile, in criticizing the Left after 9/11, another British writer distinguished Orwell from present-day leftists:

> If your enemy is prepared to use terrorist tactics to blow up thousands of innocent civilians, what steps are you prepared to take in your defense? If, in addition, your country harbors thousands of citizens who actively support this action, what are you going to do about it? These, you feel, are the kinds of questions Orwell would have been asking last autumn, and it is worth pointing out, that no one on the anti-war Left has got around to asking them. . . . The ironies of last autumn—Muslims bombing other Muslims in the name of anti-imperialism, Americans dutifully attacking a regime they had previously encouraged—would not have been lost on him, and whatever he said would have brought little comfort to either side.[31]

Writing in the September 2002 *Austin-American Statesman,* another professor invoked Orwell to castigate both opponents of the Bush administration's anti-terrorism activism and its over-ardent supporters. Under the headline. "We Need An Orwell For Our Times," the columnist called for policymakers to heed Orwell's example:

> We need a new Orwell. We need a way to navigate between two undesirable outcomes. Opposition to U.S. policy can not be nearly knee jerk anti-Americanism . . . but we need disciplined and militant opposition to any hint of American Caesarism, and to the idea that success to the U.S. means the triumph of our culture everywhere. Like Orwell, we need to see beyond warfare to a global society that is better than before the war began.[32]

Orwell's claimants were not content to limit themselves to arguments about his likely positions on current events. Writers also raised all over again the question of Orwell's posthumous positions on earlier historical controversies. For instance, the conservative British critic Noel Malcolm argued that Orwell the Cold Warrior would surely have been pro-American and pro-capitalist during the Cold War:

> Had Orwell survived his TB . . . what would his position have been during the cold war? Of course he would have fought against McCarthyism, and he would no doubt have criticized, in his cussed and incisive way, crudest forms of Manichaean-style anti-communist ideology. But in the end he would surely have been as firmly pro-NATO, and for the same reasons.[33]

Malcolm also maintained that Orwell would have been on the side of the Americans and the West—and that he would have rejected the politics of equivalence:

> One thing at least is clear. Orwell was an anti-totalitarian: . . . So, had he lived through the 1950s and '60s, there can be little doubt as to which side, so to speak, Orwell would have been on. Not that he was an admirer of capitalism: he wasn't. But he had had no patience with facile, moral equivalentism, and he could see the difference between a dole queue and a gulag.[34]

Two old antagonists, Christopher Hitchens and Norman Podhoretz, also re-entered the fray in 2002–03. Hitchens maintained on PBS that Orwell would have probably been hostile to activist or interventionist American policymaking:

> It's possible he might have repudiated politics completely and become despairing. That's likely even. I think it's incredibly unlikely he would have become religious. He had a very settled view against the religious mentality. But on the crucial questions that exercise neo-conservatives—their claim, that he would have been understanding of McCarthyism, at least sympathetic to the Vietnam War, and that he would have been friendly to Zionism—Orwell had written firmly on all three points while he was still alive. He was against McCarthyism, against witch-hunting of Communists. He was against the restoration of European

colonialism in Asia, which meant the American continuation of the war in Indo-Chino for the French. One of the reasons why I think he was inadequate as a writer about the United States was that he never quite saw how interesting and important a subject it was. He was suspicious of its imperial designs, its global and megalo intentions. If we're simply asking ourselves what he might have thought, the record is clear long before he died that he would have had no trump with anything as ghastly or irrational or stupid as the American intervention [in Vietnam].[35]

Hitchens made a related prediction in another essay: "I believe Orwell's biggest surprise, surveying the 1990s, would be the ambivalent position in the United States, and the amazing conflicts within its state and society."[36] Hitchens added in his book *Why Orwell Matters* that Trotskyism is the only political tradition worthy to claim Orwell, whose work is "the most English form in which cosmopolitan and subversive Trotskyism has ever been cast"[37]— a conclusion quite similar to John Newsinger in *Orwell's Politics* yet stated by Hitchens more unreservedly and bluntly.

Writing in the *Jerusalem Post*, Podhoretz called on President George W. Bush to stand firm in support of Israel and "resist political speech that defends the indefensible." Opening his column with a quotation from Orwell, Podhoretz then congratulated President Bush for having been vigilant after September 11, "though not sufficiently." Podhoretz argued that the war against terrorism is really a defensive war waged in response to the war against Israel. And so he urged on President Bush one of Orwell's "famous dicta": "[T]here comes a point where the primary duty of an honest man is to restate the obvious." If Bush stood firm, predicted Podhoretz, "the ghost of George Orwell will smile down upon him and he [Bush] will bask in the assurance that he is helping to create the conditions out of which a better and a safer life will almost certainly emerge for millions upon millions of people."[38]

Such arguments provoked some Left-liberals to condemn "right-wing critics like Podhoretz" for doing "damage to Orwell" by engaging in "fatuous exercises of the 'if Orwell were alive today' variety."[39] But other liberals threw up their hands and dismissed Orwell too. As the headline of a column by a former Orwell admirer lamented: "Farewell, George: Why I Can't Worship at the Altar of Orwell Anymore." The writer, John R. MacArthur, publisher of *Harper's* magazine, confessed:

> I've always thought myself obliged to exalt Orwell, whatever my gut told me. In the small corner of the media that I inhabit, one could say that it's politically correct to love Orwell. Michael Barone invoked Orwell to excuse civilian casualties in Afghanistan caused by U.S. bombing. Barone is the conservative journalist at *U.S. News & World Report*. Maybe it's the absolutist coldness [of Orwell] that enables the merciless political right to treat Orwell like its prized pig; [that is] why Barone can casually resort to him to justify the dismembered corpses of the innocent. . . . For the duration of Bush's war on terrorism, Barone, William Bennett and their friends are free to use Orwell for anything they please. As far as I'm concerned, they can have him all to themselves.[40]

But MacArthur's is a decidedly minority view. As another headline that ran a few months before the Orwell centennial year put it: "Orwell's Shadow: George Orwell Is Everywhere. There Is No Escape."

Although the "If Orwell Were Alive Today" predictions peaked during the 1984 "countdown," these claims and counterclaims from 2002–03 demonstrate that the question continues to be asked, if less widely and less passionately—or at least less obsessively. In another sense, however, the predictions are more speculative today then ever—not to say unmoored from reality. For now that a younger intellectual generation dominates the cultural scene—a generation whose members never had any personal contact with Orwell— the speculations about "Orwell alive today" have acquired a new tone and tendency: today's paeans and predictions are even less restrained than those of two decades ago.

# VI

Whatever the claims and counter-claims about Orwell, he is indeed uniquely attractive as an ideological patron and political mentor. Unlike two of his contemporaries, Ignazio Silone and Arthur Koestler, both of whom have been tarred by recent scandals,[41] Orwell's reputation still stands high, despite attempts since 1996 by a few leftists to condemn him for cooperating with British and American intelligence services in the early days of the Cold War. In fact, among contemporary British intellectuals who have been admired and claimed by the Right, Left, and Center, only Isaiah Berlin compares; among postwar American intellectuals, only Lionel Trilling. And both Berlin and Trilling (who coveted Berlin's status) are much narrower figures than Orwell—they are intellectuals rather than men of letters. And they are little known to the wider public or outside their native countries.

Both Trilling and Berlin were ultimately skeptics and political liberals—and their reputations have undergone sharp revision. Trilling has been attacked by both his late wife Diana and his son James for his psychological weaknesses; former acolytes such as Norman Podhoretz have chastised his lack of backbone. Meanwhile, Berlin has been recast as a scholarly lightweight, an intellectual celebrity, a brilliant talker yet shallow thinker who flattered the rich and powerful.[42]

Amid all this, Orwell remains standing as an intellectual model, perhaps the leading twentieth-century exemplar of the public intellectual[43]—the repeated attempts of the far Left to blacken his reputation notwithstanding. And however fatuous or bathetic, W.W.G.O.D. is part of his attraction—and a powerful sign of his enduring appeal.

# 17

# Ecce "Orwell," or Why I Am So Famous

## I

Nietzsche once wrote a little book in which he half-seriously spoke of himself in Christ-like terms. The book, *Ecce Homo* (1895), included a rhapsodic chapter combining self-parody with self-glorification titled "Why I Am So Famous."

By contrast, Orwell practiced severe self-restraint in discussing literary reputation, remarking only in "Why I Write" (1946) that the first motive of most writers (presumably including himself) was "egoism," including the wish "to be remembered after death."

But Orwell's well-known reserve apparently did not extend to the youthful conversation of Eric Blair. For Blair's great dream, recalled Jacintha Buddicom, his dearest childhood friend, was to become "a famous writer." Eric fantasized that his *Collected Works* would be enshrined in a blue leather-bound edition and that all the volumes would stand neatly in a row on his bookcase. Remarkably, Orwell has achieved that exceptional feat, and not only in English, but in all of the major world languages. And it is not just his "collected" works that are still in print, but rather the monumental twenty-volume, 8,500-page *Complete Works of George Orwell.*

# II

How did such an outsized posthumous reputation befall a man who declared that he didn't "care tuppence for the opinion of posterity?" How did Orwell acquire the role of "Orwell"? More prosaically, what were the decisive factors? What are the distinctive features of Orwell's controversial and multifaceted reputation? Fourteen years ago, in a previous study, I posed a similar set of questions—and speculatively proposed seven answers. Let me review them here, adding seven additional contributing factors that have emerged more clearly since the 1980s. Thus, in this chapter we step behind the scenes for a backstage glimpse of how Orwell became "Orwell."

First, Orwell was "a political animal," a man "who could not blow his nose without moralizing on conditions in the handkerchief industry," as Cyril Connolly once remarked. It is not surprising, then, that Orwell has elicited strong, politically motivated responses from readers. He was a socialist and a journalist deeply involved in the issues of his time, and in turn, ideological and generational politics have figured heavily in the formation of his reputation. By contrast, issues of race have had virtually no bearing on his reputation's development; and only since the mid-1980s has gender politics come to exert some influence.[1]

Second, the claims of literary-cultural groups to Orwell as a model or forerunner (e.g., the *Partisan Review* writers, the so-called Angry Young Men, the cultural critics of the British New Left) have influenced the development of his reputation. With other writers such as Edith Sitwell or T. E. Hulme, links with the fine arts or with avant-garde *littérateurs*, rather than with Left/Right politics, are more prominent. The association of Orwell's name not only with liberal or dissident Left writers (Dickens, H. G. Wells, Samuel Butler, Ignazio Silone, Arthur Koestler, Albert Camus, André Malraux) but also with conservative and/or explicitly religious writers (Swift, Dr. Johnson, Kipling, George Gissing, Chesterton, Waugh) has helped confuse his reputation and highlight its conservative aspects.

Third, Orwell has been the object of selective critical attention. Marxist and psychoanalytic criticism has influenced the emergence of certain issues about him and his work. Yet, doubtless because of his reputed "plain" style and "straightforward" meaning, structuralist and poststructuralist critics have largely ignored him. Moreover, while *Animal Farm* and Orwell's essays are widely included in the pedagogical and literary canons, seldom are his works taught elsewhere in the academy, contributing (along with the media's preoccupation with *Animal Farm* and *Nineteen Eighty-Four*) to the odd split between his critical and public reputations.

Certain distinctive aspects of his life and afterlife constitute a fourth reason why Orwell has been the occasion for such unique acclaim and argument. Orwell's practice of compartmentalizing his relationships, often behaving quite differently with one group of politically minded friends than with another, has facilitated the development of confusions about his work. The delay in the publication of a full biography until 1980 (written by Bernard Crick) also contributed to the controversies about his politics and to the advent of a variety of Orwell images.

A fifth reason for Orwell's influence, stature, and wide appeal—the reason that many literary admirers treat as the *most* significant—is his vigilance about maintaining the integrity of the English language. His attention to language abuse anticipated and has fed the preoccupation with the topic today, thereby keeping his writings current. More importantly, his singular yet plain style has drawn to him intellectual admirers while simultaneously making him an anthologized "model stylist" for beginning writers. The physiognomic fallacy, according to which "the style is the man," has let Orwell the plain stylist be taken, perhaps too readily, for an honest and open man. Good prose is like a mirror: it reflects the man who writes it—or so some readers assume. Orwell's much-praised "pure" style has even made some observers uneasy about criticizing him, as if they asked themselves, "How can I, with my pedestrian English, criticize a writer of such wonderful prose?"

But it is Orwell's doubleness as paragon and propagandist—"Orwell" as *Doppelgänger*—that generates debates and diverse views. He is both "St. George," the Defender of the King's English, and the diabolical author of Newspeak. It is this extraordinary, Janus-faced combination that sustains controversy. On the one side is Orwell the propagandist, who could abuse language in the service of what he saw as the truth. As a propagandist at the BBC, Orwell learned to perfect the launching of catchwords as slogans. And these slogans became battle-certified during the Cold War, which is one reason why everybody wants to steal his mantle. His legacy is in part his language: Newspeak, Thought Police, Big Brother. Even his name has become an adjective: Orwellian. On the other side is the Orwell who constructed a plain-man persona that could speak in the purest English prose of the twentieth century. Common sense for the common man. No one has ever done it as well.

The timing of Orwell's death is a sixth decisive factor in the formation of his reputation. Orwell's early death made it especially inviting to canonize and claim him. (Perhaps his posthumous celebration reminds some hostile critics of his own acid comment about Lenin's saintedness: "one of those . . . who win an undeserved reputation by dying prematurely.") Orwell's image as a quixotic idealist made him an intellectual youth hero, especially in Britain in the 1950s, even as (like Kipling and Dickens) his Sancho Panza side seemed to speak to his readers' deepest desires and to give voice to sentiments or ideals that attract so many of us (the "good bad" book, love of country, defense of the underdog).

But it was not so much that Orwell died "young": he died at precisely the "right" historical moment. Indeed, if Orwell had lived even until 1955, and certainly if he had lived into the 1960s, he would have had to take sides on numerous political issues: the Cold War, McCarthyism, de-Stalinization, Hungary, Suez, Algeria, the Campaign for Nuclear Disarmament, the New Left, Vietnam, the student movement. Inevitably, as happened with Bertrand Russell, Koestler, Sartre, Camus, and others in those decades, Orwell's positions (or lack thereof) on such issues would have compromised him in the eyes of some of those groups that today claim him as a patron saint. His patriotism, his democratic socialism, his anticommunism: these and other aspects of his work would all have come under attack. Never could he have won or maintained his current stature on so many different fronts. "If Orwell Were Alive Today" would never have become a press headline, perhaps never much of a speculation at all.

A seventh factor is the diversity of Orwell's work, which has further contributed to the plurality of images of him by widening his fame and lending support to the impression that there are many different Orwells. When adolescent readers outgrow the "amusing" *Animal Farm*, they can turn to the gruesome *Nineteen Eighty-Four*, then return to both works in more mature years and fully appreciate them as political satires. Orwell's readers also encounter the plain man of the essays, the truthteller of *Homage to Catalonia*, the vehement devil's advocate of *The Road to Wigan Pier*, and the salty journalist of the "As I Please" columns.

Yet numerous authors have written in diverse genres and are known by different books. What is unusual in Orwell's case is the disagreement among readers as to which is "the best" of his works, or even as to what criteria to apply in reaching such a decision, a dispute which probably says as much about variable aesthetic standards as it says about Orwell's work. *Nineteen Eighty-Four* is widely regarded as Orwell's "towering" but "flawed" masterpiece; *Animal Farm* is his "best executed" book, a little gem, though often criticized as ending in a sterile negation; *Homage to Catalonia* is described as his "moving" and "inspiring" book; *Burmese Days* is called his "best novel." There are even votes for his other books. To Henry Miller, *Down and Out in Paris and London* was Orwell's "best book"; to John Wain, *Coming Up for Air* was Orwell's "central" book; and a *Time* reviewer asserted that Orwell "never wrote a kinder or more human novel than *Keep the Aspidistra Flying*." Still other critics have considered Orwell's essays his finest work.

The eighth and perhaps single most easily overlooked factor accounting for Orwell's fame has, fittingly enough, to do with a date. George Steiner has noted that, in titling his last book *Nineteen Eighty-Four*, Orwell became the only writer in history ever "to put his signature and claim on a piece of time." If Orwell had named his dystopia "The Last Man in Europe," as he had originally planned, the book quite probably would have had less impact, at least in the long run. The title Orwell eventually chose invited correlations between world events and the book's events, produced an immediate association in the public mind between "Orwell" and a date in the near future, and generated the "countdown to 1984" mentality. Although the reputations of many writers have benefited from posthumous events like centennial celebrations, the long countdown to 1984 kept public attention continuously, if intermittently, focused on Orwell, reaching a climax as 1984 approached. In seizing a calendar year as his own, Orwell not only etched his own name in history but blackened a segment of time. This unprecedented feat is undoubtedly a significant and overlooked reason why *Nineteen Eighty-Four* has probably had, as *U.S. News & World Report* wrote in 1984, "greater impact than any novel since *Uncle Tom's Cabin*."[2]

But now that the title date of Orwell's last work has come and gone, a ninth reason for Orwell's enduring prominence becomes ever more apparent: the ethos of the man and writer. The fact is that intellectuals' fascination with and controversies about Orwell have endured long after the passing of 1984—and even after the collapse of Soviet communism and the disappearance of the Cold War referents that allegedly gave *Animal Farm* and *Nineteen Eighty-Four* their polemical cachet and political relevance. A principal cause is Orwell's moral stature. It is a quality of being that is chiefly perceived in the reading experience when one is confronted with his attractively frank literary persona. That is, readers' intense identification with Orwell is not merely attributable to his artfully "plain," indeed "pure" prose style. Rather, readers identify passionately with Orwell's voice, his character, his life story. The living voice of Orwell, the man within the writings, compels attention, if not always admiration. As one writer expressed it: "To read Orwell is to want to know him and even to be him."

A tenth, related factor is that, even as new biographies of Orwell appear and the new millennium casts new perspectives on his oeuvre, the man remains something of a mystery. Unlike every other major writer of the twentieth century, not a line of his work is capable of marring seriously his reputation today—despite the publication of his *Complete Works* in twenty volumes. And yet he stands as a puzzle for posterity. Not only is his reputation ambiguous, but so too is his life. This oddity recalls another statement of his friend Cyril Connolly: "The living dislike puzzles: the unborn worship them. . . . Beware not to deprive posterity of all speculation, of its right to model you in its own image."[3] Whether inadvertently or intentionally, Orwell took Connolly's admonition to heart. And because Orwell has remained a mystery, a figure that succeeding generations find incapable of pinning down in a political pigeonhole—and also a man and writer on whom they can project a great range of their needs and aspirations—he allows himself to be rewritten constantly. Indeed, the rewriting of history is an ironic leitmotif of Orwell's afterlife.

But an eleventh factor is also at work here: Orwell's human appeal as a regular fellow, a "common" man, even a failure. Orwell seems to embody several different, well-defined archetypal roles with which millions of readers can identify. It is as if he himself were a literary character in one of his novels: the lonely schoolboy, the ambivalent cop, the tramp-*philosophe*, the frustrated schoolteacher, the idealistic soldier. These are among the key roles that Orwell plays—and these roles, in turn, play him and our perceptions of him. It is as though "Orwell" were a great character actor: the myth of "Orwell" has to do with the impression that he inhabits these roles naturally, indeed that their roles are quintessentially "Orwell." And virtually all of them are "ordinary," even his trademark "decent."

A twelfth reason, which has been crucial for the postwar, and especially posthumous, development of Orwell's reputation, is one that I first discussed in *The Politics of Literary Reputation*, yet which has emerged more clearly in the last decade. Orwell became the most famous literary Cold Warrior partly on account of official government sponsorship of his work—which began (with his approval) during his lifetime. Intelligence services of both the British and American governments organized and financed the film adaptations of *Animal Farm* and *Nineteen Eighty-Four* and those books' translations into more than a dozen foreign languages.

For instance, Orwell conferred with the Information Research Department (IRD) of the U.K. about the Russian translation of *Animal Farm* as well as its translations into Chinese, Burmese, and even Telegu. He also enthusiastically cooperated with the American-approved German translations of *Animal Farm* and *Nineteen Eighty-Four* that were serialized in 1949–50 in *Der Monat*, the U.S. occupation army magazine. After Orwell's death, American government agencies such as Voice of America, the United States Information Agency, and the State Department energetically promoted Orwell's work, with Dean Acheson even writing in 1951 that works like *Animal Farm* and *Nineteen Eighty-Four* "have been of great value to the Department in its psychological offensive against Communism."[4] The CIA (with Howard Hunt as the agent in charge) secretly purchased the film rights to both books and had these film adaptations distributed globally in the mid-1950s. (The studios also altered the endings of both films; not only do the animals rise up against their pig tyrants and liberate themselves, but Winston and Julia die unbowed in a love embrace as Winston decries Big Brother's tyranny.)[5]

Thirteenth, now that the last century has receded into history, and even though Orwell did not live to see its second half, it truly seems as if Orwell spoke to every major issue of his time: poverty, war, racism, colonialism, totalitarianism, utopia, the Bomb, technological determinism, mass culture, religious unbelief. And he did so in a variety of forms and genres and roles. Not only was he a prolific journalist and columnist, but he was also a skilled essayist and novelist. Quoting Orwell is like quoting scripture; one can find a passage to support practically any political position. Orwell is the number one choice for an intellectual godfather, the preferred ancestor to gild one's intellectual pedigree. Illustrating this fact was the caricature devoted to his intellectual heirs apparent that ran in the *New York Times Book Review* in June 2002. An adult Orwell crawls along with two little boys—Hitchens and Andrew Sullivan—sitting on his back for a ride. The point was clear: Next to the "Big O," the current generation of intellectuals look like small fry. Whether standing or crouching or even kneeling, Orwell—or, rather, an outsized "Orwell"—towers over his potential successors. He remains every intellectual's big brother.

Finally and quite simply: Orwell was right. That is, not only did he address virtually every major political and social question of his day, but his stands on all the significant ones seemingly have been borne out by the verdict of time. In other words, at least on all of the big political issues facing him and his generation, and which indeed ultimately came to dominate the twentieth century—imperialism, fascism, and communism—he has been proven right. This is the well-argued thesis of Hitchens's *Orwell's Victory.*[6]

# III

The question of Orwell's distinctive reputation also raises complicated questions about how historical "emergence" and artistic originality bear on the making of reputations. When does a writer's work "enter" on the stage of History? How does one's "moment of entrance" relate to reputation?

The processes are more complex than they might seem, for the relationship of a writer's work to his reputation-history is not just a matter of dates. Books that seem to appear "at the same time" frequently enter history framed by radically different patterns and conditions. For instance, although *Animal Farm* and H. G. Wells's *Mind at the End of Its Tether* both appeared in 1945 and talked gloomily about the future, the two books' preoccupations and approaches indicate that they really belonged to different eras, the pre- and post-totalitarian, which reflects the fact that Wells was more than thirty-five years older than Orwell.

Or consider *Nineteen Eighty-Four* and James Burnham's *Struggle for the World* (1947). Both appeared at roughly the same postwar moment and both depicted the same superpower alignments. Both had tremendous initial impacts. Yet Burnham's book was soon forgotten. The reverse is true if one compares any of the popular books on the Spanish Civil War with *Homage to Catalonia*, originally remaindered even before Orwell's publisher, Seeker & Warburg, had recovered its advance, and yet a classic since its 1952 republication. Or compare *The Road to Wigan Pier* with James Agee's *Let Us Now Praise Famous Men* (1941). Both dealt with "invisible" poverty in outlying areas. Orwell's book had an immediate impact; Agee's book was little noticed. Both are classics of their kind today.

Thus, we need to see "spatial time" not merely as a concept applicable to fictional worlds and to literary criticism, but to our own world and to cultural criticism. The foregoing differences in historical emergence lend force to Edward Said's injunction in *The World, the Text, and the Critic* against "an irreducibly serial, filiative conception of sociohistorical time." Cultural phenomena are "a family of ideas emerging . . . in discourse," not best understood as if they were "human beings born on a certain day; the past is not a set of such births, and time does not move like a clock, in discrete movements."

There is, in other words, a synchronic dimension to reputation, what George Kubler in *The Shape of Time* calls "the mechanics of fame." Kubler concerns himself chiefly with how contingencies involving series and sequence bear on the artist's achievement—e.g., by "inserting" the artist into a phase (early, middle, late) of a reigning aesthetic mode (whether genre, style, national/regional tradition, *Zeitgeist*, etc.). Kubler sees art history and artistic style not as uniquely individual accomplishments, but as "a linked succession of prime works with replications, all being distributed in time as recognizably early and late versions of the same kind of action." "[W]ithout a good entrance," says Kubler, even the gifted artist is "in danger of wasting his time as a copyist, regardless of temperament or training." Thus a Renaissance "great man" is less a "universal genius" than simply a highly talented person "bestriding many new tracks of development at a fortunate moment in that great renovation of Western civilization, and traveling his distance in several systems without the burdens of rigorous proof and extensive demonstration required in later periods."[7]

One might speculate as to whether the success of Orwell's plain-man style, so welcome as a refreshing change from the aestheticism of the 1920s and in line with American tastes for "tough-guy" writers like Henry Miller and Ernest Hemingway in the 1930s, helped make writers similarly styled in the '50s (e.g., the Angry Young Men) seem, given Orwell's priority, artificial and worn.

To discuss further the mechanics of Orwell's historical entrance would require extensive comparison and contrast with other "candidates" of a similar kind for literary repute, a difficult task beyond my intentions here. Such considerations also raise large questions of historical "mood" and social structure, important to acknowledge yet hard to investigate empirically. It is clear, for example, that intellectuals continue to quote Orwell not just because of the timing of his death but for other reasons associated with his "moment of entrance," among them the enduring fascination of Left intellectuals with the Thirties as a golden age of idealism and political commitment, and with Orwell's attractive dual image as an opponent of right- and left-wing totalitarianism and as a conservative defender of native traditions.

The foregoing reflections do not account fully for Orwell's afterlife in the limelight, for "why he is so famous." But they do help explain why he has gone down in history and not the memory hole, why "Orwell" still occupies a prominent habitation and name in Western culture—more prominent perhaps than even the young Eric Blair had dared to hope.[8]

# Epilogue

## Our Orwell, Right or Left?

### I

So what can I say about Orwell after having scrutinized and weighed the responses of his enthusiasts and enemies? What can anyone say about George Orwell's politics as we pass the centenary of his birth? If he was, as he claimed, a "democratic socialist," exactly how may we understand his unorthodox radicalism? And if we do forthrightly admit that he was a radical, what value does he possess for liberals and conservatives in the twenty-first century?

If one writes in an inescapably ideological age and about a much-coveted political symbol like "Orwell," it often appears nearly impossible to adopt a middle stance between detached analysis and impassioned advocacy. The former pole seems an academic cop-out in violation of the spirit of Orwell's forthright admission (and my own view) that all criticism is ideological. Yet the latter pole strikes many readers as a thinly veiled attempt to claim Orwell's mantle for one's own camp—precisely the task that Orwell disavowed, nay castigated, in his essays on Dickens, Swift, and others.

That tension is one reason I alternate between the academic and the *engagé*

approach to Orwell's politics, circling around him with the scholar's detach-
ment and the partisan's enthusiasm. Another reason is that I am more com-
fortable with reproving claimants of Orwell's mantle like Norman Podhoretz
than with making a "case" for Orwell.[1] In fact, I would rather—and I will to
some extent—make the case *against* the conservative and liberal Orwells, much
as Orwell did with Dickens in his 1939 essay "Charles Dickens."[2] But I do so
only to clarify the misconceptions about his politics, before returning at the
close to explain why he is best understood as a radical—as he claimed himself
to be—yet one with a strong and enduring appeal to conservatives as well as
liberals.

# II

Probably no writer of the twentieth century has collected such a vast array of
seemingly incompatible admirers and detractors as Orwell. Without question, his enigmatic reputation has arisen for many reasons: he himself was not
only a socialist but a fierce "conscience of the Left"; his political positions
evolved throughout his life (from "Tory anarchist" to Independent Labour
Party member to Labour Party supporter); he never worked out his political
thought in any systematic treatise; and he died at the moment when the Cold
War was dawning, whereupon he became ripe for claiming by intellectuals of
the Left and Right.

This last factor is a useful starting point for considering any argument about
Orwell's politics. Few tasks are thornier, or more useless and misleading, for
contemporary historians than putting political intellectuals into well-defined
ideological categories. In fact, the numerous, shifting meanings that "liberal"
and "conservative" have accreted should make us cautious about ideological
terminology, especially in the context of twentieth-century Britain. Of the
three great political traditions—conservative, liberal, radical—only the last is
English. Indeed, as George Watson has argued, such a vocabulary, imported
from the continental (especially French) tradition of ideological "spectrum"
politics, is historically inappropriate to the liberal British political heritage.
The political usage of "conservative" and "liberal" derives from France and
Spain, and the terms were not applied to the English-speaking countries be-

fore 1825. (Even Edmund Burke was a Whig, not a Tory.)[3]

It may even be that postwar events have rendered archaic the modern ideological categories of Right and Left. Their entry into the English political lexicon around 1930 invited the "reclassification" of figures from the Victorian age—men who had not thought in terms of sharply dichotomous, near monolithic, party-line ideological taxonomies. Thus, Dickens and others soon became writers "well worth stealing" by Marxists and Tories alike, as Orwell noted in "Charles Dickens." In many ways the labels "reactionary" and "progressive" don't fit Orwell at all either. Nevertheless, the irony is that he has fallen victim to the very same oversimplifications from the 1930s that he so clearly saw through. These difficulties notwithstanding, Orwell was in some respects, as he called himself, a "political writer," and it is important and appropriate to discuss him in relation to a political tradition.

Let us proceed inductively, as Orwell might have: Which political writers did Orwell himself most strongly resemble? Malcolm Muggeridge and Hugh Kingsmill, both of them staunch conservatives in their mature years, argued that Orwell was most like William Cobbett.[4] Both Orwell and Cobbett were romantic radicals and patriots who loved the England of their childhoods; both were nostalgic populists who hated class oppression and the modern industrial world; both were tribunes of the poor, capable of looking at the worker's lot from his own standpoint. Both were also champions of the underdog, standing always on the side of the oppressed and pressing for radical reform to improve the lot of the common man.

A political writer even more frequently linked with Orwell is Dickens, who exerted crucial influence on the formation of Orwell's political consciousness. Orwell was a nineteenth-century meliorist who turned skeptical and pessimistic given the specter of a totalitarian future.[5] Like Dickens, Orwell was chiefly a moral critic, inveighing against social and economic injustice, rather than an ideological one.

Indeed we might better see Orwell as a "moral radical" than a political radical. He was not a moralist per se, but rather a "moral perceiver," in Francis Hope's phrase, and "to understand him is to ask not how he would have solved a problem but how he would have seen it."[6] This insight is shrewd. Invariably Orwell saw problems and advanced socialist claims in ethical terms that all Englishmen could sanction ("justice," "liberty," "honesty," "decency," "fair play").

Orwell did go to the root of things. But he wrote as a novelist and journalist, not as a theorist. The theorist abstracts, essentializes, and systematizes. The storyteller's gift is for narrative and telling detail. The Dickens of *Hard Times* and the Orwell of *Animal Farm* stir readers' imaginations to sympathize with human suffering.

All this recalls the remark of Richard Rees, a cultural conservative and Orwell's close friend and literary executor, that Orwell was not really a political writer at all but a "metapolitical writer" for whom politics was the "education of the human soul."[7] Dickens also put his faith in education, and Orwell is perhaps best seen in this tradition of the "metapolitical writer" less concerned with either policy or philosophy, let alone with strategies of agitation or political theory, than with the radical humanist's question of how forms of government shape the lives of individuals.

As such, despite their many affinities, Orwell does not ultimately resemble closely those political writers whose life work was spent in defining non-Marxist radicalism in systematic fashion (for example, the tradition represented by Robert Owen, G. D. H. Cole, Harold Laski). Nor should he be mistaken for an anarchist, though he shared with anarchists (from Winstanley and Godwin to his friends V. S. Richards and George Woodcock) a hatred of centralized power and a belief in the small community and the primacy of individual conscience. The shortcomings of the modern industrial state, Orwell thought, were not ineradicable and lay primarily in its class structure.

Nor, finally, is Orwell a liberal. Despite his worries about collectivism and invasive state power, he did not believe in laissez-faire economics. Nor did he share the doctrinaire Benthamite distrust of intervention by the state. Liberals from Fox to Bentham, whether they be Utilitarians (Bentham, James Mill), classical economists (Malthus, Ricardo), or Manchester School free traders (Richard Cobden, John Bright), are distinguished by a privatizing individualism quite alien to Orwell's instincts.

Orwell's convictions lie much closer to the latter-day English liberal tradition from John Stuart Mill to Keynes, given its Gladstonian view that principle ought to count for more than power or expedience, and its belief that moral issues cannot be excluded from politics. Although it is these beliefs that make Orwell resemble a "nineteenth-century liberal," in George Woodcock's characterization, Orwell was more impatient with gradualist approaches and more hopeful about the virtues of democracy than these liberals.[8] The liberal protest against injustice was too weak for Orwell. He had passionately identified with the poor during his "down-and-out" years in Paris and London (1928–30) and with the Spanish underclass during his 1936–37 visit to Spain; he became the "conscience of his generation," in V. S. Pritchett's phrase, precisely because he could support neither a liberal politics devoted to incremental reform nor a revolutionary politics committed to romantic apocalypse.[9]

So Orwell was not a "political writer" like most English utopian socialists, Marxists, anarchists, or liberals. Indeed it is his empirical, literary, "metapolitical" cast of mind, which registers perceptions rather than devises programs, that marks Orwell as a rebel, rather than a revolutionary, to use the distinction made by Camus in *The Rebel*. The rebel is one who asserts human dignity not by affirming a doctrine but merely by saying "no."[10] Orwell was chiefly "a man against," as Arthur Koestler put it in his obituary. "A revolutionary makes compromises to hang onto power; a rebel is a rebel, he is against; and he [Orwell] was against everything that stank in society."[11]

Orwell himself once remarked that most revolutionaries "are potential Tories, because they imagine that everything can be put right by altering the *shape* of society; once that change is effected, as it sometimes is, they see no need for any other. Dickens has not this type of mental coarseness." Yet this is not coarseness, but rather the rage for order. Orwell lacked it too. Unlike the theorists and revolutionaries, Orwell the storyteller and rebel knew that the task of building and maintaining an egalitarian society was slow and steady work, an ongoing, messy, inefficient, very human affair.

# III

Seeing Orwell in a line roughly traceable to Cobbett and Dickens and in all these guises—as moral radical, storyteller, metapolitical writer, and rebel— both sharpens our understanding of Orwell's place within the English radical tradition and highlights the conservative streak in his outlook. For though he was unafraid to think to the root of problems, he aimed always, like Cobbett and Dickens, to extend what was valid in the past and deepen English culture; he had little desire to raze or extirpate. "By revolution we become more ourselves, not less," he declared at the close of *The Lion and the Unicorn*.[12] He was no policymaker, and only in this work did he ever even propose in outline any socialist program.

*The Lion and the Unicorn* (1941) is the key book for understanding Orwell's Pickwickian radicalism. In that work he was, for once, a "revolutionary"—though certainly an unorthodox one. He was a "revolutionary patriot" and delivered a Jacobin threat: "I daresay the London gutters will have to run with blood. All right, let them, if it is necessary."[13] During the first two years of the war, Orwell thought it might be necessary: he called for an English socialist revolution whether Britain defeated Hitler or not. It would be a revolution unlike that of 1789 or 1917, a specifically English revolution emergent from the radical, democratic spirit of English popular culture.

Even after his hopes for such a revolution dimmed, Orwell made it clear after the 1945 Labour Party victory that he expected Attlee and Bevan to use their mandate to put a radical program into effect (including, for example, the redistribution of wealth, the abolition of public schools, and national health care). Like the great English radicals from Mill to Bevan, he sought drastic and permanent change rather than the mere amelioration of the common man's lot. Moreover, unlike the Victorians, he understood the need to change the economic basis of society. He was not content like Dickens simply to issue calls for moral reform and a "change of heart." And yet, how to achieve economic change? Orwell had no faith in systems; he admitted in effect that he had no better call than Dickens's to make: "Economic injustice will stop the moment we want it to stop," he declared in *The Road to Wigan Pier*, "and if we genuinely want it to stop the method adopted hardly matters."[14]

In many ways Orwell's scrupulous tendency to criticize his own side makes him more a critic of revolution than a revolutionary. Here again, conservatives and neoconservatives have found him an inspiration and an ally. And here too, Orwell resembles earlier English radicals, such as Cobbett and Dickens. For Orwell never compromised his radical criticism to accommodate radical sectarian orthodoxies. Nor did he conceive it solely in terms of intellectual controversies, let alone political theory. Although neither a peasant like Cobbett nor a lower-class boy like Dickens, Orwell came to his radical convictions not through books but via an odyssey of experience that brought him into contact with the lives of the underclass and working man: tramping in London, dishwashing in Paris, meeting miners and unemployed men in Wigan, fighting in Catalonia. This participant-observer experience was unique among intellectuals of his generation. Orwell had his romantic, Quixotic side, but it is wrong to see him as a utopian idealist with a will to abstraction, a radical "with both feet planted firmly in the air."[15] This characterization applies to many radicals of his generation, but not to George Orwell. Orwell was a radical and a self-declared democratic socialist, but he was never a progressive or a Marxist.

Orwell's antitotalitarianism and radical faith emerged together in Spain. His hatred of Left orthodoxy combined with a populism that had little to do with intellectual theorizing but rather was borne of "a consciousness of the deeply moral, emotionally expressed egalitarianism of the common people [of Spain] in the midst of a revolution."[16] Orwell the "revolutionary patriot" was a socialist, but he was no progressive. Nor was his patriotism simply a habit of mind undergirding support for the traditional institutions of church and state, as it was for English Conservatives. "Patriotism is actually the opposite of Conservatism," wrote Orwell in *The Lion and the Unicorn*. Similarly, in *The Road to Wigan Pier*, he insisted that his severe criticism of the progressivist valorizing of technology and modernity should not be read as support for conservatism.[17]

Nonetheless, the fact is that the Orwell physiognomy has undeniably conservative features, and conservatives of all shades have been fair in noting them and identifying with Orwell on that basis. Christopher Hollis, a prominent British M.P. and Catholic conservative, depicted his fellow Old Etonian as a lover of the land who espoused a precapitalist, agrarian cultural conservatism.[18] Those aspects are indisputably present in Orwell's life and work. Yet they more accurately amount to what Conor Cruise O'Brien called Orwell's "Tory growl" rather than a full-fledged conservative politics. For nowhere does Orwell insist, as have conservatives from Burke and Robert Peel through Kenneth Pickthorn and Quintin Hogg, on reason rather than majority will as the foundation for law, on possession of private property as the basis for individual self-determination, on the sacred importance of tradition, and on legislation in accordance with the "natural order" that inheres in things.

Furthermore, such conservative elements in Orwell's radicalism are not necessarily in conflict with his radicalism; indeed, insofar as he did value continuity with the past and the folkways of English life, they can be seen as sustaining and nourishing it. The English radical tradition has typically possessed a backward-looking, rustic strand, beginning with Cobbett's and Dickens's romantic populism and continuing on with Morris, Blatchford, Tawney, and Bevan. This is the non-Marxist tradition of the Tory radical, with special emphasis on the class implications of "Tory," which betrays a deep nostalgia for the English past. And this strand of the socialist tradition spotlights Orwell's conservative streak. For it rebels against party orthodoxies and abstract theorizing and proclaims the moral free agency of the individual, even as it scoffs at reverence for Tradition and Continuity for their own sakes. It considers patriotism not merely an abstract love of one's country but the preservation of a specifically English love of decency and democracy. Edward Thomas captures nicely the special place of Orwell, with his self-described "lower-upper-middle class" heritage, within this nondoctrinaire, antimodern English radical tradition:

> He was not a root-and-branch man. He belonged, not to the minority who want to topple an entire civilization, but to the larger number who would eradicate the chief injustices of their society but do not desire to abandon altogether the traditional moulds of life. Where Orwell wanted change, he wanted it whole-heartedly and actively. Evolutionary and historical theories of society are not his chief concern, and people who think in these terms are inclined to see in him a heroic dead end. Political writing was for him not a branch of knowledge but a form of action in defense of standards of which he felt reasonably certain, and this certainty seems to have been rooted in an unequivocal reaction to concrete experience. Just as his conservatism is founded on love of concrete objects and ways from the past, not on abstract veneration for tradition, so it is a feeling for particular injustices, not a doctrine of progress, that makes him a revolutionary.[19]

Needless to say, such a characterization of "radical" might seem rather Pickwickian. But to me it sums up well Orwell's peculiarly English radicalism. And so it is no surprise that independent radicals beholden to European neo-Marxist theory (Raymond Williams, Isaac Deutscher) long ago denied

Dear Reader:

Thank you for purchasing this ISI Books title. Since 1953, the **Intercollegiate Studies Institute** (ISI) has fostered in successive generations an appreciation for, and a deeper understanding of, America's tradition of ordered liberty. **ISI Books** serves the Institute's broader national program by publishing books, guides, and other resources that consider afresh those perennial ideas which have shaped Western culture and the American experience.

If you would like to learn more about ISI and ISI Books, please fill out this postcard and drop it in the mail.

**Name:**

**Address:**

**City/State/Zip:**

**Country:**

**E-Mail:**

**Phone:**

**I received this card in the book titled:**

A UNIVERSITY IN PRINT
*The imprint of the Intercollegiate Studies Institute*

*Call 800-526-7022 or visit us at www.isibooks.org.*

# BUSINESS REPLY MAIL

PERMIT NO. 44 WILMINGTON, DE

INTERCOLLEGIATE STUDIES INSTITUTE, INC.

PO BOX 4431

WILMINGTON, DE 19807-9957

Orwell title to the word "radical" and dismissed him as a pathetic "dead end" for the hard Left. But other independent, anti-Marxist radicals have taken him as a model and guide. In *The Politics of Literary Reputation*, I concluded that, of all Orwell's prominent contemporary admirers on the Left, the two who most resemble him and have carried on *his* radical humanist tradition are not Englishmen at all—but the American Irving Howe and the Canadian George Woodcock, both of whom were independent, heterodox radicals strongly sympathetic to cultural conservatism.[20]

# IV

However interesting the construction of a political tradition pointing backward and forward from Orwell himself, my inductive, "Orwellian" approach to Orwell's complex politics may not satisfy Orwell's most vocal admirers on the Right. After all, one can cite examples of conservative writers whom he esteemed and with whom he is justly compared (Swift, Johnson, Kipling, Gissing, Chesterton, Waugh). And one can name numerous conservative and neoconservative admirers of Orwell at *National Review*, *Modern Age*, *Commentary*, and elsewhere. So armed, one can proceed to fit Orwell into a conservative or neoconservative tradition. The fit strikes me as Procrustean, downplaying as it does the significance of *The Lion and the Unicorn* and ignoring Orwell's clear self-declaration as a "democratic socialist." But the Right's rejoinder is that radicals overvalue *The Lion and the Unicorn* and undervalue *Homage to Catatonia*, *Animal Farm*, and *Nineteen Eighty-Four*, works which they consider not only anti-Stalinist but also anti-socialist. And here I step back and assume a more detached, academic stance, before returning at the close to a personal reexamination of Orwell.

One notices that the aforementioned claims to a "radical" versus a "conservative" Orwell tend to focus on different works and different periods of Orwell's life. This is another reason why, however much we insist on carefully defining political terms, quoting chapter and verse from an author's work, or citing biographical evidence about his life, rival legitimacy claims to Orwell will probably be staked for a long while to come. Such claims involve what Robert Nozick has called "the rhetoric of historical entitlement."[21] No matter how different Orwell may seem from his predecessors or successors, one can always search history for "process" and "value" continuities that will link others to him—and thereby make him their distinguished heir or ancestor.

Radical admirers of Orwell have associated him with a radical tradition mostly via process continuities. They argue that, although Dickens and Irving Howe take positions very different from his on some issues, the radical tradition has undergone a natural evolution in response to events, so that the apparent differences are superficial. They are matters of political readjustment rather than realignment. Some radicals and Left-liberals (Julian Symons, Bernard Crick) also stress value continuities, arguing that Orwell and socialism continue to share the same underlying values, for example, the socialist belief in decency and justice for all.

Conservatives (Hollis, Russell Kirk) and neoconservatives (Podhoretz, Irving Kristol, Leopold Labedz) exclusively emphasize value continuities. They argue that radicals of the nineteenth and late twentieth centuries do not share Orwell's "fundamental" (that is, anticollectivist) convictions; and even though the self-description "conservative" or "neoconservative" was not Orwell's, the values and policy stands of the Right fairly characterize his views from the standpoint of the Victorian and postwar ages (for example, love of nature and liberty, hostility to collectivism, hatred for intellectual fashions and Left orthodoxy).

These radical/conservative arguments then get linked to arguments about the formal/value continuities or discontinuities of Orwell's career. Radicals and Left-liberals (Hitchens) typically seek to minimize the extent of Orwell's "evolution." And so they argue that Orwell did not change, or that the change was only apparent, or that he did change but not significantly. Conservatives (Kirk) and neoconservatives (Podhoretz) usually maintain that Orwell changed significantly—either midway (after *Homage to Catalonia*, 1938) or near the end of his career (with *Nineteen Eighty-Four*, 1949). They do so because the rhetoric of historical entitlement is persuasive only if one can lay claim to the whole man or to the "final" man. Typically, radicals claim the "whole" Orwell (with special focus on his wartime period), conservatives the "final" Orwell. The claim to the whole man is obviously preferable, but it is implausible when ostensibly sharp career shifts are hard to play down or reconcile. The claim to the "final" man can be effective if it can be demonstrated that Orwell "saw the light" and ultimately arrived at a "new" position.

If, in the end, I reject the Right's claim to this "final" Orwell and honor Orwell's own statement that he died a "democratic socialist," it is less for polemical reasons than simply to pay final respect to Orwell's integrity, intelligence, and self-knowledge. For, like so many other readers of Orwell, I have strongly identified with the man, writer, and political figure. He is both elusive and attractive because he was radical in intellect and conservative in temperament. Orwell was a moral radical with a bracing contempt for radical chic. He embraced a socialist politics and a conservative ethos. Radical by conviction, conservative by sentiment, he would have agreed with Burke that a passion for innovation is the mark of an immature mind, while adding quickly that a passion for stability is the sign of an ossified one. Orwell took a courageous, dissident stance within the London Left, one which remains a model for all those who would speak the truth and publicly insist that our own side live up to our professed ideals. Faced with the smelly careerist orthodoxies of numerous academic leftists and the elitist pseudo-humanism of many neoconservatives, Orwell stands as an inspiring, ever-relevant example of how to live the intellectual life, no matter what one's political or scholarly allegiances. So perhaps, in this broadest sense, I do want to claim George Orwell after all.

# V

But if so, I present the case for "a," not "the," George Orwell. For there are many brands of radicalism as well as conservatism, and Orwell clearly does not belong to some of them. Even "case," however, is too pointed a word; instead I have merely suggested a few, less familiar characterizations of Orwell that might disclose submerged aspects of both his radical and conservative imagination. We too might then become "moral perceivers," able to appreciate from slightly different angles—historical, moral, literary, metapolitical, existential—the distinctive valence of Orwell's dissenting politics. I offer these reflections not with any hope of resolving the debate about Orwell's politics, let alone in order to pigeonhole him into a new set of categories. Rather, my own work on Orwell's multifaceted reputation and his legions of claimants makes me skeptical about any case "*for* Orwell" and about all approaches to him via conventional categories. For nothing about the blockbuster "Orwell" is conventional. And so my heightened awareness of the various roles and variegated costumes in which his audiences have clad him leaves me wary about all attempts to perceive him through the clear lens of a single tradition, political or otherwise.

If I close on a diffident note, it is because probably no one can probe bold, vivid close-ups of someone without having his own sharp, lucid, perhaps all-too-static camera shot (or freeze frame?) of that person brought into question. For my part, I have been learning in recent years to adjust my angle of vision, whereupon I see George Orwell as a more rounded, complex, paradoxical man and writer.

Perhaps we can relinquish our drive to label a significant figure. Perhaps we can become willing instead simply to see him as he saw himself and as others have seen him. Then we might come to value him in all of his diverse, divergent performing selves, even while holding that, for us, some are more equal than others. In doing so we might then prize *our* figure, and yet grant Orwell's capacity to serve as a model in various ways, which in no sense need entail a loss of esteem or even wonder. It could merely signify an enlarged awareness of the shimmering rainbow of perspectives on a life—and a greater appreciation of the spectacle of scenes from an afterlife.

# Notes

The final volumes of the *Complete Works of George Orwell* appeared in 1997–98, edited by Peter Davison (London: Secker & Warburg). This collection has superseded the four-volume *Collected Essays, Journalism, and Letters of George Orwell* (London: Secker & Warburg, 1968), edited by Sonia Orwell and Ian Angus. But *The Complete Works* did not appear in paperback until mid-2003, and thus has not, until recently, been readily accessible to the nonspecialist. For that reason, I have, where possible, first cited the 1968 volumes (as *CEJL*) for references that appear in both sources. In such cases, I cite *CEJL* by volume and page number and refer the reader to the correlative volume of Orwell's *Complete Works*, which is cited parenthetically as *CW*.

## Preface

1. Furthermore, a new biography of Orwell's second wife, Sonia Brownell, has recently appeared: *The Girl from the Fiction Department*, by Hilary Spurling (London: Hamish Hamilton, 2002).

## Prologue. The Orwell Centenary—and the Orwell Century

1. *George Orwell: The Politics of Literary Reputation* (New Brunswick, N.J.: Transaction, 2002). All references are to the Transaction edition.

2. See, for instance, the following recent articles devoted to these themes: Mario Varricchio, "Power of Images/Images of Power in *Brave New World* and *Nineteen Eighty-Four,*" *Utopian Studies: Journal of the Society for Utopian Studies* 10, no. 1 (1999): 98–114; Michael Rademacher, "Orwell and Hitler: *Mein Kampf* as a Model for *Nineteen Eighty-Four,*" *Zeitschrift fur Anglistik und Amerikanistik* 47, no. 1 (1999): 38–53; Mary Reilly, "Racine and Orwell: Classical Newspeak?" *Seventeenth Century French Studies* 22 (2000): 63–75. For an indication of the range of attention devoted to Orwell by the publishing world, see also Gillian Fenwick, *George Orwell: A Bibliography* (London: Oak Knoll, 1998).

3. Malcolm Muggeridge, *Like It Was: The Diaries of Malcolm Muggeridge* (London: Collins, 1981). See the entry for 21 January 1950.

# 1. The Hype and Hilarity of "Orwellmania"

1. The "1984" ad cost $400,000 to produce and $500,000 for the advertising slot in which it ran. See Sarah R. Stein, "The '1984' Macintosh Ad: Cinematic Icons and Constitutive Rhetoric in the Launch of a New Machine," *Quarterly Journal of Speech* 88 (May 2002).

2. These citations are from Stein, "The '1984' Macintosh Ad."

3. In another letter responding to his literary agent's news that a "reactionary" Dutch paper was serializing *Animal Farm*, Orwell answered, "I don't know if we can help that. Obviously a book of that type is liable to be made use of by Conservatives, Catholics, etc." This casual (though perhaps also cynically pragmatic) attitude toward the abuse of his work suggests that Orwell may indeed have inadvertently contributed to the misreadings of *Animal Farm* and *Nineteen Eighty-Four* that arose even during his lifetime. (See the letter from Orwell to his agent Leonard Moore, 9 January 1947, *CW*, vol. 19.) On Orwell's cooperation with British and American intelligence services to translate and distribute his last two books, see chapters 4 and 17.

4. For a different viewpoint, see Richard A. Posner, "Orwell Versus Huxley: Economics, Technology, Privacy, and Satire," *Philosophy and Literature* 24, no. 1 (2000): 1–33. See also Richard Posner, *Public Intellectuals: A Study in Decline* (Cambridge, Mass.: Harvard University Press, 2001).

5. Arthur Eckstein, "George Orwell's Second Thoughts on Capitalism," in *The Revised Orwell*, ed. Jonathan Rose (Lansing, Mich.: Michigan State University Press, 1992), 191–205. The quotes from Orwell's essays are cited in Eckstein. See also Orwell's essay "Why Socialists Don't Believe in Fun," originally published in a December 1943 issue of the *Tribune*. This article was printed under the byline "John Freeman" and originally titled, "Can Socialists Be Happy?" Previously a "lost essay," it is included in Peter Davison's edition of Orwell's *Complete Works* and printed for the first time there under Orwell's name (*CW*, vol. 15).

6. See S. Carter, "A Do-It-Yourself Dystopia: The Americanization of Big Brother," *Communication Abstracts* 24, no. 6 (2001): 743–93.

7. "Consumer totalitarianism," Adorno said, referred to consumerism as the historically regnant "third totalitarianism," which has outlasted and ultimately triumphed over fascism and socialism. Or as Sabine, the Czech émigré painter in Milan Kundera's *Unbearable Lightness of Being*, puts it during her exile in sunny California: "My enemy is kitsch, not Communism." It possesses an "authoritarian power," Kundera's narrator observes, so mighty that "none among us is superhuman enough" to overcome it. Even the Gulag is merely "a septic tank used by totalitarian kitsch to dispose of its refuse." See Milan Kundera, *The Unbearable Lightness of Being*, trans. Michael Henry Heim (New York: Harper and Row, 1984). See also Theodor Adorno, *Aesthetic Theory*, trans. Robert Hullot-Kentor (Minneapolis, Minn.: University of Minnesota Press, 1997).

## 2. Ma Bell and Big Brother

1. Today, however, the fight is between the Bells (having entered adolescence, they are no longer known as the "Baby Bells") and a coalition of long-distance phone companies. Although the explicit use of Orwell's names and phrases is missing, the war to brand the other side a greedy monster—all under the noble guise of serving consumers—continues unabated.

2. The striving (and the war of ads among the communication behemoths) goes on. For instance, Southwestern Bell Communications Inc. (SBC) ran an attack ad in 2002 describing the phone giant's rivals as "parasites" who are permitted (by state deregulation laws in force since 1996) to leave company phone lines below cost and are not required to help pay to maintain them. Voters for Choice, a coalition of competitors, replied with a name-calling ad portraying SBC as a wolf in sheep's clothing with the caption: "What if the company crying wolf today *is* the wolf?" In another ad, SBC retorts: "Some people have been saying some nasty stuff about SBC." The scene shifts to a repair crew at work in a storm. "But that's OK, we've worked in mud before." See "The Battle for Hearts and Phone Lines," *Austin-American Statesman*, 17 November 2002, J1.

3. Carter, "A Do-It-Yourself Dystopia," 743–93.

4. Jenny Madden and Ben Seymour, "Interview," *Independent* (London), 21 June 1998, 2. Zizek is the author of *The Ticklish Subject: The Absent Centre of Political Ontology* (New York: Verso, 1999) and *Did Somebody Say Totalitarianism?* (New York: Verso, 2001), among other books.

5. It is worth noting that the *Big Brother* show began on Channel 4 in the U.K. and became a big hit there before being adapted for American TV. There are also Australian and South African versions. See the web site: http://directory.google.com/Top/Arts/Television/Programs/Reality-Based/Big_Brother/. Or the official web site, whose opening graphic ends with the warning, "Big Brother is always watching": http://www.channel14.com/entertainment/tv/microsites/B/bigbrother/index.html.

6. *Frankfurter Allgemeine Zeitung*, 6 January 2002.

7. "Wort des Jahres 2000," *Deutsche Presse-Agentur*, 15 December 2000.

## 3. Glasnost, Gorby, and the Strange Case of Comrade Orwell

1. For two different historical perspectives on related issues, see Gorman Beauchamp, "Orwell, the Lysenko Affair, and the Politics of Social Construction," *Partisan Review* 68, no. 2 (spring 2001): 266–78, and John Newsinger, "*Nineteen Eighty-Four* since the Collapse of Communism," *Foundation: Review of Science Fiction* 56 (autumn 1992): 75–84. A version of this piece is included in John Newsinger, *Orwell's Politics* (London: Palgrave, 1999).

2. The quotations of the dissidents are from Jay Bergman, "Reading Fiction to Understand the Soviet Union: Soviet Dissidents on Orwell's *1984*," *History of European Ideas* 23, nos. 5–6 (1997): 173–92.

## 4. Appreciating *Animal Farm* in the New Millennium

1. The star cast of actors furnishing the animal voices includes Julia Louis-Dreyfus (Mollie the mare), Julia Ormond (Jessie the sheepdog), and Kelsey Grammer (Snowball). Peter Postlethwaite is featured as Farmer Jones.

2. As Halmi explained in a post-production interview, another animated version—before the advent of animatronics—"just wouldn't have had the proper impact. Animation was done because live action could not produce the reality. I could not do it the way I wanted to do it, to be honest to the book, until I had the technology." Gail Pennington, "*Animal Farm's* Barnyard Revolution Comes to Life on TNT Special," *St. Louis Post-Dispatch*, 3 October 1999, F7.

3. Ibid.

4. Ibid.

5. "Everything came together a couple of years ago, when the technology was not quite there," Halmi says. He notes that he and Henson's Creature Shop took advantage of existing technology to introduce new technical innovations in their *Animal Farm* adaptation, including an impressive animatronic hog for the starring role of Napoleon. Ibid.

6. Nor has Halmi been reluctant to rewrite the Bible, as he demonstrated in his version of *Noah's Ark*, which includes a band of pirates on the high seas. The pirates raid Noah's ship.

7. Although it has long been known that the CIA financed and distributed the 1955 adaptation of *Animal Farm* (as agent Howard Hunt disclosed in his 1974 memoir), new details have recently come to light. The script was reviewed by the CIA's Psychological Strategy Board, which led to the altered ending in which the "lower animals" launch a victorious counter-revolution against the pigs. (The CIA, along with the U.S. Information Agency, also subsidized the first film version of *Nineteen-Eighty Four*, which was shot with two different endings. The British version followed the novel, but the American ending showed Winston and Julia rebelling and dying in each other's arms as Winston cries, "Down with

Big Brother!). Surely these revelations about how both *Animal Farm* and *Nineteen Eighty-Four* were directly connected with the cultural politics of the Cold War may affect how future viewers respond to these film adaptations (or even how future readers encounter the books). See E. Howard Hunt, *Undercover: Memoirs of an American Secret Agent* (New York: Berkley, 1974), and Frances Stonor Saunders, *The Cultural Cold War: The CIA and the World of Arts and Letters* (New York: New Press, 2000). (Saunders mistakenly attributes the altered, heroic ending to the British version.) See also Rodden, *George Orwell: The Politics of Literary Reputation,* in which I discuss the film versions of *Nineteen Eighty-Four* at length.

8. Alex Zwerdling, *Orwell and the Left* (New Haven, Conn.: Yale University Press, 1974).

9. For a practical, pedagogical approach to *Animal Farm* that involves role play and stimulating student exchange, see John V. Knapp, "Creative Reasoning in the Interactive Classroom: Experiential Exercises for Teaching George Orwell's *Animal Farm,*" *College Literature* 23, no. 2 (June 1996): 143–56.

10. *CEJL,* vol. 4: 122 (*CW,* vol. 18).

11. Quoted in Bernard Crick, *George Orwell: A Life* (London: Secker and Warburg, 1980), 344.

12. *CEJL,* vol. 3: 222 (*CW,* vol. 17).

13. For a more nuanced detailed discussion of these and other historical correspondences, see Bernard Grofman, "Pig and Proletariat: *Animal Farm* as History," *San Jose Studies* 16, no. 2 (spring 1990): 5–39.

14. Preface to the Ukrainian edition of *Animal Farm,* quoted in *CEJL,* vol. 4: 111. (*CW,* vol. 18).

15. For a full discussion of this point, see V. C. Letemendia, "Revolution on *Animal Farm*: Orwell's Neglected Commentary," *Journal of Modern Literature* 18, no. 1 (winter 1992): 127–37.

16. But the "moral" is culturally filtered and so may be interpreted—and often has been by numerous readers of the foreign-language versions—as specifically cultural. See Kerr Douglas, "Orwell, Animals, and the East," *Essays in Criticism* 49, no. 3 (July 1999): 234–55.

17. Crick, *George Orwell: A Life,* 444.

18. Peter Viereck, "Bloody-Minded Professors," *Confluence* 1 (September 1952): 36–37. See also Steve Pyle, "George Orwell's *Animal Farm*: The Little Book That Could," *Antigonish Review* 111 (autumn 1997): 31–36.

19. See Joe McDonald, "*Animal Farm* in China," Associated Press Reports, 5 December 2002.

20. *CEJL,* vol. 4: 56 (*CW,* vol. 17).

## 5. In the Land of Little Brother

1. See my *Repainting the Little Red Schoolhouse: A History of Eastern German Education, 1945– 95* (Oxford: Oxford University Press, 2002), and *Textbook Reds: Ideology and National Self-Legitimation in East German Schoolbooks* (State College, Pa.: Penn State University Press, forthcoming).

2. *New York Times,* 9 March 2003.

## 6. I Was a Teenage Thought Criminal, or Little Brotherly Love

1. From an interview with Wolfgang Strauss, 19 December 1995.

2. *Orwells DDR* (Leipzig: JKL Publications, Zeitgut Series 71, 1997). An expanded second edition appeared in March 2003.

3. "Wie ein Käfer unter einer Lupe," *Der Spiegel* 20 (1999).

4. Haase did not quite leave the matter to rest there. By 1993, at the time of his discovery of the truth in his *Stasi* file, he had not seen his ex-brother-in-law in eight years—and had not heard from him at all since 1986. Haase immediately wrote to his ex-brother-in-law, who lived a mere thirty miles away, to tell him that he now knew the full truth. But he received no answer, and Haase thereafter let the matter drop.

5. Haase recounted one high point of his tenure: he was chosen one evening to deliver a Becher poem glorifying Lenin. The pressure during that little opportunity, Haase recalled, later made clear to him the power of the Party—and the impotence of his own feeble will: "About 130 pairs of eyes were, in that moment, fixed on me and on the portrait of Party boss Comrade Walter Ulbricht, who hung behind me on the wall. At the moment, I didn't think of my literary friend Winston Smith, who had through re-education in the jail cell of the Thought Police finally been brought to love Big Brother."

6. In 1999, Haase was rehabilitated and recognized as a former political prisoner of the SED regime. He also received compensation according to a German law for political victims. He retired in September 2000. See Haase's website at http://www.antsta.de. For a different treatment of some of these issues in a French context, see Helene Roger, "Le Big Brother au temps des Small Brothers," *Cysnos* 11, no. 2 (1994): 147–63.

## 7. Politics and the German Language

1. Instead, in October 1993, after a surreal twenty-month trial, Mielke received a six-year jail sentence—not for any of his actions as *Stasi* chief but for a murder charge dating back sixty-two years. The self-appointed four-star general—Mielke used to wear 250 medals emblazoned on his uniform—was convicted on the basis of Nazi documents that investi-

gators uncovered in his own office—documents that he himself had discovered and saved, so proud was he of them. The 1993 decision was controversial; the only evidence against Mielke was the Nazi documents, which Mielke claimed were trumped up. He had been convicted in absentia by a Nazi court in 1935 of killing two policemen in August 1931.

2. Since 1977, the Society for the German Language, based in Wiesbaden, has also selected a Word of the Year. Among the winners of Word of the Year honors for the last dozen years are the following: 1991: *"Besserwessi"* (know-it-all western-German); 1992: *"Politikverdrossenheit"* (fed up with politics); 1994: *"Superwahljahr"* (super-election year); 1997: *"Reformstau"* (reform congestion); 1999: *"Millennium"* (millennium).

3. Following what it called Orwell's "intention to expose inhumane propagandistic uses of language," the National Council of Teachers of English (NCTE) began making annual awards in Orwell's name in 1973. See chapter 15.

4. "Unwörtler lassen nicht spassen," *Frankfurter Allgemeine Zeitung*, 3 February 1999. The preference of the Unword jurors for targeting right-wing cant may have reflected the perceived need to combat new right-wing Orwellian lingo—i.e., a neo-Nazi *Szenesprache*—that arose during the 1990s. Its Unwords were often crude and laconic. For example, the word "Oi"—a Cockney greeting meaning "Hey!"—has also had another meaning on the German scene: it alludes impishly to the English fascist name for the Nazi fitness slogan "Strength through Joy." (An early German LP of neo-Nazi rock was titled "Strength through Oi.")

5. For instance, Ignatz Bubis, president of the Central Council for Jews in Germany, accused Walser of "spiritual arson" and "latent anti-Semitism."

6. The Society for the German Language (GDS) has not participated in the Unword contest since 1994. After the jury criticized Chancellor Kohl for his expression "collective amusement park," the GDS publicly censured the jury, whereupon the Unword jury accused the GDS of not wanting to offend political conservatives and formed itself as an independent board, formally titled Linguistic Criticism in Action for the Unword of the Year. (The jury consists of the chairman Schlosser, three language scholars, and journalists.) Now the GDS only participates in the annual selection of the Word of the Year. Charges of the Unword jury's liberal bias persist. For instance, "culture lite" received 70 percent of the public votes for Unword of the Year in 2000. Yet the Unword jury selected the right-wing extremist expression "nationally liberated zone."

7. *Bunte*, 31 January 2002.

8. *Süddeutsche Zeitung*, 11 November 1991; *Economist*, 14 September 1991.

9. On these and other Orwellianisms, see *Süddeutsche Zeitung*, 19 December 1992, and *This Week in Germany*, 20 December 1991, 7 February 1992, 14 February 1992.

10. *Frankfurter Allgemeine Zeitung*, 27 January 1999.

11. *Deutsche Presse-Agentur*, 25 January 2000; *Frankfurter Allgemeine Zeitung*, 26 January 2000.

12. *Frankfurter Allgemeine Zeitung*, 24 January 2001.

13. *SDA – Basisdienst Deutsch*, 22 January 2002.

14. *Deutsche Presse-Agentur*, 22 January 2002; Associated Press Worldstream, 22 January 2002.

15. *Deutsche Presse-Agentur*, 29 July 2001; see also *General-Anzeiger*, 23 January 2002, and *Süddeutsche Zeitung*, 21 December 2002.

16. As many Germans are well aware, Orwell partly based Newspeak on his experience at the BBC as a broadcaster combating Nazi rhetoric. Of course, to a certain extent Newspeak was a satire first on Basic English and its philosophy of simplifying the English language by narrowing it to just a few hundred words. But the propagandistic, deliberately manipulative language of Newspeak is clearly also indebted to the wartime rhetoric of Nazism, to which Orwell was exposed on a daily basis during his stint at the BBC from 1941 to 1943. That was also the time at which he conceived his vision of *Nineteen Eighty-Four*, and he was certainly well aware of what was happening in East Germany after the war.

17. Not only Germans, of course, have held this view. Partly inspired by Orwell, the Hungarian-born British literary critic George Steiner warned in his essay "The Hollow Miracle" (1959) that language has a "breaking point," whereupon lies and sadism settle "into the marrow."

## 8. Unwords and Unfreedom in the Citadel of Unlearning

1. Wilhelm Liebknecht, "Wissen is Macht, Macht ist Wissen" ("Knowledge Is Power, Power Is Knowledge"), 1872. The speech appears in his *Kleine politische Schriften* (Frankfurt am Main: Röderberg-Verlag, 1976).

## 9. Portrait of a Defiant DIAMATnik

1. The essay is collected in *Berliner Schriften* (Berlin Writings), ed. Andreas W. Mytze (Berlin: Verlag Europäische Ideen, 1976), 49–50.

2. Even more revealing of this slide into public resignation and inner emigration was the indifferent response of most GDR citizens to the revolutionary events of 1968 in neighboring Czechoslovakia: the "Prague Spring." Here too, Havemann was an outspoken voice in the wilderness. For example, when his two sons were arrested and convicted for "traitorous actions against the state"—i.e., for painting a few walls with the name "Dubcek"—Havemann's name was prominently introduced by the state prosecutor as a Socrates who had "poisoned" his own sons' *Weltanschauung*. Invited by the defense attorney to testify at his sons' trial, Havemann was refused admittance when he arrived, supposedly because the courtroom was full. Peering inside as the trial was beginning, the

professor pointed to a row of seats completely empty. He was informed that the seats were reserved for a "delegation of businessmen." The courtroom door was then closed; when the guilty verdict was announced, his sons were led away. They were granted no contact with their father, who had waited five hours outside. He had not been permitted to communicate with them for months.

Havemann said to the court usher: "When I was sentenced to death during the Nazi period, the court permitted my parents to attend the proceeding. They also received permission to speak to me for a half-hour afterwards."

The usher replied: "Yes, but you see, we don't live in the Nazi period any longer." See Havemann's *Fragen, Antworten, Fragen: aus der Biographie eines deutschen Marxisten* (Munich: R. Piper, 1970), 202-203.

## 10. Amid the Rubble of "Orwell's Reich"

1. Humboldt University was not closed down, and it remains today the ranking institution of higher education in eastern Germany. Jürgen was not so fortunate: he was dismissed, along with 200 of his Humboldt colleagues, in late 1991.

## 11. Of Laughter, Forgetting, and Memory Holes

1. That book would become *Repainting the Little Red Schoolhouse*.

2. She did, however, keep her job; her teaching contract, due to expire in mid-1992, was extended. She survived the political and scholarly *Überprufung* required of all East German faculty.

3. *George Orwell* (London: Fontana, 1984). This final chapter appears in the second edition only. Already in the 1971 edition, however, Williams could write: "[I]f the tyranny of *1984* ever finally comes, one of the major elements of the ideological preparation" will have been its "way of seeing 'the masses.'"

4. Kundera even coins a term invidious to Orwell for the practice of reducing experience to its political aspect and thereby distorting it: "Orwellizing" the past. Kundera observes that his Prague acquaintances reduce and impoverish their years under Czech communism to the single dimension of politics: "In their talk of forty horrible years, they were all *Orwellizing* the recollection of their own lives, which, a posteriori, in their memories and in their heads, were thereby devalued or even completely obliterated (forty *lost* years)." See *Testaments Betrayed: An Essay in Nine Parts*, trans. Linda Asher (New York: HarperCollins, 1995).

5. These quotations are from Bergman, "Reading Fiction to Understand the Soviet Union."

## 12. Biographies and Biographers

1. See Spurling, *The Girl from the Fiction Department*, 122, 195, xii. Spurling also claims that, even after the publication of *Nineteen Eighty-Four*, Orwell was "no great catch from a commercial or literary point of view." She says that "the situation would only change after his death, with the paperback publication of *Animal Farm* and *Nineteen Eighty-Four*" (102). But *Animal Farm* had already been a Book-of-the-Month Club selection in 1946 and had sold more than a half-million copies; a few months before the Orwells' marriage in October 1949, *Nineteen Eighty-Four* was selected by the Book-of-the-Month Club and also as a Reader's Digest condensed book (earning Orwell more than $40,000 immediately). Spurling does not mention any of these facts, which make clear that Orwell was becoming, long before the paperback editions, a wealthy man.

   On Sonia, the CIA, and Clark Gable, see Saunders, *The Cultural Cold War,* 294. For a harsher portrait of Sonia from another friend, see David Plante, *Difficult Women: A Memoir of Three* (London: V. Gollancz, 1983). For Michael Shelden's dismissive review of Spurling's biography, see "Was Mrs. Orwell a Gold Digger?" *Daily Telegraph*, 31 May 2002. "There is no myth of the Widow Orwell," writes Shelden. "[H]er friends seem to want to rewrite history." But other readers agree with Spurling and accuse Shelden himself of "blackening Sonia's name." See Mark Bostridge, "Biography," *Independent on Sunday* (London), 26 May 2002.

2. Bernard Crick, "Orwell and the Business of Biography," in *More Adventures with Britannia: Personalities, Politics, and Culture in Britain,* ed. William Roger Louis (Austin, Tex.: University of Texas Press, 1999).

3. For a sensitive treatment of these issues, see Roger Averill, "Empathy, Externality, and Character in Biography," *Clio* (fall 2001).

4. Peter Stansky and William Abrahams, *The Unknown Orwell* (New York: Knopf, 1972) and *Orwell: The Transformation* (New York: Knopf, 1979). Their biography closed, however, with Orwell's departure from Spain in 1937; it thus covered Orwell's life only up to the age of thirty-four.

5. Jeffrey Meyers, "How True Is Life To Biography?" *Partisan Review* (winter 2001). The quoted passage is based on the preface to his Orwell biography.

6. Tzvetan Todorov, "Politics, Morality, and the Writer's Life: Notes on George Orwell," *Stanford French Review* (1992). This essay originally appeared in *Lettre Internationale* (spring 1989).

7. Mrs. Trilling told me that Sonia Orwell had written a letter to Lionel to protest the introduction. Interview with Diana Trilling, June 1990.

8. Steven Marcus, "George Orwell: Biography as Literature," *Partisan Review* (spring 1993).

9. See my *George Orwell: The Politics of Literary Reputation*, chapter 2.

10. Quoted in *CW*, 20: 241, 318–25.

11. On the children's books, see Tanya Agathocleous, *George Orwell: Battling Big Brother* (New York: Oxford University Press, 2000) and Richard Jennings, *Orwell's Luck* (Boston: Houghton Mifflin, 2000).

12. D. J. Taylor, *Orwell: A Life* (New York: Henry Holt, 2003); Scott Lucas, *Orwell* (London: Haus Publishing, 2003); and Gordon Bowker, *Inside George Orwell: A Biography* (New York: Palgrave Macmillan, 2003).

## 13. Orwell, Marx, and the Marxists

1. Dennis J. O'Keefe, "Homage to Orwell," *Policy Review* 17 (summer 1981): 129–34.

2. Richard Rees, *George Orwell: Fugitive From the Camp of Victory* (Carbondale, Ill.: Southern Illinois University Press, 1961), 6.

3. Zwerdling, *Orwell and the Left,* 120.

4. Crick, *George Orwell: A Life*, 305.

5. Isaac Deutscher, "*1984*—The Mysticism of Cruelty," *Russia in Transition and Other Essays* (New York: Grove, 1960), 263.

6. Crick, *George Orwell: A Life*, 189–91.

7. See *The Road to Wigan Pier* (New York: Harcourt Brace Jovanovich, 1956), part II.

8. "Marx and Russia," *Observer*, 1 February 1948, 3 (*CW*, vol. 19).

9. See especially *The Road to Wigan Pier*, part II.

10. *The Road to Wigan Pier,* 177.

11. *CEJL*, vol. 3: 229 (*CW*, vol. 16).

12. *CEJL*, vol. 1: 357 (*CW*, vol. 11).

13. *CEJL*, vol. 2: 236 (*CW*, vol. 16).

14. *CEJL*, vol. 3: 224 (*CW*, vol. 16).

15. *CEJL*, vol. 1: 357 (*CW*, vol. 11).

16. *CEJL*, vol. 3: 298 (*CW*, vol. 16).

17. *CEJL*, vol. 4: 268 (*CW*, vol. 19).

18. "Marx and Russia," 3 (*CW*, vol. 19).

19. *CEJL*, vol. 4: 468 (*CW*, vol. 20).

20. George Orwell, *Animal Farm* (New York: Harcourt, Brace, 1974), 24.

21. *CEJL*, vol. 3: 64 (*CW*, vol. 15).

22. Rees, *George Orwell: Fugitive From the Camp of Victory,* 145.

23. *CEJL,* vol. 2: 265 (*CW,* vol. 13).

24. Audrey Coppard and Bernard Crick, eds., *Orwell Remembered* (London: Ariel Books, 1984), 155. Rees's remark is in an extract from Melvyn Bragg's BBC-TV special devoted to Orwell, *The Road to the Left,* broadcast on 10 January 1971.

25. Eduard Bernstein, *Evolutionary Socialism: A Criticism and Affirmation* (New York: Schocken, 1961 [1899]), 174.

26. *Ibid,* 174.

27. For the relation of Bernstein to Fabianism, see Peter Gay, *The Dilemma of Democratic Socialism: Edward Bernstein's Challenge to Marx* (New York: Columbia University Press, 1952), 174.

28. *The Road to Wigan Pier,* 216.

29. *CEJL,* vol. 2: 86 (*CW,* vol. 12).

30. *CEJL,* vol. 2: 95 (*CW,* vol. 12).

31. "The English Civil War," *New Statesman and Nation,* 24 Aug. 1940: 3 (*CW,* vol. 12).

32. "Vessel of Wrath," *Observer,* 16 January 1944: 4 (*CW,* vol. 16).

33. Rees, *George Orwell: Fugitive From the Camp of Victory,* 8.

34. *CEJL,* vol. 1: 258 (*CW,* vol. 10).

35. On this point, see David Wykes, "Orwell's Adlerian Memoir: Such, Such Were the Joys." Unpublished essay, 1983.

36. *CEJL,* vol. 2: 87 (*CW,* vol. 12).

37. "The English Civil War," *New Statesman and Nation,* 24 August 1940: 3 (*CW,* vol. 12).

38. Review of Alec Brown, *The Fate of the Middle Classes. Adelphi* 12 (May 1936): 127–28.

*39. CEJL,* vol. 2: 77–78 (*CW,* vol. 12).

40. Cyril Connolly, *The Condemned Playground* (New York: Macmillan, 1946), 150.

41. *CEJL,* vol. 1: 448 (*CW,* vol. 12).

42. *CEJL,* vol. 1: 276 (*CW,* vol. 11).

43. *CEJL,* vol. 3: 365 (*CW,* vol. 17).

44. See Harry Pollitt, review of *The Road to Wigan Pier, Daily Worker,* 17 March 1937: 5.

45. George Woodcock, "George Orwell: Nineteenth Century Liberal," *Politics* 3 (1946): 385.

46. See Kate Carr, "The Nightmare of Mr. Orwell," *Daily Worker,* 16 June 1949: 3; Thomas Spencer, "Prisoner of Hatred," *Daily Worker,* 19 October 1950: 3; Samuel Sillen, "Maggot

of the Month," *Masses and Mainstream*, August 1949: 79–81.

47. Raymond Williams, *Politics and Letters* (London: New Left Books, 1979), 384.

48. Williams, *Politics and Letters*, 388–91. The interviews were conducted by Perry Anderson, Anthony Burnett, and Francis Mulhern of the editorial committee of *New Left Review*.

49. A. L. Rowse, "The Contradiction of Orwell," *Contemporary Review* 26 (October 1982): 185–186. Rowse's remarks recall his 1947 review of Orwell's *English People*. Orwell, said Rowse, suffered "from the mean absurdities of intellectuals," while striking the pose "of a good man struggling with adversity. In middle age this old Etonian of the Left has seen that there is something to be said for his country." A. L. Rowse, "Pity the Poor English," *Sunday Times*, 19 October 1947, 3.

50. Williams, *George Orwell*.

51. Raymond Williams, *George Orwell: A Collection of Critical Essays* (Englewood Cliffs, N.J.: Prentice-Hall, 1974), 8.

52. Lucas's book presents Orwell as "both the origin and the icon of an intellectual and political network which, proclaiming itself the protector of freedom, tries to limit and even quash dissent." In an accompanying short biography, *Orwell*, Lucas argues in terms that directly echo Williams: "Orwell was never really a socialist, and, in spite of his interest in 'clear writing,' he remained as confused in his politics as he was talented in his prose." Each of these quotes is taken from the advance notice for each book released by Lucas's publishers.

53. Geoffrey Wheatcroft, "Saved from Friend and Foe," *Spectator*, 8 June 2002, 39–40.

54. *CEJL*, vol. 2: 18 (*CW*, vol. 12).

## 14. Orwell, the Catholics, and the Jews

1. *CEJL*, vol. 4: 13 (*CW*, vol. 17).

2. Charles Brady, "Virtuous Skeptic," *America* 75 (20 July 1946): 364.

3. Christopher Hollis, "George Orwell and His Schooldays," *Listener* 51 (4 March 1954): 383.

4. *CEJL*, vol. 1: 50 (*CW*, vol. 10).

5. George Orwell, *A Clergyman's Daughter* (New York: Harcourt, Brace, 1960), 24–28, 67–78.

6. *CEJL*, vol. 4: 496 (*CW*, vol. 20).

7. T. A. Birrell, "Is Integrity Enough? A Study of George Orwell," *Dublin Review* 449 (autumn 1950): 51, 65.

8. Christopher Hollis, *A Study of George Orwell: The Man and His Works* (Chicago: Regnery, 1956), 40.

9. *CEJL*, vol. 1: 101 (*CW*, vol. 10).

10. See, for example, Neville Braybrooke's "The Two Poverties: Leon Bloy and George Orwell," *Commonweal* 58 (14 August 1953): 449–51. Hollis compares Orwell to Chesterton in *A Study of George Orwell*, 175. Non-Catholic intellectuals have also made similar comparisons. Lionel Trilling compared Orwell with Peguy and Chesterton in his introduction to *Homage to Catalonia* (New York: Harcourt, Brace, 1952).

11. See, for example, Orwell's review of Chesterton's *Criticisms and Opinions of Charles Dickens* in *Adelphi* 7 (December 1933): 224–25; also "The Christian Reformers," *Manchester Evening News*, 7 February 1946, 2, and *CEJL*, vol. 1: 383–85 (*CW*, vol. 11).

12. On Orwell's possible anti-Semitism in *Down and Out*, see especially the attitude of Boris the Russian toward Jews and the story of Roucolle the miser.

13. Muggeridge, *Like It Was*, 376. Of Orwell's funeral, Muggeridge noted, "the congregation (was) largely Jewish and almost entirely unbelievers."

14. *CEJL*, vol. 3: 85; 4: 513 (*CW*, vol. 16; 20).

15. *CEJL*, vol. 3: 89; 3: 152; 4: 399 (*CW*, vol. 16; 16; 19).

16. See *CEJL*, vol. 1: 4 (*CW*, vol. 19) and *CEJL*, vol. 4: 360 (*CW*, vol. 19). Orwell admits his "natural hatred for authority" in "Why I Write." In "Such, Such Were the Joys," he claims that he hated God and empathized with the unpopular and disparaged figures of the Scriptures: "You were supposed to love God, and I did not question this. Till the age of about fourteen, I believed in God, and believed that the accounts given of him were true. But I was well aware that I did not love him. On the contrary, I hated him, just as I hated Jesus and the Hebrew patriarchs. If I had sympathetic feelings toward any character in the Old Testament, it was towards such people as Cain, Jezebel, Haman, Agag, Sisera; in the New Testament my friends, if any, were Ananias, Caiaphas, Judas, and Pontius Pilate."

17. *CEJL*, vol. 3: 332 (*CW*, vol. 17).

18. *CEJL*, vol. 3: 332 (*CW*, vol. 17).

19. *CEJL*, vol. 1: 515 (*CW*, vol. 12).

20. *CEJL*, vol. 3: 175 (*CW*, vol. 16).

21. *CEJL*, vol. 2: 241 (*CW*, vol. 14).

22. *CEJL*, vol. 2: 148 (*CW*, vol. 12).

23. *CEJL*, vol. 4: 322, 4: 374 (*CW*, vol. 19; 19).

24. *CEJL*, vol. 4: 400 (*CW*, vol. 19). T. R. Fyvel, *George Orwell: A Personal Memoir* (New York: Macmillan, 1982), 140.

25. Grandfather Blair had been vicar of Milbourne at St. Andrew in Dorset. Orwell also did attend church regularly for a period during his early thirties, convincing the parish rector (and perhaps even himself) that he was a devout believer. When contrasting it with Catholicism, Orwell sometimes demonstrated a veiled affection for Anglicanism, "the old dog . . . the poor old C. of E." In gestures like his request to have an Anglican burial service, one senses in Orwell a strain of Tubby Bowling, the hero of *Coming Up for Air*. Bowling possessed at times "that peculiar feeling—it was only a feeling, you couldn't describe it as an activity—that we used to call 'Church.' The sweet corpsy smell, the rustle of Sunday dresses, the wheeze of the organ and the roaring voices, the spot of light from the window creeping slowly up the nave." *Coming Up for Air* (New York: Harcourt, Brace, 1950), 34.

But Orwell's affection was never for doctrine. It evoked in him the specter of Reverend Hare and his High Anglicanism in *A Clergyman's Daughter*. If anything, Orwell was more like schoolmaster Victor Stone, who likes vestments, hymnal choirs, and May Queen processions. These things he associated sadly with the past—with vanishing English traditions, with peaceful country churchyards, and with his boyhood. "[I]t was a good world to live in," says Tubby Bowling, "so different from the world I live in now that you might have a bit of difficulty in believing I ever belonged to it." (*Coming Up for Air*, 38, 39.) Orwell liked the forms of worship. And surely this half-concealed fondness for old ritual has also suggested to some observers the element of the Catholic in him.

26. Alan Sandison, *The Last Man in Europe: An Essay on George Orwell* (New York: Macmillan, 1974), 6. Sandison's study addresses Orwell's affinities with Protestant belief rather than Catholicism, however.

27. V. S. Pritchett, "George Orwell: An Appreciation," *New York Times Book Review*, 5 February 1950, 22.

28. Letter from Richard Rees to Malcolm Muggeridge, 8 March 1955. Quoted in Malcolm Muggeridge, "The Knight of the Woeful Countenance," in *The World of George Orwell*, ed. Miriam Gross (London: Wiedenfeld and Nicolson, 1971), 167. Geoffrey Ashe cast Orwell as a kind of Christian socialist. Orwell "transcended socialism," wrote Ashe. "[W]hile unable to budge an inch toward Christian orthodoxy, he clung to Christian values and recognized their origin." See "A Note on George Orwell," *Commonweal* 54 (1951): 193.

29. *Studies: An Irish Review* 46 (summer 1957): 256.

30. Frank Getelein, "The Testimony of an Honest Man," *Commonweal* 57 (20 March 1953): 607.

31. Birrell, 50. See also Evelyn Waugh's laudatory review of *Critical Essays* in *Tablet* 186 (6 April 1946): 176.

32. *CEJL*, vol. 3: 265 (*CW*, vol. 16). Getelein, "Testimony of an Honest Man," 607. In his notebooks, Thomas Merton remarks of Orwell: "You find it everywhere—the obsession with immortality." *Conjectures of a Guilty Bystander* (Garden City, N.Y.: Doubleday, 1966),

142–43. For a detailed treatment of the topic, see Erika Gottlieb, *The Orwell Conundrum: A Cry of Despair or Faith in the Spirit of a Man?* (Ottawa: McGill-Queens University Press, 1992).

33. Orwell cited Graham Greene as an example of a leftist Catholic. *CEJL*, vol. 4: 512. (*CW*, vol. 20) See also "The Christian Reformers" (footnote 11). The correspondence between Catholicism and conservatism was closer in Britain, given journals such as the *Tablet*, than in America. In the 1940s, journals such as *Commonweal* and *America* took liberal stands on many political issues. The easy correlation of Catholicism with conservatism becomes even more tenuous and complicated in the 1950s, with the rise of neoliberalism and neoconservatism.

34. See Russell Kirk, *Beyond the Dreams of Avarice* (Peru, Ill.: Sherwood Sugden, 1991 [1956]), 181–82.

35. Will Herberg, "The Sense of Decency," *America* (5 November 1955): 159. Christopher Hollis, *A Study of George Orwell*, 114, 153.

36. Melvyn New, "Orwell and Antisemitism: Toward 1984," *Modern Fiction Studies* 21 (spring 1975): 81–105. The interpretation may not be so farfetched: T. R. Fyvel claims that Orwell once told him that the likeliest figure to stage a hopeless revolt against a totalitarian regime would be a Jewish intellectual. "Wingate, Orwell, and the Jewish Question," *Commentary* 11 (February 1951): 137–44, esp. 143. See also T. R. Fyvel, "The Quiet Eye of George Orwell," *Guardian*, 28 August 1982, 9.

37. Trilling, introduction to *Homage to Catalonia*, viii–xi. "The Partisan Review Award," *Partisan Review* 16 (October 1949): 967. Philip Rieff, "George Orwell and the Post-Liberal Imagination," *Kenyon Review* 16 (winter 1954): 49–70.

38. In his historical study of *Partisan Review*, James Gilbert calls Orwell's "Letters to London" "particularly important in the evolution of *Partisan*." See *Writers and Partisans* (New York: Wiley, 1968), 246–50, 274–80.

39. *CEJL*, vol. 2: 59 (*CW*, vol. 12).

40. Orwell, *A Clergyman's Daughter*, 61.

41. *CEJL*, vol. 2: 18 (*CW*, vol. 12).

42. Recounted in Cyril Connolly, *The Evening Colonnade* (New York: Harcourt Brace Jovanovich, 1975), 346.

43. See, for instance, Peter Faulkner's "Orwell and Christianity," *New Humanist* (December 1973): 270–73. Faulkner writes that Orwell became "a thoroughgoing and convinced Humanist. . . . Of all modern writers he is the most unequivocally and consistently humanistic." Also see Nathan Scott, "The Example of George Orwell," *Christianity and Crisis* 19 (20 July 1959): 7–10, and Max Cosman, "Orwell's Terrain," *Personalist* 35 (1954): 41–49.

44. Norman Podhoretz, "If Orwell Were Alive Today," *Harper's* 266 (January 1983): 30–37;

Irving Howe, "Enigmas of Power," *New Republic* 188 (year-end issue, 1982): 27–32.

45. Brian Wicker, "Books," *Commonweal* 89 (10 January 1969): 475.

## 15. Canon Fodder for the King's English

1. On these issues, see Samir Elbarbary, "Language as Theme in *Animal Farm*," *International Fiction Review*, 19, no. 1 (1992): 31–38; James Miller, "Is Bad Writing Necessary? George Orwell, Theodor Adorno, and the Politics of Language," *Lingua Franca*, 9, no. 9 (December-January 2000): 33–44.

2. K. Davidson, letter to the author, 23 May 1983; A. R. Davis, letter to the author, 13 May 1983; K. M. Galvin, letter to the author, 12 May 1983; H. F. King, letters to the author, 10 June 1983 and 18 September 1989; G. M. Lambert, letter to the author, 13 June 1983.

3. James Squire and Roger K. Applebee, *Teaching English in the United Kingdom: A Comparative Study* (Champaign, Ill.: National Council of Teachers of English, 1969): 96.

4. M. T. Fain, letter to the author, 7 July 1983.

5. On Woodhouse's covert activities for British intelligence, see Saunders, *The Cultural Cold War*, 168-76.

6. See Saunders, *The Cultural Cold War*, 293–96.

7. Lawrence Schwartz, *Creating Faulkner's Reputation: The Politics of Modern Literary Criticism* (Knoxville, Tenn.: University of Tennessee Press, 1990), 182.

8. Zwerdling, *Orwell and the Left*, 129. Arthur Koestler, "A Rebel's Progress," *Observer*, 29 January 1950: 4.

9. David Caute, *The Great Fear: The Anti-Communist Purge Under Truman and Eisenhower* (London: Secker and Warburg, 1978), 404, 600; Squire and Applebee, *Teaching English in the United Kingdom*, 204.

10. Schwartz, *Creating Faulkner's Reputation*, 3, 5, 138, 209.

11. Ibid., 210.

12. Albert B. Friedman, "The Literary Experience of High School Seniors and College Freshmen," *English Journal* 44 (1955): 423.

13. Dwight Burton, *Literature Study in the High Schools* (New York: Holt, Rinehart and Winston, 1964), 46.

14. James Knapton and Bertrand Evans, *Teaching a Literature-Centered English Program* (New York: Random House, 1967), 19–21.

15. "Censorship in the English Classroom: A Review of Research," *Journal of Research and Development in Education* 12 (spring 1976): 655–61.

16. Fain, letter to the author.

17. E. D. Hirsch Jr., "Cultural Literacy," *American Scholar* 54 (1983): 34–46. See also Hirsch's *Cultural Literacy: What Every American Needs to Know* (Boston: Houghton Mifflin, 1987).

18. Linda Cookson, *Introduction and Study Questions for Nineteen Eighty-Four* (London, 1983): 310.

19. Frank Thompson, *Cliffs Notes to Orwell's* Animal Farm (Lincoln, Neb.: Cliffs Notes, 1967): 52.

20. Fred Hechinger, "Censorship of Books on Upswing in U.S., Report Shows," *Lexington Herald,* 2 November 1981: 10; L. J. Davis, "Onward Christian Soldiers," *Penthouse* (March 1982): 30–31.

21. Ronald W. Sousa, "On the Politics of Reading, or William Bennett Reclaims George Orwell," *Ideologies and Literature* 3 (1985): 2–8. See also Chester Finn, "Higher Education on Trial: An Indictment," *Current* 48 (October 1984): 57–80.

22. Sousa, "On the Politics of Reading," 8.

23. Ibid., 172. See also Michael Scrivener and Louis Finkelman, "The Politics of Obscurity: The Plain Style and Its Detractors," *Philosophy & Literature*, 18, no. 1 (April 1994): 18–37; Eugene Goodheart, "Orwell and the Bad Writing Controversy," *Clio—A Journal of Literature History and the Philosophy of History* 28, no. 4 (summer 1999): 439–43.

24. Mina Shaughnessy, *Errors and Expectations: A Guide for the Teacher of Basic Writing* (New York: Oxford University Press, 1977), 193, 157.

25. Stewart Justman, "Orwell's Plain Style," *University of Toronto Quarterly* 53 (winter 1983–84): 200. See also Miller, "Is Bad Writing Necessary?" and Andrei L. Reznikov, "Dangerous Language Litter: George Orwell on Clichés in the English Language," *Proverbium: Yearbook of International Proverb Scholarship* 18 (2001): 291–97.

26. Orwell, "Exclusive Club," *Observer,* 6 February 1949: 3 (*CW*, vol. 20).

27. Susan Hardy Aiken, "Women and the Question of Canonicity," *College English* 48 (1986): 288–301.

28. Glenn Robinson, letter to the author, 12 October 1989.

29. Hugh David, "Impolite Letters," *Encounter* 71 (December 1985): 62–66.

30. Ibid.

31. The most famous—or notorious—recent Doublespeak Award winner is President William Jefferson Clinton, recognized for "unwanted fame for his language skills at misleading the public by fudging, fibbing, and dodging." His grand jury testimony statement was cited as especially noteworthy: "It depends on what the meaning of 'is' means. If 'is' means 'is and never has been,' that is one thing. If it means 'there is none,' that was a completely true statement." Gene Amole, *Denver Rocky Mountain News,* 20 February 2000.

32. See chapter 13, note 52, on Lucas's book.

## 16. Ecce "Orwell," or Why I Am So Famous

1. George Woodcock, *The Crystal Spirit: A Study of George Orwell* (Boston: Little, Brown, 1966), 53.

2. Judith Shulevitz, "What Would Orwell Do?" *New York Times Book Review*, 8 September 2002.

3. Ben Wattenberg, host of the PBS program, "The Orwell Century," March 2002.

4. Shulevitz, "What Would Orwell Do?"

5. Among my exchanges with Hitchens were volleys about Orwell's posthumous politics. When I demurred that "we can't predict what Orwell's stands might have been in the 1950s and '60s," and then allowed that Orwell might well have gone the way of some of his conservative friends, including his literary executor Richard Rees and his close friends Anthony Powell and Malcolm Muggeridge (both of whom he had placed in charge of his funeral arrangements), Hitchens replied:

> We don't know what Orwell would have said about McCarthyism or about the Vietnam War? I disagree, because he actually pronounced on both of them before he died. There was a proposal for a witch hunt in Britain in the 1940s for cleansing of the Civil Service of subversives, and he wrote and publicized and campaigned for principles that there should be no tribunals, no secret evidence, no arraignments of people for their political views if they are working for the government. If the people are suspected of actual treason, he said, these are the safeguards they should have before any hearing.
>
> He was also opposed to the witch-hunt mentality. But no one was more anticommunist than him, nobody. And he'd been a victim himself of a communist in the Civil Service, who tried to prevent him from being published.

6. The PBS program was "Think Tank with Ben Wattenberg," a weekly PBS series devoted to public affairs.

7. W. H. Auden, "George Orwell," *Spectator*, 16 January 1917, 86.

8. Geoffrey Wheatcroft, "The Defeat of the Left," *Atlantic Monthly* (October 2002): 35.

9. Florence Stratton, "Orwell's *1984*—Our Reality," *Catholic Worker* (January-February 2003): 5.

10. Newsinger, *Orwell's Politics*, x, 157–58.

11. Ibid., 158.

12. Jonah Goldberg, "Orwell's Orphans," *National Review*, 6 February 2002.

13. Ibid. See also Simon Caulkin, "Too Complicated For Words," *Observer*, 2 December 2001: "Orwell's target today would almost certainly be business and the English language."

14. Nat Hentoff, "Berlin, in 1936, China, in 2008?" *San Diego Union-Tribune*, 2 July 2001.

15. Anthony Arblaster, "Orwell: The Man Who Was Ahead of His Time," *Tribune*, 4 October 1968: 2; Philip French, "Bloody, but Alive," *Financial Times*, 3 October 1968.

16. Richard Rees, "George Orwell," in *The Politics of Twentieth-Century Novelists*, ed. George Panichas (New York: Hawthorn, 1970), 98.

17. Ben Pimlott, "Would George Orwell Recognize Tony Blair's England?" *Financial Times*, 21 July 2001: 4.

18. George Scialabba, "Curious George," *Washington Post*, 20 October 2002.

19. Podhoretz, "If Orwell Were Alive Today," 32.

20. Ibid., 37.

21. Christopher Hitchens, "An Exchange on Orwell," *Harper's* (February 1983): 56–57.

22. Mary McCarthy, *The Writing on the Wall* (San Diego: Harcourt Brace Jovanovich, 1970), 168–69.

23. Rupert Murdoch, 'The Century of Networking." Cited in Newsinger, *Orwell's Politics*, 157.

24. Henry Porter, "England, Our England," *Guardian*, 28 July 1993: 2. See also Wheatcroft, "Saved From Friend and Foe."

25. Noel Malcolm, "The Truth About Orwell's Politics," *Daily Telegraph*, 14 August 1995. Other columnists compared Mayor Richard Daley to Napoleon of *Animal Farm*. Headlined "Orwell Alive in the Council," one columnist began:

> The Chicago city council has been called a zoo, but at Wednesday's meeting it looked more like a farm. *Animal Farm*, to be precise.
>
> To paraphrase: "All Mayor Daley's Appointments Are Just Recommendations, But Some Appointments Are More Recommended Than Others." I think I saw that painted on the Council chamber wall.
>
> President pro tem may sound good, but it's a ceremonial position that gets one staffer and a paltry budget of $4,000, compared with $456,002 for the budget committee and $105,304 for the police committee. In Animal Farm-speak: Big budgets good, small budgets bad.
>
> Considering Daley's conquests, I've suggested before that he is Chicago's Alexander the Great. Now he's looking more like Napoleon. (Cate Plys, "Orwell Alive in the Council," *Chicago Sun-Times*, 28 July 2001.)

26. Graham Greene, "Well, As It Happens, Orwell Was Right about War," *Ottawa Citizen*, 12 October 1999, A18.

27. Norman Solomon, "I Dreamt of Orwell," *Boston Globe*, 27 February 2002.

28. William Walker, "Coming Soon to a Video Camera Near You," *Toronto Star*, 12 May 2002.

29. Adapted from an essay by Daniel Kurtzman at www.TomPaine.com.

30. Lee Congdon, "Newspeak Totalitarianism," *Austin Review* (July 2002): 4.

31. D. J. Taylor, "Left, Right, Left, Right," *New Statesman*, 20 May 2002.

32. Gary Chapman, "We Need An Orwell For Our Times," *Austin-American Statesman*, 19 September 2002.

33. Noel Malcolm, "Orwell's Critics, Down and Out," *Sunday Telegraph*, 26 May 2002. See also Pimlott, "Would George Orwell Recognize Tony Blair's England?" 4.

34. Ibid.

35. Quoted from *Think Tank with Ben Wattenberg*, "The Orwell Century," March 2002.

36. Christopher Hitchens, "George Orwell," *American Enterprise* (November-December 1999): 56.

37. Hitchens, *Why Orwell Matters* (New York: Basic, 2002).

38. Norman Podhoretz, "Facing The Plain Truth," *Jerusalem Post*, 5 April 2002.

39. Matthew Price, "Beating a Dead Elephant," *In These Times*, 5 March 2001. Price's references to Podhoretz pertained to the latter's Orwell comments during the 1980s and '90s.

40. John R. MacArthur, "Farewell, George: Why I Can't Worship At the Altar of Orwell Anymore," *In These Times*, 10 June 2002.

41. Revelations about Koestler's mistreatment of women—his alleged rape of Jill Craigie, among other assaults—have destroyed his reputation as a humanist and champion of the dispossessed. Silone's radical credentials have been soiled by evidence that he was an informant to the fascists in the 1930s as well as knowledgeable about CIA funding of the Congress for Cultural Freedom (and other anti-Soviet postwar activities of the Western intelligence services in the "cultural Cold War").

42. On Trilling, see my edited volume, *Lionel Trilling and the Critics: Opposing Selves* (Lincoln, Neb.: University of Nebraska Press, 1999), and Norman Podhoretz, *Ex-Friends: Falling out with Allen Ginsberg, Lionel and Diana Trilling, Lillian Hellman, Hannah Arendt, and Norman Mailer* (San Francisco: Encounter, 2000). On Berlin, see Christopher Hitchens, *Unacknowledged Legislation: Writers in the Public Sphere* (New York: Verso, 2000) and Michael Ignatieff, *Isaiah Berlin: A Life* (New York: Metropolitan, 2001).

43. In *Public Intellectuals*, Richard Posner refers to Orwell as "the exemplary figure" of "the best public-intellectual work of the last century" (73).

## 17. W.W.G.O.D.?

1. On Orwell's "androcentrism," see Daphne Patrai, *The Orwell Mystique: A Study in Male Ideology* (Amherst, Mass.: University of Massachusetts Press, 1984).

2. The previous nine paragraphs are adapted from my *George Orwell: The Politics of Literary Reputation*, 94-96.

3. Cyril Connolly, "Reputations" (1950), collected in *The Evening Colonnade*.

4. Dean Acheson, "Participation of Books in Department's Fight Against Communism," 11 April 1951, National Archives Records Administration, 511.412/6-2 851.

5. See *George Orwell: The Politics of Literary Reputation*, 202n, 291–93, 434, 448. On the *Animal Farm* film, see Saunders, *The Cultural Cold War*.

6. This was the title of the original British edition of *Why Orwell Matters*.

7. George Kubler, *The Shape of Time: Remarks on the History of Things* (New Haven, Conn.: Yale University Press, 1962), 87–88.

8. An ongoing indication of Orwell's "enduring habitation" is that one still encounters "Orwell" quite often in the lyrics of rock and punk bands. Although no prominent touring bands are currently associated with Orwell's work, songs about him and *Nineteen Eighty-Four* are still widely played on radio stations. Among his "fans" are several of the leading British groups and stars from the 1970s to the 1990s, including David Bowie, Sting and the Police, the Jam, and the Clash (who were originally known as "the 101-ers").

## Epilogue: Our Orwell, Right or Left?

1. See the exchange between Podhoretz and Hitchens in the January and February 1983 issues of *Harper's*.

2. See "Charles Dickens" in *CEJL*, vol. 1: 458 (*CW*, vol. 12).

3. George Watson, "Left and Right," in his *Politics and Literature in Modern Britain* (London: Macmillan, 1977), 85–97.

4. Malcolm Muggeridge recalls his and Kingsmill's judgments in *Like It Was*.

5. Gordon Beadle, "George Orwell and the Victorian Radical Tradition," *Albion* 13 (1976): 290–92.

6. Francis Hope, "My Country Right or Left," *New Statesman* (19 December 1969): 892.

7. Rees, "George Orwell," in *The Politics of Twentieth-Century Novelists*, 86, 88.

8. George Woodcock, "George Orwell, Nineteenth Century Liberal," *Politics* 2 (December 1946): 51.

9. V. S. Pritchett, "George Orwell," *New Statesman and Nation* (28 January 1950): 96.

10. Albert Camus, *The Rebel* (New York: Vintage, 1956), 1–10.

11. Koestler, "A Rebel's Progress," *Observer,* 29 January 1950, 4.

12. *CEJL,* vol. 1: 421 (*CW,* vol. 12).

13. *CEJL,* vol. 1: 441 (*CW,* vol. 12).

14. *The Road to Wigan Pier,* 171.

15. Franklin D. Roosevelt famously defined a radical in those terms in a 1939 speech.

16. *CEJL,* vol. 2: 134 (*CW,* vol. 12).

17. *The Road to Wigan Pier,* 147.

18. Hollis, *A Study of George Orwell.*

19. Edward Thomas, *Orwell* (New York: Barnes and Noble, 1968).

20. On Irving Howe's conservatism, see Samuel Hux, "Uncle Irving," *Modern Age* (spring 1985).

21. Robert Nozick, *Anarchy, State, and Utopia* (New York: Basic, 1974).

# Index

## A

Ackermann, Anton, 120
Afghanistan, 228
    Taliban fighters in, 92
Alexeevna, Liudmila, 33, 159
Allied bombings of Germany, 126
America
    academics in, 85, 154, 165
    al-Qaeda and, 92, 228
    Caesarism and, 245
    Capitalism of, 13, 46
    civil liberties in, 244
    communication industry in, 15
    empire and, 201
    foreign policies of, 208
    government of, 257
    imperialism of, 236
    intellectuals and, 249
    intelligence agencies of, 175, 249
    intervention of, 238, 247
    involvement in Vietnam of, 236
    Jewish liberals and, 205
    invasion of Iraq and, 225
    Left and, 139, 205

literary scene of, 139, 257, 260
    mass media and, 8
    neoconservatives and, 218
    newspaper and cable industries of, 16–17
    press of, 8, 195
    public of, 23, 197
    publishers of, 60
    readers in, 41, 197
    schools of, 210, 213, 218
    West Berlin and, 113
American Newspaper Publishers
    Association (ANPA), 17
Andreev, German, 33
Andropov, Yuri, 32, 34, 220
Anglo-American
    capitalist democracy, 243
    Catholics, 225
    classrooms, 210–11
    intellectuals, x, 4, 225, 241
    intelligence agencies, 212
    Left, 32, 139, 178–79
*Animal Farm*, x, xvi, 4, 7, 11, 30–31, 36–37, 41–52, 75–76, 80, 142, 160, 166, 168, 170, 172, 174, 177, 179, 183–